THE MINISTER AS
MARRIAGE COUNSELOR

Charles William Stewart

THE MINISTER AS
MARRIAGE COUNSELOR

Abingdon Press

NEW YORK — NASHVILLE

To Alma

PREFACE

The purpose of this book is to provide the practicing minister and the training student with a source book in the increasingly complex field of marriage counseling. There is a need to move beyond the description of techniques and anecdotes toward the preparation of texts and study materials that show ability to integrate and build on psychological and sociological principles. And these works should aim at a unique group, ministers, who have a special role and relationship with people in society.

There are other books on pastoral care and counseling; there are other marriage counseling texts. This book attempts to bring the minister into relationship with the emerging profession of marriage counseling. The purpose is to enable him to develop a professional approach to the sweethearts, husbands, wives, and children in his "care." Some will shy away from the word "professional," but this is the direction in which ministers should move. The days of the "lick-and-a-promise" session with a couple to be married and of the solemn prayer and little else over the quarreling couple are rapidly drawing to a close.

This book is dedicated, therefore, to helping the minister sharpen his counseling skills, to his growing perception and awareness of marriage problems, and to the mustering of the couple's and family's resources to deal with these problems appreciatively and intelligently.

I am presenting one interpretation of marriage counseling as it may be practiced by a minister. This interpretation, put quite simply, is that the counselor does not do personal counseling with the couple who come to him with a marriage problem, but rather helps them to understand their marriage relationship. He helps them to change their role pictures and to adjust to them so that there will be more harmony and less friction in the marriage. The implications of this kind of counseling are that the personalities of each partner will be modified somewhat; however, the focus of the counseling is on the marriage. There are other interpretations of marriage counseling, as is readily apparent to the reader as he surveys the field: the client-centered and the psychoanalytic, to name two of the more prominent. However, for reasons stated in the text, I have preferred to work within a "role-relationship" theory, while recognizing the contributions and integrity of other approaches.

No study of this kind is accomplished alone. I wish to acknowledge my profound debt to Paul E. Johnson, my teacher of pastoral counseling, whose insight and professional encouragement have meant much to me along the way. Also, I would like to express my appreciation to James A. Galvin, M.D., and Arthur E. Shirey, Ph.D., who read the prospectus of the book and offered valuable suggestions at the beginning; and to Mrs. Evelyn Gaskill, MSW, and to Mrs. Ethel Griffith, MSW, of Marriage Council of Denver, who read the completed manuscript and whose competence as marriage counselors sharpened my own emerging conceptions of theory and practice. Attorney Edward Sherman was of much help in clarifying several legal points. To Miss Carol Onsgard and to Mr. Claude Guldner, my thanks for their labor in typing the manuscript. And finally there is one's family. My parents, Catherine and Peter Stewart, offered my sister and me an excellent example of a Christian home. And my wife, Alma, and our children have been a haven in time of discouragement and a profound stimulus, not only to counsel couples and families in distress, but to attempt to bring a book to birth out of the process. Their influence is too great to put in these few words.

It is hoped that this manuscript will be of help to the seminary student and the minister in the field, not to provide answers, but to generate the questioning and questing mood, that they become better "shepherds of souls" with couples and families. If it does that, it will be well worth the while.

CHARLES WILLIAM STEWART

CONTENTS

I. The Minister—A Key Person in Marriage 11

II. The Field of Marriage Counseling 21

III. The Counseling Process 29

IV. The First Interview 41

V. Premarital Counseling—Its Goals 50

VI. Premarital Counseling—Its Structure and Flow .. 60

VII. Marriage Counseling—Its Nature and Goals...... 79

VIII. Estrangement and Reconciliation 94

IX. Divorce and Post-Divorce 114

X. *Family Counseling—Its Nature and Goals* 132

XI. *Family Counseling—Its Structure and Flow* 145

XII. *Group Marriage Counseling* 160

XIII. *A Pastoral Counseling Center* 180

XIV. *Family Life Education in the Church* 190

XV. *Epilogue* 204

APPENDIX 209

SELECTED BIBLIOGRAPHY 211

INDEX 215

I

The Minister—A Key Person in Marriage

WHAT IS HAPPENING TO MARRIAGE?

Never has so large a proportion of the population in the United States been married. It was reported that 3,500,000 men and women in this country were married in the one year 1956. Yet never have the chances for failure in marriage been so great. In that same year (1956) there were 400,000 divorces and annulments, with approximately 100,000 more men deserting their families without benefit of legal arrangement. Before 1850, divorce action was relatively unknown in this country. Some families were abandoned by fathers, but this was not formalized by a legal divorce. In 1946, a post-war year, between one third and one fourth of all marriages contracted ended in divorce. Surveys revealed that in addition, another one fifth or one sixth of all couples living together were living in a state of "psychological divorce"—under the same roof but separated from each other emotionally.[1] In the recent study of marriage by David and Vera Mace, the authors report dourly that half of those married today are living together unhappily.[2]

Though these figures might connote pessimism—and many a minister has used them for a dramatic punch line to a sermon—a closer look reveals the rapidly changing patterns and satisfactions of marriage and the positive as well as negative forces at work. Marriage is in flux—we are moving from a work-centered, paternalistic, inner-directed pattern to a leisure-centered, companionate, outer-directed pattern. The minister, rather than harking back to the good old days when dad was on the throne and could demand work and obedience from his wife and chil-

[1] I am indebted for these figures to James H. S. Bossard. See June 24, 1956, *New York Times Magazine*. Also, Skidmore, *et al., Marriage Consulting*, Ch. 1.

[2] *Marriage, East and West.*

11

dren, needs to be aware of changing family patterns and behaviors and to see the positive values which may accrue from them. More broadly, the church, without surrendering the centralities of its gospel, can emphasize what needs to be conserved while recognizing what needs to be changed in the light of the emergence of a new social system.

With this flexible, yet faithful, approach let us consider some of the current changes in the American couple and family.

1. The family is mobile both socially and geographically. Though Vance Packard has overstated the case for status in *The Status Seekers*, he has put his finger on class distinctions which most equality-loving Americans do not like to admit. Middle-class white Protestant families are motivated to better themselves. This involves moving to a "good neighborhood," putting their children into the "best schools," and going to the "right church." It may involve dad's quitting his job and moving the family to a new community where he gets a job with greater opportunity (i.e., a chance to move to a larger income bracket). This social and geographical mobility, a mark of an industrial organizational society, makes for ambition and wanting the best for one's family, but it also makes for a sense of "rootlessness and insecurity." Many Americans move away from their parents and parental homes and except for annual visits are "familyless." This sparse kinship system militates against stable marriages and depth of family feeling, while putting couples completely on their own early in marriage with little backing from their own parents.

2. Men and women in America are striving to live on equal terms. The male and female roles are in a fluid state in mid-twentieth century. In traditional cultures where roles are established and stable, a man learns the male role fairly simply from his father, as a woman does from her mother. But since the passing of the Nineteenth Amendment in 1920, women have been released from a servile role to take their place alongside men in business, industry, politics, and the professions. Women have been confused at times, wondering if this new freedom meant they were to dress, smoke, and drink like men, and give up childbearing and homemaking. Men have fought back but found their domain growing narrower and narrower, and finally sought retreat at male clubs and the golf course. The masculinized woman and the effeminate man are parodies of equality. The goal of being a companion and helpmate to

her husband has appeared more possible to the liberated woman, as has the possibility of being a real husband and father appeared to the man. These patterns are not learned from parents, however, but must be worked out in the give-and-take of the immediate generation.[3]

3. A new leisure is offering families opportunity to be together. With the coming of the seven-hour workday and the four-day work week, Americans are faced with leisure time as was formerly available only to the very wealthy. This time can be misused for poor pursuits, rather than building healthy marriages and families with positive orientations. Reuel Denney points out that it is the middle class's pressure for bigger and better superhighways, on which larger, more powerful automobiles may be driven, that moves the government to spend tax money there rather than for art galleries, libraries, and university scholarships.[4] Mass-produced hobbies or commercialized recreation run second best to family use of leisure, which helps ease tensions and produces greater understanding and harmony. Reading, listening to music, and conversation can help develop the individual as well as increase the family's enjoyment of living.

4. The loss of authority by parents has led to a feeling of uncertainty in dealing with children, and makes it difficult for youth to find adequate standards of conduct. The shock which Western culture has undergone has been not a surface tremor, but an earthquake which has shaken the foundations of institutions. The parents' right and duty to say "Thou shalt not" is one of the institutions which has been shaken, but so has the church's authority to preach and absolve. Take the publication of the Kinsey reports as one vortex of the moral maelstrom. Parents realize that many young people have sexual experience of all sorts before marriage. How should they react to their children? Should they keep them from dating or going out unchaperoned? No, the young people are prone to put pressure on mother and dad to do what their contemporaries do. Parents must capitulate, but their teen-agers still want guidance in interpersonal behavior and many parents fail to perceive this point. As one psychiatrist said, "These kids can engage in intercourse, but they can't love." Youth are frank about sexual talk, but they need guidance

[3] M. F. A. Montague, "Marriage, A Cultural Perspective," in V. W. Eisenstein, *Neurotic Interaction in Marriage.*
[4] "Individualism and the New Leisure," *Esquire*, L, 4 (1958), 78.

in the intimate give-and-take of relations with the opposite sex. But many parents are uncertain as to their own values in this realm, let alone their capacity to communicate them to their youth. Both youth and parents need opportunity to work out common understanding at this point.[5]

5. There is a quest for meaning on the part of youth, couples, and families in the face of a turbulent, even dangerous, world. While recognizing the ostrich-like run for security in the trend of many back to the church, the honest critic of culture must also admit that a genuine quest for meaning motivates some. This is not the search for "pie in the sky" of former days nor "piousity on the fly" of some today. A search for a depth in oneself and of a genuine sharing of one's life at the level of meaning moves the searcher. The rise of personal groups within churches in America and in Europe is demonstration of the fact that many Christians today are not satisfied with worship "en masse" nor "punch and cookie conviviality," but want to merge their lives with a God of meaning and a religious community in which they share their lives at a level of spiritual quest. In marriage and family living this kind of quest is going on, as we shall cite in a later chapter, and it appears to be a good omen.

Sociologists see these trends within the American family as indicating both disorganizing and reorganizing forces.[6] In the nineteenth century the traditional functions of the rural family were to produce a living on the farm, to confer status upon its members, to reproduce itself, to educate the children in the skills necessary to make a living, and to provide physical and emotional security to its members. Most of these functions have been lost with the rise of an urban industrial society. The husband and father's occupation has been in the factory or business; he has derived his status from his job and this has been passed on to the dependent members of the household. Children have been thought of not as additions to the work group on the farm, but as providing emotional satisfactions to their parents. The education and socialization of the child has moved outside the family to be taken up by school, church,

[5] Ernest Burgess, "Address to American Orthopsychiatric Association," in *Readings in Marriage and the Family*, ed. J. T. Landis and M. G. Landis (Englewood Cliffs, N. J.: Prentice-Hall, 1952), pp. 21 ff.
[6] Robert Winch, *The Modern Family*

peer group, and television. The function of providing emotional security, however, has increased in importance. In an increasingly complex and competitive society, the father and working mother have felt isolated and looked to the home to provide them with love, acceptance, and esteem. Therefore, the urban and suburban family has been thrust back upon itself to find meanings and purposes for living. The centripetal forces tearing at the bonds of family life have forced husbands and wives, parents and children to find security in their own relationships. With these demands upon each member to give of himself, to meet expectations of other members, and to satisfy needs for companionship and meaningful group participation, some marriages and families have not been strong enough to stand the stress. Others, however, have not only met the needs of its members but are charting new courses for the democratic family life of tomorrow. To say that the family is in flux, then, does not connote pessimism necessarily; it may merely reflect the dynamic changing character of marriage and the family of today and show the challenge facing us in the period ahead.

A BEGINNING CASE[7]

Let us now turn to a beginning case of marital difficulty as it confronts the modern minister. In the details of the problem the reader may become identified and see from the beginning the central position the minister occupies in marriage and family relations. We shall return to the case in Chapter II and use it as illustrative material for our study.

Larry, twenty-one, a college junior, and Priscilla, nineteen, a freshman, come to the pastor at the end of a church youth camp. They have been stimulated by the intellectual and devotional atmosphere of the camp, and want to talk about their religious position. The counselor notes, however, that there is something personal at the back of their theological inquiry, and he has a memory that Larry has been going steady with Cora, another girl aged nineteen, throughout the year.

[7] It should be noted that the case studies in this book are drawn from middle-class Protestant urban families. There will be variations of marriage and family patterns from other classes, ethnic groups, and geographic locations. However, the principles of counseling are a constant factor in the work.

When Larry and Priscilla settle down to talk about themselves, they ask for individual conferences back at the church. Priscilla tells that she is in love with Larry but that there is an obstacle to their being engaged. She says she is married to another boy, John, an ex-Marine, who lives near her. They have eloped to another state without her parents' consent; however, she reports they have never consummated their marriage but live at their separate homes as before, so she can go on to school. Priscilla says she now sees the error of her ways but that she loves Larry, who is more of her religious persuasion and the type of man she would like for a husband.

Larry comes in the next hour to tell the counselor his side of the story. It seems he and Cora have been going together for a year, and that at Christmas—it is now June—they had sexual relations and Cora became pregnant. He realizes now that though Cora wants to get married, he does not love her but loves Priscilla. He wonders what he can do in this desperate spot in which he finds himself. Will the counselor see Cora and try to make her see he does not love her, and that it would be foolish to marry?

When the counselor goes home, he is called on the phone by Cora, who explains that she loves Larry and wants desperately to marry him. Will the counselor get him to accept his obligation? Phone calls come too from Cora's mother, who is upset by the news of Cora's pregnancy, and from Priscilla's mother, who now knows of the elopement and wonders what she should do with the situation.

The counselor is in the middle of a network of stresses coming from three young people and from the mothers of two of them. What is he to say and what is he to do? Though this situation may seem extreme, it actually happened. It may not be duplicated, perhaps, but other situations just as complicated will come to the minister-counselor's door. How will he handle them? What will be the focus of his counseling and the thrust of his helping operations?

THE KEY POSITION OF THE MINISTER

That these young people came to the minister tells us something about his focal place in marriage. Traditionally, the minister, priest, and rabbi have married the majority of persons. Though with the separation of church and state it is possible to be married by the justice of the peace or the judge, the majority of young people when questioned about who will perform their marriage think of a minister. Sometimes individuals who have been married by a civil officer and have had the marriage fail come to the church for the second marriage with a wistful quest for "stability in this one."

How will the minister handle the couples who come to him for help? The minister has something unique to offer as a marriage counselor. He touches the marriage and the family at a particular place and in a particular way. Over twenty years ago Dr. Leland Foster Wood pioneered in the Department of the Family in the Federal Council of Churches. Said he, "The growth of interest in educational and spiritual preparation of young people for marriage, of which pre-marital counseling is a part, constitutes one of the most striking developments in our time." [8] In the decades following, Roy Burkhart, David Mace, Granger Westberg, Seward Hiltner, Wayne Oates, J. C. Wynn, and others have continued the frontier study of marriage counseling from the minister's frame of reference.

Today, with the tremendous activity in the area of marriage counseling, the pastor needs to see this aspect of his work from fresh perspective. Rather than being seen as just an additional job, his association with marriages and families can be seen as a central orientation, that is, to give guidance to his total task of shepherding.[9] He ministers not just to individuals but to families, and he binds kinship groups to a larger family, the church. In this kind of role he has certain advantages and certain disadvantages. Moreover, the way in which he confronts his shepherding task makes a difference in his total impact upon the families of his parish. Let us consider these ideas in closer detail:

A. Advantages

1. The minister can prepare couples for marriage. Social workers invariably covet the opportunity the minister has to counsel couples before marriage. This preparation for marriage is no longer considered icing on the wedding cake but an absolute necessity. Methodist and other denominations take this counseling so seriously as to publish manuals to guide the pastor in this phase of counseling.[10] Later chapters (V and VI) will elaborate on premarital counseling.

2. As pastor to his parishioners, the minister should be close to their

[8] *Pastoral Counseling in Family Relations* (New York: Federal Council of the Churches of Christ in America, 1948), p. 2.

[9] J. C. Wynn, *Pastoral Ministry to Families.*

[10] Henry Bullock, ed., *The Pastor's Manual for Premarital Counseling.*

problems. This is not always so. Earl Koos, in his study of an East Side New York block in 1945, found that in fifty-seven emergencies the priest was consulted twelve times and the clergyman four times, as compared with twenty-nine times for the bartender and thirty-one times for the druggist.[11] Granted that middle-class families might react differently, there is a natural reluctance to consult a professional helper in family problems. With the increase of interest in counseling and psychotherapy some of this reluctance seems to be disappearing, and the pastor who is alert is being consulted about many problems.

3. The minister has access to his families' homes and the parishioners have access to him. The pastor visits in the home, not just in crises as does the social worker, but on friendly visits in normal times. The parishioners feel they "know" their parson because of frequent contact in the church. To see him for counseling is not to start cold but to begin with a person whom they feel they know. This reserve of "rapport" and "good will" is all to the minister's credit when he begins counseling.

4. People look to the minister as a model of a "good man," a Christian, and to his home as an example of Christian family living. The minister's field is the realm of values. He is supposed to know about God, about the way to salvation, about the use of prayer. His relationships with his family are open to view and are looked to for models of meaningful relationships. Dr. Leland Foster Wood says:

> Marriage Counseling is an inescapable function of the pastor since he maintains standards of marriage, administers the sacraments, is called during family crisis . . . and is involved in the attitudes and responsibilities of the members of the family throughout the total life span.[12]

These are to his advantage.

B. Disadvantages

We would not be honest if we did not recognize that the minister has certain disadvantages in the field of marriage counseling.

1. First is his lack of training. The problems are there, as any student pastor in his first parish will be ready to tell you, but the minister is

[11] *Families in Trouble* (New York: King's Crown Press, 1946), p. 86.
[12] "Marriage Counseling and the Ministry," *Marriage and Family Living*, VI (1944), 74.

generally untrained to handle them. In a study of four Oregon communities Wade and Berreman reported only 11 per cent of the Protestant ministers could meet the qualifications of the American Association of Marriage Counselors. (See next chapter for these standards.) This means that nearly 90 per cent of the ministers are performing a function for which they are not qualified.[13]

2. The minister's tendency without training is to judge or reassure. Because the minister preaches from the pulpit, he may try to function the same way in face-to-face relations. He creates a certain moral image in his prophetic role, and the parishioner may hesitate coming to him with a problem for fear of being "preached at" and judged. On the other hand, those who come may want punishment and may be disappointed if the minister does not administer a verbal spanking. These distortions in role image may need correction before counseling can begin.[14]

3. The parishioner may be afraid to shock the minister by the recital of his misdeeds. This is the opposite side of the image of the minister as a good man. Many ministers have had little brush with the "seamy" side of life, and the fear of the parishioner is justified. On the other hand, the minister need not have tasted all the "seven deadly sins" to understand the weakness to which flesh is heir. Again this stereotype of the "holy Joe" may need correction before the minister can adequately function as helper.

4. The minister works with couples and families other than as counselor. He is preacher, priest, organizer, and administrator. In Sunday morning worship, in an adult class, at a board meeting, he meets the parishioner and works with him at other levels. After Sunday morning services, the couple in counseling greet the preacher with embarassment. He knows certain things about them, and it is not the same as last Sunday. Too, he may be working in an administrative way with an adolescent on the youth fellowship cabinet and also seeing him in counseling. Feelings get mixed up with plans for the church as a whole, and this should be recognized.[15]

As a point of orientation, the minister can ask himself: What kind

[13] Quoted in Skidmore, *et al., Marriage Consulting,* p. 68.
[14] A. Tingue, "The Minister's Role in Marriage Preparation," *Marriage and Family Living,* XX (1958), 11-17.
[15] Wayne Oates, "The Pastor as Marriage Counselor," *Marriage and Family Living,* XVII (1955), 62-67.

of person am I? Am I trying to enact the role of "father" with my parishioners? Do I think of them as children who must be controlled, told the "right way" to do things, punished when they wander from the path, and in general kept dependent? Or am I attempting to function as a democratic guide to the people of the parish? Do I think of them as growing, emerging personalities who engage in some childish behavior but in general have infinite possibilities to become mature people? Do I see their families as experiments in democratic companionate living which I can help in growth? In the latter case, it is not distressing to see independence develop, whether in counseling or other parish relationships. Rather it is a sign of growth in Christian thinking and living.

The role of the minister is up for intelligent scrutiny and review.[16] In thinking of marriage counseling as one specialized function of the pastoral task, we shall be concerned not just with techniques and skills; rather we shall be interested in encouraging the student in seminary as well as the parish minister to take a closer look at himself in his understanding of his personality, of his own marriage—if he has taken unto himself a wife, and of his family—if children have blessed him. Further, at each step of the way the minister should examine his motivation for helping. Is it perverse curiosity about others' sex lives? Is it prudish desire to control or to manipulate people? Is it feelings of wanting to work out one's own problems by counseling? [17] "Physician, heal thyself" may still be said to the clergyman whose own neuroses block his helping operations. It is better not to counsel than to be of harm to the client. This is a primary axiom of counseling.

In the following pages it is posited that the beginning counseling of the student will be supervised, either by a teacher, another counselor, or another minister. The errors of investing parishioners with the distortion of one's own problems will be diminished the more supervision is possible. The other helping professions do not allow counseling in the realm of marriage without supervision. The ministry to be competent and qualified must rise to this professional level.

[16] H. R. Niebuhr, *The Purpose of the Church and Its Ministry* (New York: Harper & Bros., 1956).

[17] For an excellent discussion of this point, see R. Ekstein and R. S. Wallenstein, *The Teaching and Learning of Psychotherapy* (New York: Basic Books, Inc., 1958), ch. 9.

20

II

The Field of Marriage Counseling

WHAT IS MARRIAGE COUNSELING?

Before one gets very far in the field, he becomes aware of the complexity of marriage counseling. Many counselors are involved in the business of helping couples and families; many kinds of help are being offered to marriage partners and family members, and the common designation may be "marriage counseling." Is there any way to set up some guideposts before we embark on our journey so that we may not get lost in a jungle of terms? Is there direction so that we do not go down wrong pathways in our seeking to learn the structure and function of counseling in marriage?

Perhaps the best beginning would be to answer the question "What is marriage counseling?" Here is a preliminary definition: *Marriage counseling is a process in which a counselor helps persons, couples, or families to make plans and to solve problems in the area of courtship, marriage, and family relations*. It is a phase of the general sphere of counseling; however, the problems dealt with are in the area of relationships surrounding marriage and the family. The area is divided generally into three divisions: (1) premarital counseling, (2) marriage counseling, and (3) family counseling. In premarital counseling one deals with the engaged couple before marriage; in marriage counseling one deals with the married couple; in family counseling one deals with the father and/or mother and their children. Family counseling may also deal with in-laws or grandparents, so that several generations of a family may be seen. The entire field may be designated marriage counseling since marriage is the focus of the helping operation. In premarital counseling one deals with the families of both partners. In marriage counseling one may also talk about the family out of which both partners have come, as well as the feelings they have about establishing a family. And in family counseling the kinship patterns of wife, husband, and siblings make of the therapy a series of multiple relationships which must be understood.

WORKERS IN THE FIELD

Let us return to Larry, Priscilla, and Cora, whose predicament engaged us in the first chapter. They surely need help you say. But to whom shall they turn? What will be the nature of the help offered them in each case? And what specific function can and should a "religious helper" perform for them? Answering these questions may point out the specific workers in the field of marriage counseling, as well as showing the kind of help each worker offers to the clients who come to him.

Suppose Larry takes Cora to a physician. He can expect the general practitioner to examine her, to give her a pregnancy test if there be any doubt that she is "with child," and to question her in order to get a symptomatic picture of her condition. This is counseling, surely, for the physician has a certain manner which he brings to his task, and he may reassure or fail to calm Cora's fears, depending on his manner. Information is being sought primarily at this point by Larry and Cora; later they may seek further medical help during the pregnancy, the birth, and the pediatric care of the child. Other medical problems which may bring them to the physician or his ancillary helper the nurse are: the methods of birth control; the incapacity to have children; physical matters which prevent them from being healthy persons, let alone adequate partners.

Suppose Larry and Cora seek out a social worker at the city's Family and Children's Service. They are fully conscious of Cora's pregnancy now, and they want to know what steps to take before the baby arrives. The social worker has certain knowledge of homes for unwed mothers, such as the Florence Crittenton Homes, to which she can help Cora find access. She is also aware of adoption procedures and the steps through which to go in placing the child when it is born. The social worker uses a case work approach, which enables her to get at the dynamics of why Cora and Larry engaged in premarital sexual intercourse, as well as their attitudes toward the child and toward the institution of marriage at this point in their lives. The social worker works with a staff and has the consultative help of other professionals as well as the knowledge of agencies and institutions which can be of greatest help to the couple.

Suppose Larry and Cora see their educational advisor regarding dropping out of college until after the baby is born. It is true that information regarding academic procedure is being sought, but Larry's concern centers also in obtaining a job in order to pay for Cora's having the baby. Cora is concerned about her classmates not discovering that she is pregnant, and so she wants to drop out. Furthermore, she is anxious about whether she will be able to finish school after the baby arrives. The teacher, who may have taught the couple in the education for marriage course, is a logical person to whom they can turn. He knows he is involved in the counseling process when he deals not just with the academic problem but with the feelings which color the adjustment which will have to be made.

Suppose Larry becomes so distraught over his predicament that he is losing sleep and worrying so that he cannot keep a meal on his stomach. He might seek out a physician skilled in psychosomatic medicine or go to a psychiatrist. He will talk to the psychiatrist, for instance, about his anxiety states and how this situation has aroused them. The therapist will not be satisfied with handling the symptoms but will attempt to get back of the behavior to the basic trends in his personality structure. This might involve him in a treatment process over a considerable length of time, certainly longer than the crisis in which he finds himself at present. The goal of the psychiatrist will be to help Larry, not just with the problem, but with becoming a more mature person, who can choose a wife with his whole self and enter marriage with the capacity to love his wife and his child wholeheartedly.

Or, suppose that Larry and Priscilla seek out a lawyer regarding annulling her marriage to John. They go to the lawyer to gain legal information and to secure legal aid in proceeding to the courts to get the annulment. However, there is also much feeling regarding the steps they are taking, for Priscilla is guilty at having done this without her parents' consent, and Larry is anxious over the situation he is in with Cora. The lawyer may very much be counselor-at-law to them.

However, when this trio sought help they chose a minister whom they knew through intimate contact in a Christian group. The preliminary concern which Larry and Priscilla brought to the pastor was theological and was dealt with on that level. However, when they felt they could confide in him, they unfolded the story presented in·Chaptel I. Why did they come to a minister? Certainly because they were involved in an ethical problem as to how to proceed. But more than that, they each were experiencing guilt at the betrayal of their standards and the disappointment of their parents. Furthermore, they needed to express this sense of guilt and to find some way to obtain forgiveness for the hurt which they had inflicted upon others by their actions. As we pointed out in the last chapter, the minister is in the heart of the marriage and family situation in a parish. And by the nature of his role he will be involved in counseling with couples, children, and families. He takes his place with the other workers in the field as a legitimate member of the marriage counseling team.

THE PROBLEMS

The case of Larry, Priscilla, Cora, and John does not open up all of the problems with which marriage counseling deals, though the reader may feel that not many are left untouched. Just to enumerate them and comment on them briefly may help to give the impression of the nature of the field. Then as we go on to discuss premarital, marriage, and family counseling in later chapters, these problems can be dealt with in fuller detail.

There are first those problems which the couple faces before marriage: dealing with dating from the casual "date" to the going-steady stage; the courtship period with its increasing intimacy and ambivalences; and finally the engagement period when the couple makes the commitment to marry, and their relationship moves beyond the two-group and involves both of their families and the larger community.

Secondly, there are the problems of early marriage, which involve the marital adjustment between man and wife: sexual, interpersonal, and spiritual. The problems of emotional immaturity which the person brings into marriage are magnified as he either accepts or does not accept the responsibilities of his marital role, and these may need dealing with.

Thirdly, there are the problems of family life, which arise when the first child comes into the home, either through birth or adoption. The conception of the child, the carrying of the child during pregnancy, the inability to have children, the nurture of the child from infancy through adolescence, and the education and discipline of the child are the areas in which the problems of relationship between father, mother, and child may form.

Fourthly, there are the problems which center in the rupture of marriage and the family. Extramarital interest in another partner, the desire for freedom from the marriage and/or the family which eventuates in separation or desertion, and the whole area of divorce and remarriage pose some of the more difficult problems which one faces in marriage counseling.

Finally, the problems of the second generation, either in-laws or grandparents, may be brought to the attention of the counselor. In-laws may become "outlaws" to couples when they attempt to extend their parental dominance into a new family and fail to recognize the adult status of their children. Or grandparents may act other than in a "grand" manner when they attempt to prescribe their systems of discipline for their children's children, unasked for and unwanted.

Other problems, like financial difficulties or cruelty of one spouse to another, may be subsumed under one of these categories. They shall be broken down in more detail as we deal with counseling couples or families. Our approach at this point is to show how these problems cluster around a particular phase of marriage or family living, and how couples may go through one phase successfully only to come to another phase of their lives where the problems are different.

INTERPROFESSIONAL CO-OPERATION

The case of the college students should have made the reader aware of the fact that no one counselor is completely adequate or skilled to deal with all of the problems of marriage and family living. In the first place he cannot have studied in all the fields so that he has all the information needed to help the couple. Again, he cannot have prepared himself professionally to pass the bar, become ordained, become licensed as a physician, or certified as a teacher to do all that needs to be done with a couple. One college teacher of education for marriage, rather than obtaining a Ph.D., took one year's training in a medical school, one year's legal training, and one year's training in sociology of marriage and the family beyond his B.D. The Ed.D. and Ph.D. degrees are now being granted in marriage counseling as a comparatively new thing. However, most writers and practitioners of marriage counseling recognize it as a multiprofessional and multidisciplinary approach.[1]

The marriage counselor today needs to work with other professions within a clinic in which the professions of medicine, social work, ministry, law, and education are represented (see Chapter XIII). He needs to relate himself to groups like the National Council on Family Relations, and others in which these various professions are represented and in which the contributions which they have to make to the growing understandings of marriage and the family in the United States may be shared by all. If the minister is seeking further training in marriage counseling, it should not be for the purpose of setting himself up as a lone "expert" in the field in his community, but as one helper among many who can bring a particular strength to the counselor's role, as he works with couples or families in trouble.

The minister should recognize that he is probably a "part-time" marriage counselor, while others are giving full time to the profession. Some ministers today are being employed in larger city churches as full-time counselors. A minister in this position will serve as much time as a social worker dealing with these kinds of problems. But for the majority of ministers working alone in a parish, only part of the working day will be spent counseling with couples and families in difficulty. Such a minister needs to recognize, therefore, the limitations which this sets upon him time-wise and energy-wise. A close working relationship with those from other disciplines and other groups will strengthen the work which he can do in the time which he can allot to marriage counseling.

[1] See Skidmore, *et al., op. cit.* Also *Marriage and Family Living* (Journal).

AN EMERGING PROFESSION WITH STANDARDS

In recent years there has been emerging a new profession to which individuals give full time in marriage councils[2] and for which they receive the designation "marriage counselor." The standards for these persons, as well as for those of other professions who give part time to marriage counseling, have been established by a multiprofessional group: The American Association of Marriage Counselors, founded in 1942. The purpose of this group is "To establish and to maintain professional standards in marriage counseling. This purpose shall be furthered by meetings, clinical sessions, publications, and research in this field."

The group has recognized standards for the following classifications of members:

1. Fellow. A minimum of five years as a Member of the Association and significant contributions to the field of marriage counseling.
2. Member. Recognized professional training and at least two years' experience in marriage counseling in accordance with accepted ethical standards.
3. Associate Member. Professional training in a field related to marriage counseling, or significant contributions to the field.
4. Affiliate in Training. A graduate major in marriage counseling, or from one of accepted professions, who is in training in an accredited Marriage Counseling Service.[3]

Professional ethical standards are becoming of increasing importance to psychologists, for example. Clinical psychologists are working in many states to change the statutes so that nonmedical people passing qualifying committees of psychologists may be licensed to practice psychotherapy. They report that unqualified individuals, forbidden by such laws to list themselves in telephone books as psychologists, are flocking over into the marriage counseling field and so listing themselves. Since the

[2] For example, The Marriage Council of Philadelphia; American Institute of Family Relations, Los Angeles; Menninger Foundation, Marriage Counseling Service, Topeka; Merrill-Palmer Institute of Human Development and Family Life, Detroit; and Marriage Council of Denver.

[3] Write to American Association of Marriage Counselors, 27 Woodcliff Drive, Madison, New Jersey, for specific membership requirements.

27

public has become aware of the field through national mass media, marriage counselors, too, need accrediting bodies and recognition by state laws as professionals, so that innocent people can be protected from the tealeaf readers and quacks. The American Association of Marriage Counselors is the agency to provide such accreditation.

If the theological student or the parish minister is to consider the field of marriage counseling seriously, he should be able to meet the qualifications of other workers in the field. As the field develops from one of lusty childhood to growing adolescence, those who work with marriages and with members of the family will increasingly be asked to meet the standards of such a group as the American Association of Marriage Counselors. Surely the theological student, who works in a clinical setting in a hospital, and the parish minister, who goes beyond his theological education to get additional training at one of the multi-professional marriage counseling training centers, can consider applying for the associate membership in the A.A.M.C. Only 8 per cent of this group at present are clergymen. It is to be hoped as the competency of other professions increases, that the knowledge and skills of the clergyman, so actively engaged with marriage in his parish, will increase in a comparable way.

III

The Counseling Process

One of the peculiar marks of twentieth-century Western culture is the emergence of the professional "listener to people's troubles." Counseling of sorts has been going on since man dwelt in caves, but of a common-sense garden variety of which no one would have thought of making a profession. Professor John McNeill chronicles the history of pastoral care from the prophets in the eighth century B.C. in Israel to the present day.[1] These "cura animorum," at times priests, at times physicians, brought ethical principles and intuitive understanding of individuals to bear on the problems confronting them. But it has remained for the present century—particularly since the epochal work of Sigmund Freud and his followers—to make of counseling a scientific study with a body of principles and techniques. The industrial revolution as well as the scientific movement has brought this to pass. With the increasing tempo of living, the emotional and psychic life of persons has come under increasing stress. The depersonalization brought about by living in cities and working in large organizations has eroded away some of the built-in tension relievers. The mass media of communication have surfeited individuals with entertaining stimuli but left them with little time to communicate with one another. Changing community mores and understandings of the place of husband and wife in society, as well as of what constitutes proper ways of rearing and educating children, have left many confused. Whereas these difficulties might have been talked through in unhurried Victorian days, today the anxious and confused person seeks out a counselor, an "expert" in human relationships, to "listen" to his problems. For many the hour or so a week

[1] John T. McNeill, *A History of the Cure of Souls* (New York: Harper & Bros., 1951).

29

with the professional listener is the only chance that they have to engage another in meaningful conversation.

THE GOALS AND METHODS OF COUNSELING

For purposes of presentation let us characterize counseling in three ways: (1) that which is counselor-centered, (2) that which is client-centered, and (3) that which is centered in the relationships between counselor and client. One immediately should add that these categories are ideal types, and that in the counseling typology breaks down. In the hurly-burly atmosphere of helping another, counselors use procedures from all three types. This means that their counseling procedure is eclectic, that is, it borrows from several methods, depending on the situation. However, for the purposes of presenting counseling approaches, this typology may be helpful.

A. Counselor-centered Counseling

Counselor-centered counseling proceeds on the premise that the client needs information, legal aid, medical care, or advice as to the handling of his affairs and seeks out an "expert" in the area who can help him (see Fig. 1). The counselor is an "authority" in this area and can

Figure 1

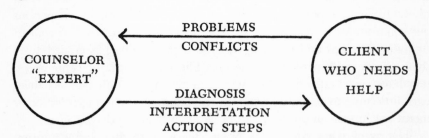

diagnose his case, interpret his life situation, and provide action steps which he can take out of his dilemma. In many cases individuals may legitimately seek such counselor-centered help from the physician, psychiatrist, teacher, lawyer, or social worker. In our highly specialized society we have designated certain areas to certain professions, and if one wants help in that area, he seeks out that professional.

The client may want simply to get "information." "Where can I go to have my baby away from the eyes of the community?" Or, "How can I get an annulment from this marriage, since I don't love this man?" One is immediately aware that these questions are not just intellectual queries but are heavy-laden with feelings. The counselor who has certain knowledge and skill can lend them to the client. But he must also be aware of the feelings of the client and of the meanings of these events to him. The client tends to make of the counselor who answers his questions an authority and develops dependency feelings toward him. This is necessary, as in the instance of the physician who must care for a woman through her pregnancy. His is the responsibility for the health of the mother and the successful birth of the child. When the helping operation depends on the knowledge given and the skills employed by the helper, the focus is properly on the counselor.

But as Robert Kahn and Charles Cannell point out, the general practitioner is becoming aware that the diagnostic interview depends not just on his expert knowledge, but on the patient's ability to communicate his symptoms and his general state of being to the physician.[2] This means in the diagnostic or social history type of interview the use of the question is controlled. The above authors differentiate between a primary question and a secondary question. The former is any question which introduces a new topic or asks for new content. The latter (or probe) is intended to elicit more fully the information already asked for by a primary question. In elaborating this position the authors draw on insights from the client-centered (see next section) group of counselors, pointing out that the accepting and permissive counselor allows the client finally to produce his own answers to the questions he raises, without biasing him through the direction of the interview.[3]

The psychiatrist is most nearly an example of the counselor-centered counselor. One should qualify this to say that the psychiatrist does not advise or judge but establishes a relationship of authority. It should be pointed out also that psychotherapy differs from counseling in that it involves a prolonged period of treatment, from six months to five

[2] *The Dynamics of Interviewing,* pp. 3-5.
[3] *Ibid.,* pp. 205-32.

or more years. And that the goal is a total or partial reorganization of character, the therapist helping the client to work out new patterns of living through systematic analysis and working through of unconscious conflicts. This requires extensive training on the part of the psychotherapist, to enable him accurately to diagnose personality difficulties and to treat them intensively. He is an expert *par excellence* and skilled in working with the neurotic and psychotic individual. We shall deal with the psychiatric concepts and procedures in the course of elaborating "relationship-counseling." But suffice it to say, certain emotional problems fall rightly to the psychiatrist's authority and skill. Furthermore, the "dependency" feelings built up by the client upon such an authority can be skillfully handled by the psychotherapist.

The reader may rightly expect that the minister when he begins counseling may fall into a "counselor-centered" pattern. But unless he has been specially trained—either in law, medicine, social work, or psychiatry—he does not possess the knowledge or the skill to function at this level. "But what of his special knowledge of theology and ethics?" you ask. "Does this not give him some authority?" Certainly, the minister has certain specialized knowledge and is looked upon as an authority in moral and religious realms. "Should I marry Cora?" Larry wanted to know. "I love Priscilla but she is already married. What should I do?" The minister might be expected to answer such questions. But in the realm of values the answers are not of an informative sort. They involve the person's total life commitment, and here the client is the most significant authority. For this reason counseling has generally proceeded on the premise that the individual should become capable of making his own decisions and running his own life. The next two approaches proceed on this premise—where the individual needs more than information, where he needs understanding of himself and his social environment.

B. Client-centered Counseling
The diagram of the counselor-client relationship according to Carl Rogers and his followers is shown in Figure 2.

The client converses about his feelings, attitudes, and values, which *in toto* make up his self-picture, to a receptive listener. The counselor attempts not to diagnose but to understand the frame of reference of the

Figure 2

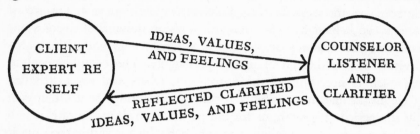

client,[4] and by accepting and reflecting the statements of the client to help him understand himself. Then as he understands himself, the client is helped to accept himself with his strengths and weaknesses, and to choose and set goals which are within the realm of his possibilities. The therapist's intention is to lay aside his own self temporarily in order to empathize completely with the client. Says Carl Rogers:

> I will become . . . another self for you—an alter ego of your own attitudes and feelings—a safe opportunity for you to discern yourself more clearly, to experience yourself more truly and deeply, to choose more significantly.[5]

The client is the "expert" concerning his own feelings, attitudes, and values, and the locus of responsibility for directing his life remains with him. Through counseling he is able to understand his feelings and to integrate his feelings, ideas, and behavior around the kind of person he thinks he is and wants to become. Moreover, he begins to accept responsibility for himself within a psychological climate where the counselor does not attempt to do his planning for him. The presence of an understanding person who is *for* him allows him the opportunity to take stock of himself, to see his life pattern more clearly, and to set out for goals which he both wants and is able to realize.

The client's interior life is the primary focus in this approach, much as it is in psychotherapy. Insight is a goal for the client, although adjustment to certain "givens" within the environment or the client's

[4] See E. Harold Porter, Jr. *An Introduction to Therapeutic Counseling* (Boston: Houghton Mifflin Company, 1950), pp. 1-86.

[5] *Client-Centered Therapy*, p. 35. See also Rogers' *Counseling and Psychotherapy* (Boston: Houghton Mifflin Company, 1942), for his earlier formulation.

personality are allowed for. It needs to be said that certain persons who do not have the capacity for self-determination or have lost it are not able to be helped by this approach. This would include very young children, the mentally retarded, the psychotic (mentally ill), or the severely socio-pathic (delinquent) personality. The counselor-centered approach is necessary in these instances, where the psychiatrist/psychologist assumes responsibility for the client during the acute episode, for the period of growth, or for the period of institutionalization.

Client-centered counseling is an approach which is within the capacity of the minister to learn, and it certainly should be part of his counseling skills. Many ministers have found its "inner release" theory and techniques helpful in dealing with the personal problems of parishioners. However, there are certain limitations in the approach which have come under discussion in recent years.

The client-centered approach is basically centered in the person finding the source of growth and self-orientation entirely within human powers. One must grant that the initiative and motivation for change rests with the client. But one goes on to point out that the "core" of the person is his relationships. He develops his capacity to choose by way of the nurture of his parents in infancy and childhood. Moreover, the decisions he makes involve him in a community of persons whose influence is from the simplest to the most profound. So that when he chooses, he does so according to a scale of values and a frame of orientation. For many people decision-making brings them to the centering truths and goods of religion. As Gordon Allport[6] and others point out, even the person who denies belief in God can be said to have a religion. Client-centered counseling is an excellent technique for personal counseling with individual problems. However, in the area of the values, goals, and beliefs which center in the family it may need to be supplemented by another approach which takes these variables into account.

Particularly is this so for the pastoral counselor. The minister is not just another "listener to people's problems." He comes into the counseling room representing certain "goods" for the client. He is a value-bearer and he cannot escape the role into which he is cast. The client sees him through "God-tinted" glasses; that is, the minister symbolizes what

[6] *The Individual and His Religion* (New York: The Macmillan Company, 1950).

the client understands and feels about God, the Ten Commandments, Jesus Christ, the good life, and the church. If one takes simply the client-centered approach, he misses the complex of feelings, attitudes, and particularly the values which cluster around his representative role. For this reason, we are presenting a third approach: relationship-centered counseling with theory and techniques drawn from psychiatry and social work but adapted to the unique role of the minister.

C. Relationship-centered Counseling

Relationship-counseling is a collaborative relationship between seeker and helper, established in order to understand the seeker's role image and behavior within his social system and to help him to change or adjust the problems of conflict. The counselor transcends individual psychology and counseling in order to explore the dynamics of the relationship between the client and the significant people in his environment. The therapeutic relationship is a microcosm through which the attitudes, feelings, values, and behaviors are seen, understood, experimented with, and perhaps changed for life in the macrocosm-society.[7]

Let us spell this out in more detail. Perhaps the best way is in terms of role definition, role expectation, and role interaction. *A role is an interpersonal relationship within a social system like the family, consisting of an actor or ego, and a social object or alter-ego.*[8] Role expectations are those demands which the actor places upon a social object. A husband expects his wife to "keep" the house, for example. These demands are his "rights" and her "duties." Similarly, the wife expects her husband to bring home a paycheck to finance the marital venture. The role interactions are "those overt actions of each partner . . . oriented to or affected by the personality of the other partner."[9]

It soon becomes evident that the family is a complex of roles: of actors and social objects, held in dynamic tension and propelling the individuals involved into significant action.

[7] See Harry Stack Sullivan's *The Psychiatric Interview;* also Fromm-Reichmann's *Principles of Interview Psychotherapy;* also Patrick Mullahy's *The Study of Interpersonal Relations* (New York: Hermitage House, Inc. 1949), for explanation of this point of view.
[8] Talcott Parsons, *The Social System* (Chicago: The Free Press of Glencoe, Illinois, 1951).
[9] Robert Huntington, "The Personality Interaction Approach to Study of Marital Relationships," *Marriage and Family Living,* XX (1958), 43.

Figure 3

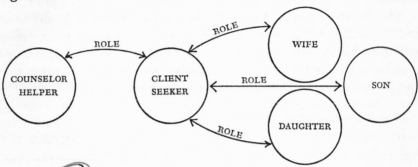

The goals of relationship counseling are: (1) to help the client to understand his role image—that is, his picture of his role—the role expectations of others in his social orbit, and of his role behavior in his present social context, for example, his family; (2) to see the conflict between his role expectations and his actual behavior in the role, both from his own viewpoint and from that of the significant people in his environment; (3) to develop alternative ways of handling himself, and either to change or adjust his role image and behavior. The difference between client-centered and counselor-centered counseling and this approach can be put in this way: the former employs intrapersonal oriented categories (within the person), the latter uses interpersonal oriented categories (between persons). Were a husband to tell a psychiatrist "I hate to put the children to bed," the therapist might respond by saying, "What else do you hate?" The emphasis is on the psychic life of the client. A relationship counselor would respond, "You think it's your wife's job?" and he is immediately involved in role relationship and definition.

Says Marie Kargman, "The emphasis of this approach is on getting the client to make explicit the definition of the role which he is taking as well as his expectations of alter ego, and then to evaluate his definition and his expectations in those areas where he is having marital difficulty, using normative patterns as a frame of reference." [10] The implications are that the counselor provides those normative patterns either verbally

[10] See Marie Kargman, "The Clinical Use of Social System Theory in Marriage Counseling," *Marriage and Family Living*, XIX (1957), 263-69.

in conversation or non-verbally through providing an identification figure.

The concept of role is central, too, in the counseling relationship itself. The seeker role is specific; the person is motivated to talk to an understanding person in order to improve his relationships, whether marriage or family, educational, vocational, or social. He comes to a specific person to talk about his difficulties in interpersonal behavior. He is unable to bear the total responsibility for making his decisions and working through his difficulties. He wants to share this responsibility with another, and the relationship counselor allows this. Together they approach the difficulties and engage in two-way communication, with both counselor and client responding to one another at the level of honest appraisal and search.[11]

What specifically is the counselor's function here? It is in the very beginning to teach the seeking client his role.[12] The client comes to the helper confused, often embittered, about his place in a social system like the family. By structuring the counseling relationship, the helper tells him what is and what is not possible and how they may set goals and proceed toward them together. The counselor is well aware of his own role, that of "professional friend." [13] He is both more and less a friend; he is confidant to the client's distresses, but he is not related to the client socially. His objectivity is nurtured by a professional outlook, while his friendship provides the basis of the relationship.

Tele is the term given by Jacob Moreno for the two-way process of communication of client and counselor. Like the telephone there is a speaker and a receiver in both seeker and helper; the emotional process flows both ways. If the counselor empathizes with the client's feelings and attempts to get into his frame of reference, so also does the client move out toward the counselor. The client may be said to identify with the personal beliefs, standards, and values of the counselor. The counselor not only teaches the client his role in counseling, but also helps the client understand his role in society. Then the helper supports the seeker while he attempts to change his role picture and his role behavior.

[11] Jacob Moreno's term is *tele*. We shall elaborate this concept in further paragraphs. See *Group Psychotherapy* (Journal), 1945.

[12] See Kahn and Cannell, *op. cit.*, p. 62.

[13] John Macmurray's phrase found in Karen Horney's *Are You Considering Psychoanalysis?* (New York: W. W. Norton & Company, Inc., 1946), p. 223.

In this process the counselor is very much aware of what the psychoanalysts call *transference,* a process at the unconscious level. By transference we mean those role behaviors coming out of early childhood which are so much a part of a person that like carbon paper, they make of later human contacts a carbon copy of earlier relationships. "You remind me of someone I used to know." We have all heard this upon meeting a stranger. But when a person is in an intensive relationship like counseling, and he "acts out" feelings, attitudes, and behaviors *as though* the counselor were a parent, brother, or lover, this is transference. The transference of feelings may be a means of helping the counselor to know how the client relates to the significant persons in his circle. He may fall back on earlier integrations of role behavior and approach the counselor as a parent; or, as we shall observe in later chapters, he may be frustrated in his marriage and approach the marriage counselor as a lover or a potential mate.[14] This can be of help in the client's understanding of his role behavior. But as we have indicated, the counselor must be trained to understand these feelings and to handle them, lest he lose objectivity and fail to be of help to the client.

More than once a well-meaning pastor has through his gentle, understanding approach to a distraught wife been subtly placed in a romantic role. Rather than dropping the client, the pastor helps her to understand the unrealistic basis of the infatuation. This may be done in a reflective clarifying way, as a client-centered counselor. But when the pastor helps the woman understand why she "fell in love" with him, he is involving her in "working through" her relationship with her husband and former lovers. The psychotherapist may be concerned with how her relationship with her father enters into her present erotic feelings for her therapist. The pastor, however, can without probing work on an objective plane on the illusionary, unrealistic nature of her romantic feelings. The strength of the pastor's own marriage or, if single, his relationship to women, plus his own religious maturity will enable him to be of real help to such a distraught person without loss of balance.

Because the minister is a symbol of religion, as we have indicated,

[14] See Robert O. Blood, "Transference and Countertransference in Marriage Counseling," *Marriage and Family Living,* XX (1958), p. 373.

the client approaches him differently than other counselors. He represents the centering values of life to the client, values which he has missed, neglected, but in most cases ardently desired. Transference operates where the client distorts the minister into the frock-coated parson whom he has known in his youth—terrible, awesome, and unapproachable. The minister corrects this distortion through the role-teaching aspects of his counseling. But he does not step out of his pastoral role or he distorts the relationship from the other direction. This has been the error of some pastoral counselors who have attempted to be completely neutral toward value in counseling. There is a value dimension, yes, even a God dimension in the relationship of pastor and parishioner which distinguishes it and which provides its strength. The parishioner wants to talk about his ultimate values, about his role, not just in the family, but in the scheme of things, and he can speak of these things only with the minister. The community is important for him, but even so is the "community of God" represented to him by the church at its best. Relating to the pastor brings him into the heart of these meaningful relationships with God and with fellow man. The pastor points beyond himself to those healing resources—worship, prayer, the sacraments, and the fellowship of believers. Not to recognize these realities in the counseling relationship is to miss the most significant aspects of the pastoral-parishioner relationship.

Marriage counseling involves understanding the social system of marriage and the family in order to counsel couples and families effectively. Marriage is a cluster of interpersonal relationships centering in the rights, duties, and expectations which individuals bring to husband, wife, parent and child roles. The minister can most effectively offer a counseling relationship to couples and families. This means he does not *probe* into unconscious personality processes or concern himself with neurotic or psychotic intrapersonal problems. Rather, he handles current interpersonal conflicts which the individual and/or couple have within the context of his marriage or his family. These conflicts are not just on the top of the head, however; they are freighted with feelings and emotions. The minister can help the parishioner within the seeker-helper relationship, and he can do it without forsaking his ministerial role. Rather, he can find the pastoral role has representative strengths which make of his helping operations something unique. To do this, however, the minister cannot operate in blissful though righteous ignorance. He will hurt rather than help persons by applying homiletical or disciplinary measures where counseling is needed. He needs first of all to train with other ministers in a clinical setting; [15] he needs to continue learning by writing up his interviews, keeping case files, obtaining the consultative help of social workers, psychologists, and psychiatrists, and by referring the client promptly when he finds he is of no help to that person. He may even need to obtain some therapeutic help himself before he has the emotional balance and objectivity to be a helping person.

More and more seminarians are unashamedly seeking out psychotherapeutic help during their period of seminary training. The author has counseled scores of theologues who want help with their marriage, and feels it is a good omen. The minister had better "heal himself" and his marriage now before setting himself up as a "healer of souls." What better time is there to do this than in the "years of preparation"?

[15] See training centers listed in Appendix.

IV

The First Interview

One of the best means of learning counseling is to examine in retrospect the verbatim account of an interview in the presence of an experienced and trained supervisor. This is the basic core of clinical pastoral training as carried out in hospitals and institutions. It has become a significant learning device in pastoral counseling courses in theological seminaries.[1] What we propose to do in this chapter is to examine an actual interview to which you, the reader, make the counselor's responses. If you have undergone this experience before, it will be possible for you to evaluate your own responses with some sort of objectivity. If you have not, it is suggested that you have a trained pastoral counselor or other helper to evaluate your responses and to help you understand your counseling attitude and method. This will be "grist for the mill" in improving your counseling techniques. It will further serve as an approach for your continuing study of marriage counseling through actual counseling experience. But first, let us establish the structure of the interview before we encounter "live" material.

THE STRUCTURE OF THE INTERVIEW

Any good counseling manual will delineate the details of counseling procedure.[2] The minister needs to be apprised of these. Because of the complexity of his pastoral role, he calls in the home, he visits in the hospital, and he sees persons at various church and community functions. He, therefore, needs to be aware of when a *counseling situation* exists

---

[1] See David Belgum, *Clinical Training for Pastoral Care* (Philadelphia: Westminster Press, 1956).

[2] See Porter, *op. cit.,* for an excellent example.

and how he should proceed once it exists. If an individual indicates the need to speak of a personal matter at the end of a pastoral visit or at the conclusion of a meeting, the minister does not begin counseling immediately. Rather he establishes with the parishioner that help is available for him at a particular time. In a similar way when the parishioner calls on the telephone, the pastor does not counsel over the phone (even though his line is private, the parishioner's line may not be). This preface to counseling which Seward Hiltner calls "pre-counseling" merely sets the stage for the interview itself.

The interview room should be private, in a place where the parishioner may sit down in a comfortable, relaxed setting. Preferable is an office or a study, if such be available. Barring this, a private room is acceptable. (Some pastors without studies report using a private church-school classroom in which to counsel.) If the parishioner comes to the minister's home, the living room may become the natural scene of the interview. However, if by dint of interruptions from children or telephone the interview suffers, it might be better to change its location immediately or to reschedule it.

The arrangement of the room is important. If the pastor counsels in an office, he may seat himself behind a desk with the counselee's chair located to the side so he can see the pastor comfortably. However, some counselors report this arrangement creates a "desk psychology." The desk is a barrier to forming an empathic relationship with the counselee; and the counselee reacts with the same anxieties as in a "job interview." Two chairs spaced at a reasonable distance and at right angles to one another make a good arrangement. A small table placed between the chairs might prove to be useful. Subdued lighting is best for the room. Glaring lights tend to destroy the feeling of privacy between counselor and counselee.

The time and *frequency* of interviews needs to be determined during the first interview. Most counselors set the limits at fifty minutes to an hour for an individual and ninety minutes for a couple. As we shall note, the parishioner who keeps you beyond this time is gratifying unconscious needs. If the difficulty has built to a crisis for the individual or couple, the pastor may want to schedule a daily interview. However, for the "garden variety" marriage problem once or twice a week is sufficient.

The role of seeker and helper should be defined in the first interview.

This is "structured" by the counselor; it is the base of operation. We dealt in the last chapter with the learning of the seeker's role by the parishioner. It behooves the pastor to begin this teaching immediately in order to make realistic the hopes and goals of the parishioner. Too, he needs to let the parishioner know how he functions as helper, so that the roles of preacher, priest, or administrator are not "transferred" to the counseling relationship.

The fee is established in the first interview, if there is to be a fee at all. With parishioners, the pastor gladly counsels as a part of his pastoral care and no fee enters into the picture. With those outside the church, however, it is more professional to accept a fee. Marriage counselors at present have a sliding scale of fees depending on the income of the couple.[3] And they report that more responsibility is accepted by couples to work on their problem if they pay for the counselor's services. The fee should not be side-stepped by the counselor but discussed freely in the first interview.

Recording the interview is another problem which faces the counselor. The name, address, and telephone number of the person or couple need to be registered at the beginning. If you are fortunate enough to have a secretary, she may do this for you. Normally any other writing distracts one's attention from the client. Some psychotherapists do take notes during the interview. The counselor-centered method may allow for this. The pastor who confronts the parishioner face to face looking him in the eye, may find that writing breaks rapport. One should, however, record the interview immediately after the hour, either verbatim or in outline (see short form at the end of this chapter). Some pastors obtain permission to tape record the interview or they may speak their impressions of the interview immediately into a tape recorder. However it is done, it is absolutely necessary for the counselor to keep records of his interviews.

The *decision about termination or referral* is usually made during or after the first interview. As we shall discuss more fully in later chapters, the pastor should size up the difficulty early so that referral is possible. If he continues with a parishioner overlong, a relationship is built up between them and referral may be next to impossible. The decision about

---

[3] For a current estimate of fees, write The American Association of Marriage Counselors, *op. cit.*

whether he can help the individual or couple is the pastor's to make. The decision about termination is generally worked out by both seeker and helper. For the records, however, the limit for the pastoral counselor may be fifteen to twenty interviews. Anything beyond that becomes psychotherapy, with the complexities and nuances of the "transference relationship" to be worked through.[4]

Confidentiality of what the parishioner tells the pastor may need to be assured in the initial interview. One should not have to remind the clergyman of the "seal of the confessional." The information divulged in the counseling room is private domain; in most states the courts cannot force the clergyman to reveal what a parishioner has told him.[5] On the other side of the coin, he should not "leak" confidences lest he destroy the helping relationship. This means that to publish this material or to use it in any public way requires the permission of the counselee. He should never use case material in sermons no matter how well disguised. This will ruin his counseling effectiveness faster than any other mistake he may make. Professional consultation on restricted material where it is solely for the benefit of the counselee is considered within the bounds of "confidence."

A PASTORAL INTERVIEW[6]

Instructions: In the following first interview, read the counselee's (Mrs. C.'s) statement and respond to it as though you were the pastor. Do not try to make a response in terms of what follows your statement, only what precedes it. Be yourself; only your honest responses will help you to study your style of counseling.

Record of Counseling Interview

Pastor:
Mrs. C: Good morning.
Pastor:
Mrs. C: Very bad. It has been raining hard. Won't you be seated?

[4] For a definition of "transference relationship," see Chapter III.
[5] This point will be elaborated in Chapter IX.
[6] Adapted from Russell Dicks, ed., "Counselor's Workshop," *The Pastor*, February, 1956, p. 20. Used by permission.

Pastor:

Mrs. C: I have something to tell you, but I don't know how to start.

Pastor:

Mrs. C: I have a serious problem. I have just discovered that my husband is being unfaithful to me.

Pastor:

Mrs. C: Yes, he has been unfaithful to me for some time. I am almost sure.

Pastor:

Mrs. C: I am quite sure. I have found lipstick on his clothes.

Pastor:

Mrs. C: I am quite sure it is another woman. I think I know her.

Pastor:

Mrs. C: No, she doesn't live here. She lives in another town where my husband works. I think I even know who the woman is. What do you think I ought to do?

Pastor:

Mrs. C: I don't believe in divorce. I was brought up in the church, and I don't believe in divorce.

Pastor:

Mrs. C: Then what do you think I should do? Do you think that I should go and tell the girl about it and have her stop this?

Pastor:

Mrs. C: Then what do you think that I should do? Should I tell my husband about it? Should I nag him? Should I try to make him admit it? Whenever I mention the subject, he flies in the air, he denies it —and he is high-tempered.

Pastor:

Mrs. C: Quite some time. Indeed, this is not his first affair. He did the same thing a few years ago, and he admitted it, promising not to do it again. And here he starts again.

Pastor:

Mrs. C: It has changed recently. I notice the change.

Pastor:

Mrs. C: I have been taking care of the home all right. I take care of the meals and everything around the house.

Pastor:

Mrs. C: Yes. I do realize that. That may be the reason.

Pastor:

Mrs. C: I doubt it very much. He never went to the church, and when I married him, instead of converting him to my ways and bringing

45

> him to the church, I stayed home with him. I realize that I made a mistake.

Pastor:

Mrs. C: I hope something can be done for him. He needs help.

Pastor:

Mrs. C: My husband does not read books, only magazines and newspapers. He even doesn't want me to read to him from the Bible. He is afraid.

Pastor:

Mrs. C: He doesn't care for any books.

Pastor:

Mrs. C: You don't think that I should confront him with his behavior?

Pastor:

Mrs. C: How then shall I go about it?

Pastor:

Mrs. C: I haven't told him that I was going to speak with you.

Pastor:

Mrs. C: (*sheds a few tears*)

Pastor:

Mrs. C: Goodbye, Pastor. I hope I may see you again.

Pastor:

THE FLOW OF THE INTERVIEW

Now, to understand the dynamics of the first interview let us turn to the sequences and interchange between Mrs. C. and the pastor.

First, there is an *introduction* and an *opening statement*. In this instance the pastor has called in Mrs. C.'s home on a rainy day. She says "good morning." Conventionally she speaks of the weather in the next statement and offers the pastor a seat. Then the real opening statement is made, "I have something to tell you, but I don't know how to start." What does this reveal about her?

It may reveal that Mrs. C. has denied she had a problem up to now. The problem has her confused, perhaps even ashamed. "Should I tell the pastor?" She thinks, "If I do tell him, will the story change his opinion of me or of my husband?" Other possible opening statements by the counselee may question the education and credentials of the counselor, as, "Where did you go to school and are you a psychologist?" Or they may reveal dependency on the counselor as, "I don't really know how to talk about this. Could you tell me how to start?" Or the counselee may intellectualize using psychological or religious terms, as, "If I could only get rid of my inferiority complex, Reverend, I'd· be all right." Or she may project the blame on another at the start, as, "I don't know why I'm here, pastor, it's really my husband who has the problem." Or she may sit in silence clenching and unclenching her fists or weeping.

There follows usually the *initial statement of the problem*. Mrs. C. blurts it right out, "I have just discovered that my husband is unfaithful to me." What does this statement reveal about the parishioner? Certainly it is a broad statement, and it projects the blame for the breakdown of the relationship with her husband upon his "suspected" adultery. As she goes on, the proof appears rather flimsy, but her unrest about his love and loyalty has genuine determinants. Another possible statement of the problem may reveal a covering up of the real problem, as, "We're in good financial shape and have many friends. I don't know why we should be drifting apart." Another may demand of the counselor an evaluation or reassurance, as Mrs. C. does in the following statement, "Then what do you think I should do? Do you think I should go and tell the girl about it and have her stop this?" Or negative and mixed feelings may be expressed, as, "I just don't agree with those ministers who just sit there and expect me to do all the work. Are they dumb or something?" Or medico-psychological complaints may be registered, as, "It's this dizziness I feel when I come into a church meeting. I don't know why I feel this way. Do you think I'm sick or is it just psychological?"

Terminating the interview brings characteristic responses from Mrs. C. Often the real feelings of the counselee do not come out until the separation from the counselor is imminent. What do the tears tell us of Mrs. C.? They may be a request for reassurance from the counselor, or more subtly, a request for more time. A burst of anxiety may be expressed by the counselee, and the pastor wonders, "Dare I let her go?" Other possible closing statements may indirectly ask, "Do I need counseling?" If the counselee has had some difficulty generating initiative to come for help, the closing statement may reveal a desire to close with one talk, as "Thank you, Pastor, you've helped me a great deal." Or there may be subtle resistance expressed by statements like "I don't want to take any more of your precious time." Or, "If you'd only tell me what I should do, I would come back."

What pleases the counselor most is a closing statement which reveals a willingness to work on the problem, as "Well, this has helped me just to get these things off my chest with someone. I'm looking forward to next time."

Now, let's look at your responses as the counselor. How did you react to Mrs. C.? Characteristically, no doubt! But what do your responses indicate regarding your style of counseling. Look at the exercise objectively (or if another counselor-supervisor evaluates the interview, he may do this for you). Answer these questions about each response:

1. Did you evaluate the counselee's statement?[7] That is, did you judge the relative goodness, appropriateness, effectiveness, or rightness of the behavior or attitude expressed? For example, when Mrs. C. questioned you about her possible course of action, did you tell her your evaluation of the situation?

2. Did you interpret the situation to the counselee? That is, did you teach her or show her the church's position, or your theological or psychological understanding of matters? For instance, Mrs. C.'s statement about divorce may have elicited your interpreting your church's stand on divorce, or your interpretation of marriage.

3. Did you support the counselee? That is, did you reassure her, attempt to reduce the intensity of her feeling or to pacify her? The weeping of Mrs. C. at the end may have called for reassurance from you. The subtle implication of this response is "There, there, things aren't as bad as you've made out," which denies her feelings, and this without your finding out the facts of the case.

4. Did you probe into the counselee's problem? By interrogation did you seek certain information, provoke discussion along a certain line, or try to uncover hidden implications? The mention of "lipstick on his clothes" may have moved you to ask, "How did you know this wasn't yours?" The probe may put the counselor in the pose of the authority who, once he has all the facts, can solve the problem himself. It may also uncover feelings faster than the counselee wants to express them, unless the counselor knows how to proceed.

5. Did you understand the counselee's expression of fact, feeling, and value? That is, did you help clarify the statements made and let her

[7] I am using the categories suggested by Porter, *op. cit.*, p. 201.

know that you perceived her situation as she told of it? Such a response you may have made at the beginning. When she said, "I have something to tell you, but I don't know how to start," you could show your understanding by responding, "Something is upsetting you, but you don't know how to begin."

Moreover, you may examine the interview for structure. Did you let her know what you have to offer in counseling? Did you invite her to come back? How will her husband know of your accessibility if you plan to see him?

Let this exercise be a sample of the kind of verbatim writing you may do of not just the first interview, but of each interview. Furthermore, the practice of evaluating each interview, using the above questions, may be a means of helping you perceive your counseling mistakes and help you to develop more "understanding" responses. After you have gained the benefit from verbatim interview evaluation, you may want to use a short form, such as follows:

Marriage Counseling Short Form
Interview Summary

Name _____ Address _____

Counselor _____ Date _____ Int. No. _____

Nature of Request (Presenting concern; previous counseling; goals)
Developing Situation (Focal anxieties; history; efforts)
Counselor's Appraisal (Appearance; tensions; health; resources)
Counseling Procedure (Role of each; plans; objectives)
Questions to consider (Needs indicated; perplexities; hypothesis)
Reasons for terminating:
           Referred to agency, institution, other
           Terminated by person
           Terminated by mutual consent
Evaluation at termination

V

Premarital Counseling—Its Goals

One of the delightful accounts in that deeply human book by Hartzell Spence, *One Foot In Heaven,* deals with the difference between Brother Spence's two-dollar and five-dollar weddings.

His two-dollar patter began like this: "Be careful how you answer these questions, young lady. It's perjury to falsify your age on a marriage record." His five-dollar opening was: "Come in, come in. So you want to get married. Well, young man, I don't blame you. You're wise to get a ring on this young lady's finger before someone else does." Then turning to the bride: "I'll bet it took some tall talking to get *you* on the dotted line." [1]

Words of advice and friendly, fatherly reassurance have long been stock-in-trade with the marrying pastor. Today, however, these sessions before marriage are being seen by the minister as a precious opportunity to help the couple face marriage with more insight and awareness of its values, both interpersonal and religious. Of course, it is fortunate if the couple has been a part of the family life education program of the church (see Chapter XIV). Then they need merely to pull together their previous learning and to "see" themselves within the social system of marriage. However, even if the couple are complete strangers to the pastor, he need not feel the days preceding marriage are too few to accomplish something of purpose with the couple.

THE GOALS OF PREMARITAL INTERVIEWS

What are the goals of the interviews which the minister arranges with the couple? If the goals are seen clearly, he can proceed with more

[1] (New York: Whittlesey House, 1940), p. 257.

confidence in the counseling itself. First, the minister arranges the procedural details regarding the wedding ceremony. Often this is all the couple wants from the interview: "Can we be married June 1? Can we use the chapel for the ceremony? Can we hire the parish hall for the reception? And will it be all right to have the rehearsal the night before at eight-thirty?" Even if the minister can answer "yes" to all these questions, as a civil servant with obligations to the state, he must ask certain questions of the couple regarding their age, their family's consent if one or both are under age, and their knowledge of the state's requirements for marriage, namely: the blood test, license, and waiting period.

Second, the minister uses the interview to make an appraisal of the couple. He has an obligation to his church and to the community not to take lightly his duties as one who "unites couples in marriage." He must appraise the emotional maturity—a basis for readiness for marriage—of the man and woman. Too, he must measure, so far as possible, the compatibility between these two highly complex personalities. This is no small order for these interviews, but it is uppermost in the counseling pastor's mind.

Third, the minister provides the couple with specific information with regard to the physical, economic, psychosocial, and religious sides of marriage. Though educational opportunity has expanded for the present generation, many young people have not been educated for marriage. Snips of knowledge from parents, conversation with boy friends and girl friends, and cursory reading are their only background. The need to fill in the gaps and to synthesize their information into a working whole provides a tremendous opportunity for the counseling pastor in these interviews.

Moreover, the pastor needs to relate the couple to a living Christian tradition and this can best be done in a face-to-face relationship. The meaning of faith to them, particularly at this critical stage of their life, needs discussion and will be gladly talked about by most couples. Too, their relationship to the church, symbolized by their being married in the sanctuary, becomes focused anew. Though marriage is not one of the sacraments of Protestant churches it is perhaps the most important rite, and the couple becomes aware of this through a perceptive pastoral counselor.

Finally, the minister opens up areas of interpersonal interaction be tween the man and woman which may be fruitfully explored before marriage. John and Mary feel that they are very much in love, so much so that they are willing to build their lives together from this moment. The marrying pastor is thankful for their love and their faith in one another. But realistically, he knows the marriage will be made or broken depending on their adjustment to the strengths and weaknesses of each other and the way they accept or reject the roles of husband and wife, father and mother. These interactions can be observed, brought into the light, and discussed with the couple before the ceremony in a way that will make the marital adjustment much easier. This does not say that the couple will not have quarrels and difficulties. But the pattern for frank discussion is established and may bring them back to the minister after marriage for further counseling.

THE TEACHING ASPECT OF PREMARITAL INTERVIEWS

In one sense premarital counseling is not really counseling; it is teaching. A lively discussion was conducted in the journal *Pastoral Psychology*[2] dealing with whether the counselor could be client-centered (Rogerian) in the premarital interviews. We are taking the position that the minister is dealing here with the education of a couple regarding marriage and family relations and not with specific problems as in personal counseling. The couple come to the pastor oriented to an event—the wedding—and a relationship—their marriage—and not to a problem. If one waits for them to bring up a problem, he may get nowhere with the couple. They may sit entranced with one another and forget the pastor is even in the room!

The couple has some understanding about marriage, gathered from many sources as we have indicated. But they are ignorant of some other areas which they will face in marriage. The counseling minister does not take too much for granted; for example the daughter of a nurse may have only a superficial understanding of the sexual side of marriage. When emotional attitudes are involved, the "nurse" mother may have feared to teach her daughter adequately. The couple have need of a

[2] See Seward Hiltner, Ed., "Consultation Clinic," *Pastoral Psychology*, II (1952), 52-58.

teacher and guide .to lead them out in exploration of the marriage relationship.

Anxiety is present in both the man and the woman as they face such a conversation. But the couple is also highly motivated to learn. After the initial "fear of the unknown" and of revealing their most intimate feelings, desires, .and goals to a "stranger," the couple launch out into the conversations with enthusiasm and seriousness. The minister's role here is not to act as an "authority," but as a catalyst or "midwife," to help the couple open up the areas of marriage so as to explore them fully. With such an empathic and helpful guide they can continue to grow into the marriage relationship.

Such teaching by the pastor is person-centered, but he need not wait on the couple to bring up an area for discussion. The question and answer approach is well suited to this kind of teaching, with the minister using the answer as a means of going further into the subject to be explored. For example, the pastor may ask the question:

P: How did you two meet?
John: Oh, we met at a dance at high school, Pastor. I took another girl; but when I met Mary, I gave her a rush and danced most of the other dances with her.
P: You really were attracted at first sight, then?

The pastor may reflect feelings and clarify statements in this way, but he is not hesitant to direct the conversation into areas which by his experience he knows need to be explored. A word of caution needs to be said, however, about prying or moving too rapidly, especially with a strange couple. Rapport needs first to be established so that the couple feel they can trust you as their minister with certain highly personal information. The entire first session may be spent establishing such rapport.

SCREENING ASPECT OF PREMARITAL INTERVIEWS

Are there any couples which you as a minister refuse to marry? And if you do, how do you determine their fitness or unfitness? It is true most churches have canon laws, disciplines, or rules of order, and these give general guidance. But the specific case often puzzles the pastor, and he is confused and bewildered after the first statement by the couple as to how to proceed. Oftentimes he says in a rationalizing way, "If I don't marry them the justice of the peace will. What difference does my refusing them make?" Lest the Protestant pastor continue to merit the "Marryin' Sam" epithet, it behooves him to have an adequate screening technique.

The best screening device is to establish a pattern of premarital counseling. The fact that each couple is required to sit down with the minister and seriously face the decision to marry gets to be known throughout the community. If strangers appear at the door of the pastor's home, they can be soon appraised of his standards regarding premarital counseling. If the couple is not willing to sit down with the minister to talk unhurriedly, they disqualify themselves from his services. This tends to eliminate those who are eloping, either from the community or a distant place, those who are under the influence of alcohol, and those who are under duress. If the woman, for instance, is being forced into the marriage, the man will hesitate to have her talk to the minister at any length. Her arm may become "untwisted" when she leaves his side for any time.

Other couples which the minister may discern as poor marriage risks after a few moment's conversation are those who represent a wide chronological age difference. Many writers say the maximum age difference should not exceed ten to twelve years. However, the emotional-mental age of both may compensate somewhat for their difference in years. A wide gap in education, as a college educated man and a woman with grammar school training, may make a poor risk. However, if the woman has educated herself and learned a great deal from experience, this may be compensated. The psychopathic personality, the sexual deviant, the former mental patient, the drug addict or seriously alcoholic person may on the face of things be considered a poor marriage risk. This may be learned often with psychological examination and the pastor may then make his decision regarding performing the ceremony.

Another screening device is insight on the part of the couple. The minister does not use legal or ecclesiastical standards alone, but professional ethical ones. He helps the Protestant man and the Catholic woman face up to some of the issues involved in a mixed marriage (these issues we shall deal with in detail in Chapter VI). He helps the young people under legal age to face some of the serious issues of being married when neither have finished high school and the man does not have a secure job. He helps the couple, both of whom have been married before, face some of the issues of adjustment to be confronted in a second marriage. Many couples, though they have defended themselves against such issues, are relieved to bring them out into the open to discuss with an understanding guide. The minister need not decline to marry the couple; he may simply ask them to delay the marriage until they have discussed more completely the problems facing them. Or, in the case of the youthful marriage the postponement may be until one or both have finished the school year, or the young man has a better paying job.

The third screening device is testing. If the minister fears emotional instability, feeblemindedness, or marked incompatibility between the individuals, he can ask them to undergo testing before continuing the counseling. All tests require psychological training to administer and to interpret. If the minister wishes to become competent in this area, he will need to learn this function in a graduate school of psychology, which offers such training. Otherwise, he will need to depend entirely upon a psychologist to test his parishioners. When the minister uses these tests, he does not test merely for curiosity's sake, but to learn something of the individuals which will help him in his counseling. It should be stated that in the case of mental deficiency or suspected psychosis, the clergyman should refer the person to a psychologist, psychiatrist, or psychiatric social worker to substantiate his suspicions. To marry such persons is to risk not only the happiness of the couple, but in the case of organic mental deficiency or mental illness, the hereditary possibilities of children born of the union.

THE USE OF TESTS

The way in which a psychological test may be used with the couple, that is, its timing and interpretation, will be discussed in the next chapter. What we are interested in now is the choice of a test, and the factors which it might be called on to test. There are basically three factors which one might test for in premarital interviews: (1) sexual knowledge, (2) compatibility, and (3) personality. The sex-knowledge inventories are devised to determine the person's basic knowledge in the sexual sphere; they get at attitudes and feelings indirectly, if at all. The compatibility tests are constructed to determine the similarity and differences between the man and woman to be married. The personality tests are devised to test the personality and temperament of the individuals approaching union.

There are two sex-knowledge inventories, designated Form X and Form Y and published by Family Life Publications.[3] Form Y has forty-eight questions in the area of vocabulary and anatomy of sex. Form X has eighty questions in thirteen areas: general knowledge; sex-act techniques; the hymen; possible causes of poor sexual adjustment; sex dreams; birth control; sterilization and circumcision; menstruation; conception; pregnancy; childbirth; superstitions; masturbation; venereal diseases; and the effect of menopause on sexual life. These tests have been devised to determine ignorance in the sexual sphere, and are better used in classroom situations than in counseling. The focus of the premarital interview is upon attitudes and feelings rather than facts. Were the pastor to use the inventory as a crutch, it could come between him and the counselees. The man or woman with neurotic attitudes regarding sex could get a perfect score on the test and be able to hide behind his knowledge of the "facts." For these reasons, in intimate matters of the sexual relationship it is better to enter gently at the couple's invitation, rather than forcing entrance by means of a test.

Experience also shows that the couple talks more freely with the physician regarding their sexual organs, the positions taken during intercourse, and the physical means of contraception. They will talk with the pastor about their attitudes and feelings regarding the sexual relationship. If there is guilt surrounding premarital relations or masturbation, or fear about entering this phase of marriage, this may be brought to the fore by one or both partners. In discussing birth control the pastor should be able to interpret the Protestant view regarding family planning and its place in the religious perspective. The place of sexual relations in a mature religious life should be possible of discussion as the couple opens up to the topic. In all of this the minister is not pruriently curious nor embarrassed, but free and mature and earnestly desirous to help.

[3] Family Life Publications, Durham, North Carolina.

In determining the compatibility of the couple three tests can be suggested: the Burgess-Cottrell-Wallin Schedule on Marriage Adjustment; the Crane Tests for Husbands and Wives; and Schedule E from the Marriage Council of Philadelphia.[4] Though the Burgess-Cottrell-Wallin Schedule is most complete, Schedule E has enough questions for the average couple. It uncovers feelings regarding engagement, relationship to families, budget, confidence and affection, sexual matters, children, and mutual interests and disagreements. These last items are perhaps nearest to basic likes and dislikes of the members of the wedding, and can be used in counseling sessions. It is recommended by Emily Mudd of Philadelphia that Schedule E be given before marriage in the premarital sessions and three months afterwards in a follow-up interview.

The minister cannot test for the personality factor unless he has been trained in testing procedures or unless he is able to obtain the services of a clinical psychologist to give such tests. The ones simplest to use are the Bernreuter, the Minnesota Multiphasic Inventory, and the Johnson Temperament Analysis.[5] The Bernreuter is perhaps the simplest to give and to score. However, it does not have the reliability of the other two tests. The Minnesota Multiphasic has a higher percentage of reliability and is used by many schools and colleges. The Johnson Temperament Analysis is recommended for use by the American Institute of Family Relations. It is meant to be used in both mate selection and courtship quandaries. It can be given to both man and woman to test themselves; but in addition it can be used as a sociometric tool in a crisscross technique. That is, A tests A; A also tests B; B tests B; B also tests A. In this way each person not only has his own picture of his temperament, but the mirrored impression he gives his intended spouse.

The traits the Johnson Temperament Analysis tries to measure placed in opposite pairs are as follows:

[4] Burgess-Wallin Schedule, Burgess, Ernest W. and Locke, Harvey J., *The Family* (New York: American Book Company, 1945, Appendix C). Crane Tests may be obtained from George Crane, Chicago, Illinois; Schedule E is available from 3828 Locust Street, Philadelphia 4, Pennsylvania.

[5] The Bernreuter may be obtained from Stanford University Press, Stanford California; The Minnesota Multiphasic at 522 Fifth Avenue, New York 18, New York; The Johnson Temperament Analysis, 5916 Hollywood Boulevard, Los Angeles 28, California.

Nervous—Composed
Depressed—Gay-hearted
Active—Quiet
Cordial—Cold
Sympathetic—Hardboiled
Subjective—Objective
Aggressive—Submissive
Critical—Appreciative
Self-mastery—Impulsive

Norms are given in the manual for high school men and women and for adult men and women (1944 edition). It needs to be said that these tests are not valid in themselves but are best used as tools supplementing the interview. Tendencies, attitudes, and propensities discovered in the tests may be fruitfully explored in the face-to-face situation of the premarital interview. The interview is the matrix in which the pastor does his most important work.

THE USE OF BOOKS

In premarital counseling the pastor often gives the couple books on marriage harmony to read and study. Such books are meant to supplement, not take the place of counseling. A moment's reflection on the part of the pastor will cause him to realize how most couples will intend to read such books but will put it off in the flurry of planning for the ceremony. Many such books are packed away in the bag to be taken on the honeymoon and unpacked again, unread, when the couple returns. A better plan is to give the books to the couple at the start of the premarital interviews, and to use them as a basis of the couple's work with you. The Methodist manual, *In Holy Matrimony*,[6] is meant to be used in such manner.

Other established manuals which can be read by the couple at this stage are:

Butterfield, Oliver M. *Sexual Harmony in Marriage*. Chicago: Emerson Books, Inc., 1955. A scientifically sound, well-written book dealing with the sexual side of marriage.

[6] Henry Bullock, ed. (Nashville: The Methodist Publishing House, 1958).

Popenoe, Paul, *Preparing for Marriage*. Los Angeles: American Institute of Family Relations (no date). A short pamphlet which deals with sexual relationships completely and wholesomely.

Wood, Leland Foster. *Harmony in Marriage*. Revised Edition. Los Altos, California: Round Table Press, 1955. One of the parson's standard "gift books," which deals with the many-sided relationships of marriage.

Stone, Abraham and Hannah. *A Marriage Manual*. New York: Simon and Schuster, Inc., 1952. A standard marriage manual by two pioneers in the field. Better as a reference than as a book for couples.

We shall return to the use of books for study in the section on education for marriage (Chapter XIV). In reality the use of such books belongs in a small group of premaritals where teaching and guidance by the minister can take place. Too often ministers have felt embarrassed to talk through feelings about sexual relations and have used a book as a crutch. This embarrassment is surely communicated to the perceptive couple, confirming their doubts about the rightness of sexual relations in the eyes of the church. How much better it is to verbalize these feelings in the counseling session. If the book blocks such free talk, perhaps it is better not to use it with the couple.

In summary we have dealt in this chapter with the goals of the premarital interviews, their teaching and screening aspects, and the use of tests and books by the counseling pastor. But some will say, "What are you to do with the couple who come to you and want to be married that day?" How can you possibly meet such elaborate goals with John and Mary Come-Lately? Surely these goals are formulated on an ideal situation, but wouldn't you agree that some conversation is possible, even if only for an hour before the ceremony? It is heartening in the present-day with the attention of the mass media upon personal and marriage problems, that couples see premarital counseling to be as essential as the bride's bouquet. The question for a minister then becomes not "Will I have time to counsel?" but, "Am I prepared vocationally to do this most important work?"

VI

Premarital Counseling—Its Structure and Flow

The doorbell of the parsonage rings. There standing outside the door are a young man and young woman. The minister knows as soon as he opens the door that they have come on an important call. Excitement shines from their eyes and their love overflows when they exclaim simultaneously, "We'd like to get married, Pastor, and we'd like you to do the honors." This is a supreme moment in their lives, and the minister with any sensitivity to human values recognizes the privilege to be asked to participate in the event of marriage. How he helps the couple prepare to be "united in holy matrimony" will reflect the degree of his concern for them. It may indeed head off later counseling with the couple. For as the veteran marriage counselor Abraham Stone said, "An hour's discussion before marriage may be more valuable than weeks of counseling later, after difficulties have arisen."

We have lifted up the goals of the premarital sessions. Our business now is to determine how these goals can be realized in the structure and flow of the interviews. An actual interview will be reported for the reader to see in detail the implications of this type of counseling.

STRUCTURE

The first questions which the minister asks the couple, after the procedural details about the wedding have been settled, concern their age, their religion if they are strangers, and whether this is a first or second marriage. If this is a youthful marriage (that is, if they are below the legal age of the state in which they reside) parental permission will have to be gotten. If this is an interfaith marriage, the minister may also want to discuss parental attitudes and their solution of this problem before going further in counseling. If one partner has been divorced, the minister may want to discuss this with the couple before proceeding with any further counseling. In any case these situations will likely entail planning additional counseling and will center on these particular facets of their relationship before going on.

We advocate at least three premarital interviews for the normal couple. Exceptions will occur, but it is better for the minister to set some standards upon which to operate, than to govern his counseling solely by the exceptions. If these interviews can be arranged one week apart, this is ideal. Quite simply, they can be arranged as follows:

Interview One
The minister sees each partner separately to discuss their romance, their common interests, their relationships to both families, their understanding of sex, and the planning of family. While one is being seen, the other, if he desires, can take the Schedule E. The couple are asked to see a physician.
Interview Two
The minister sees the couple together to discuss their budget, their planning of a home, and the values by which they live. He asks them to bring in a sample budget as a basis of discussion for this session.
Interview Three
The minister sees the couple together to discuss their interests, how they resolve conflicts, and their adjustment to difficulties. The latter part of the interview is used to discuss the religious side of marriage with the marriage ritual as the focus of discussion.

Any minister who has counseled will be able to suggest adaptations and variations of such a schedule. Rigidity in following this schedule will fail to allow for individual differences among partners and for the unique combination represented in their engagement. Let it simply be said as we elaborate upon such a structure that the practicing parson be aware of this as suggestive. With Bob Brown and Mary Jones he will determine his own timing and sequence as he perceives their unique needs and possibilities which can be productively explored.

FLOW

The first interview is a time for getting acquainted with each person and for establishing a relationship which will enable the counseling to continue within a climate of trust and honest search. The minister can sometimes do this effectively in the first minutes of the interview, merely while getting the details concerning the circumstances of the wedding. A little humor à la Father Spence doesn't hurt a bit at this point. If the minister knows the couple, or feels that rapport has been established, he can proceed to see each person privately for the personal counseling part of the interview. He takes the person to another room while the remaining member takes the Schedule E test inside his office.

In the private interview the minister has an opportunity to discuss issues of an intimate nature that might have proved embarrassing were the couple together. He may use an outline of questions—the reader will remember a question-answer approach is suggested—though it would be hoped that as he gains proficiency in interviewing, the outline would be abandoned. The questions used below have been found helpful to the author in stimulating conversation, but they are only suggestive; each minister should add or subtract questions according to his own discretion.[1]

One can preface his remarks to the individual by saying: "I believe that marriage is more than just reading a ceremony over a couple; it is the blending of two lives. If this is so, the minister who presides at the event should know something of the couple to help this take place. "Mary, I know a little about you from your church experience but not about you and Bob. Tell me, how did you meet and fall in love?"

This question should be enough to get the conversation off and running. The minister without being "nosy" can give the impression of wanting to share in this experience. This should lead to the questions:

When were you engaged? And how are you sure Bob is the right person?

Mary is quite sure—passionately sure. But she tells quite naturally of other boys she has dated. The pastor listens to this recital of "love" and measures it against infatuation, love at first sight, or rebound love. He may inquire:

Have you ever been engaged before?

[1] See Sylvanus Duvall, *Before You Marry*, for over 100 questions. I have used Duvall in some instances but the selection and order are my own. See also Granger Westberg, *Premarital Counseling*, pp. 10-17.

If Mary says "yes" and elaborates on a breakup, the pastor is aware of any bitterness, humiliation, or "carrying the torch" for the past fiancé. He may expand the discussion from love by asking:

Do you have the same interests? What do you do on dates?

He is aware of the "best foot forward" aspect of modern dating, but he also listens to see if the dating pattern has changed any since the couple became engaged. Have they found pleasure in doing little things together and have they developed mutual interests? The discussion may then turn fruitfully to their family.

How do you and your parents get along? Do they both approve of Bob?

The first question gets at some of the basic feelings of security which Mary has developed at home. She may also reveal any overdependence she has on her mother, or rebellion at parents—expressed in leaving home to be married. The second question gives you Mary's impression of whether her future husband will be accepted into her family. The old proverb says:

> A son's a son till he takes him a wife
> A daughter's a daughter all her life.

(See interview at end of chapter for an example of this.) It is important to verbalize these family feelings and to ask:

How do you get along with Bob's parents?

It's fortunate when both parents have communicated their desire to have Bob and Mary set up an independent life together, and have affirmed that they are behind them all the way in the new venture. From the talk about the family which reared her, it is quite natural to speak of the family she plans to establish with Bob. The minister may ask:

How about children? Have you both discussed the matter openly so as to understand the other?

Mary should feel enough rapport by now to talk over these intimate matters. Nervous laughter or evasion should be noticed by the pastor so that he does not proceed too fast. Some persons do not want to talk but superficially here; however, the pastor has an obligation not to side-step so important an issue as the physical relationship. He may go on:

Have you reached an agreement on the size of your family and when you want your first baby?

This should lead quite naturally into talk of planned parenthood, particularly if you ask how they are going about planning their family. The minister does not bear the total responsibility here, so he can ask:

Have you seen your doctor for a physical examination for proper contraceptive material and information? [2]

Let us hope Mary has had qualified training up to this point and can answer "yes." But it has been the author's experience that such a step is furthest from the mind of many who come to the minister to be married. Forty of the fifty states now require a health certificate before a couple is granted a license to marry, and a majority of the states now require serologic testing of at least one partner. However, birth control information is voluntarily given by physicians at the couple's request (except in Massachusetts and Connecticut where this is forbidden by law) and the minister may serve as the eye opener to the advisability of such a step. The male should be examined as well.

From here the minister speaks frankly about the sexual side of marriage with Mary, and is open to any desire to confess premarital sexual experience or any guilt concerning such adventures. Some such questions as these may gently lead such discussion:

Do you understand the purpose of sex in human life? Do you plan to be faithful to Bob in your marriage? How important is sex and sexual compatibility to you in the total marriage relationship?

The minister should emphasize sexual intercourse as a psychological and spiritual union. It serves as a "bridge" across which flows the deepest

[2] See Nadina Kavinoky, M.D., "The Premarital Medical Exam" in Clark E. Vincent, *Readings In Marriage Counseling*, p. 127.

meanings, feelings, and values in a marriage relationship. As such, it is not an end in itself for gratifying desire in marriage; it is not masturbation, but union.[3] From Kinsey's studies it is reported that premarital intercourse in both males and females occurred less frequently in the sample most involved in religious groups. However, sexual adjustment may be poor for these "virgins" until they see sex and enjoy sex as a sacramental means of expressing the deepest communion between a couple. If a minister can be accepting of Mary's statements and without embarassment talk frankly and openly of these intimate matters, he will perform a real service to her at this juncture.

He should not close this session without saying:

Do you have any questions of me?

When the couple are together and both have completed the Schedule E and their initial interview, the minister may want to speak to them both about the visit to a physician. He may want to suggest one if they do not have a family physician. Another suggestion is that they prepare a model budget to use as the basis of the next session's discussion. Some may decline to do this, but this is their option. "How do you feel about making up a model budget for next time?" might be an approach. There is considerable relief expressed by Mary and Bob at being through with their first session, but also a sense of expectancy at going on. "After all, only two more weeks of freedom."

The second interview usually follows one week later. The minister arranges to see the couple together in his office or home. He may speak initially about the progress of their wedding plans, their securing the license, and their visit to the physician. Some couples want to talk further with the pastor about the sexual side of marriage; the doctor may have awakened questions which they want to talk about. Time is allowed for such discussion—this time with the couple together. However, if the couple do not raise these matters, the minister does not question or probe.

The focus of the second interview is the budget. If Bob and Mary have worked out a budget, they may feel quite comfortable in sitting around a table or desk to discuss the various items of the budget. The

[3] See Peter Bertocci, *The Human Venture in Sex, Love, and Marriage.*

financial plan which a couple draws up is a particularly good tool to bring out the values by which the couple plan to live when married. Sometimes these values are hidden or assumed; and this honest talk brings them out in the open where they can be seen and worked through with each other.

The minister is particularly aware of the interpersonal interaction between Bob and Mary. Who takes the lead in talking out the budget? Who is adamant about spending practices? Does Mary think too much is being allowed for the car and not enough for the house? Does Bob talk Mary down concerning the amount needed for entertainment? All of these things are important in detecting the kinds of adjustment they will have to make. Furthermore, the pastor is aware of what pattern Bob and Mary set for the handling of their money. Does one person plan to be the treasurer, allowing the other an allowance? Have they divided responsibility: Mary being responsible for food and household expense, and Bob for car and capital improvements? Do they plan a joint checking account? Will there be a budget committee of two? All of these questions and observations tell you a lot about the division of authority that will take place in the marriage.

The counseling minister may have an outline of questions for this session as he did the first. It becomes easy to ask these spontaneously, however, as he looks over the budget with the couple. He may begin by asking:

How much money should you have before you marry?

Bob may have put a "nest-egg" aside for the day when he contemplates marriage. Mary too, may have been saving since the engagement was announced, though some of her money may have to be spent for gowns and other accessories. A simple wedding with more money left for "getting settled" can be advised. However, the minister may find today that many couples come to the counseling session with no savings, and are planning to do their initial buying on installment. According to a recent study, American married couples in 1956 owed a total of twenty-six billion dollars for items brought home and to be paid for later. Is it any wonder that many couples hold the attitude that thrift is "un-

American"? If the couple has no savings, the counselor accepts the fact and goes on to ask:

What is your total prospective income, including your wife's if she contemplates working?

This, of course, gives the couple their base figure in the budget. Perhaps they have already decided, as some do, to use the wife's income to make stable purchases, as furniture, appliances, or down payment on a house, or car, and to use the husband's income for current expenses. Such a procedure can be recommended, for it prevents the couple from living on an inflated budget only to have to trim their spending considerably when the wife quits working. Naturally, the family from which each has come has accustomed them to a certain style of financial dealings. To get at this, the pastor asks:

What standard of living have you been used to in living with your parents or on your own income?

This question may point up a difference in social class between Bob and Mary. Suppose Bob comes from the upper-middle class and is used to more money than Mary, who is from a lower-middle class home and for whom money never has grown on trees. They will face adjustments that two from the same strata will not. The counselor wants to know if marriage will change the amount of money each has had; Bob, for instance, will not have the clothing money he had in his home. Mary may have to spend more money on entertainment as Bob starts a new job. Are they aware of the adjustments that they need to make? Having talked this through, the method of handling money may be approached:

Who gets what and by what plan? Will you use the dole, the family treasurer, a division of spending responsibilities, a budget, or a joint expense account?

The initial reactions to these questions tells the counselor a lot. Bob may say, "Oh, I'll just sign my pay check over to Mary, and let her worry about it," or, "We'll just buy on time and let the companies do our budgeting for us." Mary may say, "Bob is an accountant and is able to balance books where I can't. I'll try to keep the checkbook balanced, but let him pay the bills." Any of these statements tell us a lot about the persons involved. If they plan a budget, a good form to suggest is *The Rubber Budget Account*.[4] This budget is not rigid but allows a couple to go over or under the amount allotted and to adjust these amounts at a monthly "budget meeting." From the couple's spending plan the counselor may move on to housing by asking:

What is your long-range policy on housing? Will you rent, buy, or build? (And, one should not forget the possibility that they may live with one set of parents.)

If Bob and Mary must take the latter option, surely the counselor will be aware of the attitudes, whether over-dependency or whatever, which living with parents points to. The writer's experience is that most young couples have a goal of renting for a short time until they have down payment enough to buy or build. The couple's plans for their home will reveal to the counselor their long-term saving habits, their ability to deny themselves immediate satisfactions for the pursuit of a distant goal, and the symbolism of money. Does it represent an end in itself or a means to an end? And are the ends worthy ends? The discussion is squarely in the realm of values at this point.

Another area for discussion is insurance. The minister asks:

What are your life insurance plans? Do you know a source of unbiased information?

Bob may not have had adequate insurance protection up until now. Many men, unless they have been in the armed services and have been forced to insure their lives, have little or no protection. Marriage, however, provides another social pressure, and Bob is now contemplating taking out a $10,000 policy. The counselor does not advise here, but merely raises the question of security to help Bob and Mary continue their planning.

The use of money is intimately connected with the total relationship between Bob and Mary. The place of each in the role-structure of mar-

---

[4] May be obtained by writing American Institute for Economic Research, Great Barrington, Massachusetts.

riage comes up when the topic of the working wife is discussed. The pastor asks Mary:

Do you plan to be employed outside the home after marriage? If so, for how long? How will this affect your budget? Your having children?

The American economy is dependent on women as part of the labor force; many American homes are built on the income from two wage earners. However, roots of conflict are here if Mary postpones having a child in order to have a more expensive house. Or if when she does get pregnant she and Bob cannot adjust to a smaller paycheck. Or if Bob somehow resents his wife's independence and carps at her poor housekeeping rather than assuming his share. Any or all of these issues may come out in premarital counseling, and it would be helpful if they did. Another facet of this problem can be put this way:

Have you faced the prospect of Mary's having a vocation after the children are grown? How will she prepare for this?

There is no reason for Mary's not going back to work, either part time or full time after the family is grown. It is not advised for the mother who has children under three, experts say, and it is preferable to wait until they are in school to take a part-time job, and in high school before she takes a full-time job. The earlier years can be used, though, to finish college courses or in obtaining skills to go on later. This may well be explored in this session on budget.

The counselor surveys each item on the budget with the couple, not in a judgmental way, but in order to see how the couple works together on such practical issues. William J. Goode concluded in his studies[5] that economic stress appeared to be a major factor in the marital failures studied. How much more useful to spend a session before marriage when a start can be made in the adjustment of two people with different financial backgrounds and experience with money. The alert pastor can be sensitive to trouble spots as they unfold in this session and help to guide the couple through these before they become too exaggerated. This session draws to a close with feelings generally pretty honestly expressed

[5] *After Divorce*, a study of 425 divorced women.

and faced by the couple and the pastor. They usually are very appreciative by now of the counseling opportunity.

The third interview brings Bob and Mary back to the minister usually with expectation, sometimes with anxiety as the wedding day approaches. If they have filled out Schedule E, the minister can look this over briefly as they are getting settled in his office or study. The focus of the first part of the session is the personality differences between Bob and Mary, the likelihood of conflict, and the ways they either use or hope to use in the marriage to resolve their conflicts. Here is the nub of their adjustment and the seasoned minister-counselor knows how valuable such a discussion can be. He may lead into it by a humorous question:

Have you two had any spats since your engagement? If so, what happened? Who apologized to whom? Who has the worst temper and who has to submit to whom?

Tension may be relieved by laughter on the part of both, as Bob tells of his losing his temper at Mary's chronic lateness for engagements. Mary appears to be the pacifier, as she relates how they usually make up. The pastor is aware of the means they have set up for solving conflicts, and asks:

Are either of you interested in changing the other person after you are married?

Mary tells of her early ambitions to change Bob's habits of sloppy dress, but that he has done better since she let up on him. Bob also states that he has become less rigid about punctuality as Mary has improved. So it becomes easy to raise the next question:

Then can you accept each other as you are?

Self-acceptance is a primary characteristic of maturity, and it should enable a person to accept another person. Though Bob and Mary may still be romantically illusioned about the other person, the process of acceptance should have begun at least before the wedding. The engagement period provides a good period to get to know each other, so the pastor asks:

Is either of you excessively dominating or submissive? Who is to be boss in the house?

Laughter again may greet this question, but the couple is surely aware that these patterns of "above and below" have been revealed in their talks so far. This may be expressed freely; it may be reflected back to Mary and Bob by the pastor. He has his observations of the budget session as well as from his review of Schedule E. He leads the couple out further:

How adjusted are you? Can you give as well as take? Can you share hardships and difficulties as well as joys?

A good area to explore here is that of sickness. If Bob has been ill and Mary has nursed him, this couple knows what you mean. Bob may have been less than his genial self, and Mary may have had difficulty with his grouchiness. But "in sickness or in health" takes on meaning since that experience. The pastor moves on to the *safety valve* aspect of their relationship with the next query:

Have either of you ever walked out on the other? What do you do for an "escape hatch" when tempers are hot? And would you seek help from a counselor if your marriage relationships were ever threatened?

This may be the furthest from this starry-eyed young couple's minds. But on reflection they recall times when they almost broke the engagement. Yes, they would seek out a counselor. In fact, could they come to see you if this ever happened? This is surely to be encouraged and even planned for, as we shall discuss below.

The second concern of the final session is to discuss the religious side of marriage. If this is a mixed marriage (between faiths or races or across cultural lines), this area certainly should have been discussed in the first interview. However, for the sake of convenience let us deal with the problem here, focusing on the interfaith marriage (Catholic to Protestant or Jew to Protestant). Suppose Mary were a Protestant girl who wants to marry Bob, who is Roman Catholic. They approach a Protestant minister with the problem, asking, "What shall we do?

One recognizes at the outset that if they have consulted a Protestant

71

minister, they have made at least a tentative decision not to be married in a Roman Catholic church. They want him to perform the ceremony. But Bob wants to continue to attend his own church. One can point out the difficulties of divided loyalties in this important area, also of the implications this has with Bob's family and friends, and also that in the eyes of the Roman Catholic Church they will be living in sin. They will need to stake out their common ground and decide now about the education of their children as Protestant.

Another approach they might take is for Mary to tell the pastor that she has decided to go with Bob to his church to be married and that she just wanted, in fairness, to tell him about this.

With respect to Mary it is well to counsel with her and Bob, even though she will be leaving a Protestant church. The antenuptial agreement should be read over:

I, the undersigned, not a member of the Catholic Church, wishing to contract marriage with .... a member of the Catholic Church, propose to do so with the understanding that the marriage bond thus contracted is indissoluble except by death. I promise on my word and honor that I will not in any way hinder or obstruct the said.......... in the exercise of h.... religion and that all children of either sex born of our marriage shall be baptized and educated in the Catholic faith and according to the teaching of the Catholic Church even though the said .... be taken away by death. I further promise that I will marry................only according to the marriage rite of the Catholic Church, that I will not either before or after the Catholic ceremony present myself with .... for marriage before a civil magistrate or minister of the gospel.

Signed ....

Signed in the Presence of Rev. ....

Place ....

Date ....[6]

If she understands all the implications of the agreement and has the understanding and acceptance of her parents, one can feel this counseling

[6] Robert O. Blood, *Anticipating Your Marriage* (Chicago: The Free Press of Glencoe, Illinois, 1955), pp. 46-47.

has helped Mary and Bob in a pastoral way toward this adjustment. Better a unified family, sociologists are saying, than one divided over religion.

Suppose both Bob and Mary have inquiring minds and are determined to do some genuine religious thinking before their marriage and afterwards. A third alternative might then evolve out of these discussions.

James A. Pike[7] suggests this as the strongest solution to the problem. Let each person rethink his religious position and what he really believes and what church or group represents that actual belief. If both then come to the same church allegiance, then there is no longer a "mixed" marriage. In this instance Mary and Bob might find the Protestant Episcopal church representing their beliefs and religious practice. This is not necessarily a compromise, but a new and fresh solution. "The chief obstacle to a successful religious intermarriage is psychological," says Algernon D. Black,[8] and I would add sociological. If the couple do not face the problems rebelliously, attempting to escape their family background, but face them with tolerance, mutual respect, and intelligent planning, there is no reason why they cannot make a successful adjustment. If sociological studies mean anything, interfaith marriage is on the increase. And with the contraction of the globe and the intermingling of people across cultures, intercultural and interracial marriages will come to the pastor. The approach to the latter can be handled in a similar fashion, though isolation from family and community in urban centers or other countries may be a necessity.[9] The important thing to remember is that once all the facts are in, the decision is the couple's, and if they are serious about it one can continue with them.

With Bob and Mary, both from Protestant backgrounds, one leads into a discussion of religion with them by saying:

Religion must mean something to you or you wouldn't have chosen to be married by a minister in a church. What does religion mean to you and to your marriage at the present time ?

[7] James A. Pike, *If You Marry Outside Your Faith*, p. 105.
[8] In Maxwell Stewart, ed., *Problems of Family Life and How to Meet Them*, p. 30
[9] See Case No. 34 in Emily H. Mudd, ed., *Marriage Counseling, A Casebook*, p. 378. Also see James H. S. Bossard and E. S. Boll, *One Marriage, Two Faiths* (New York: The Ronald Press Company, 1957).

Say that one has helped train these two, this is a choice moment for them to unfold their growing beliefs in God and how He relates to their married life. If the pastor doesn't know them, they may need to be drawn out a little more as to the difference between the marriage ceremony as a social event and a religious rite. One goes on:

What do you plan to do regarding religious practice in your home, and the religious education of your children?

Bob and Mary have high ideals for their home and intend to say grace at meals and have a devotional period together. In the "settling down period" these may be forgotten, but once the first child appears, they remember their resolves again. The determination to give their child a religious training is a good foundation on which to build.

If Bob and Mary are strangers to the pastor, he may ask:

Do you plan to attend the same church; and if so, which one?

If they are of two different Protestant denominations, this may bring them to a decision about church affiliation and attendance. Without being high pressured the minister can say, "If you have no pastor, would you consider coming to our church and making it your church home?" He owes it to them to be this hospitable.

The final aspect of this session is the review of the marriage ceremony. This is done with a copy of the ritual of the minister's denomination in his hand. One also has them read with him each part of the ritual so that they understand the nature of their vows and the symbolic meaning of their actions. Some premarital manuals have an explanation of each section to which the minister can add thoughts of his own.[10] The author's practice is to use the ceremony in a Socratic fashion to draw out the couple in discussion of meanings, rather than to preach a sermon here. If the couple has been verbal heretofore, this is not a place to "dry them up" with a homily or lecture. Good teaching proceeds as before by mutual search and consolidation of "meanings" and "actions."

The couple has completed their three sessions with the minister. One

[10] See Henry Bullock, ed., *The Pastor's Manual for Premartial Counseling,* pp. 103-109.

should say a word here about the religious nature of this counseling. God and the church have not been talked about until perhaps this latter period. But one can say if the man and woman have opened their hearts to the pastor and more deeply to one another that they have moved to the levels of genuine communication of feelings and values. One may want to formalize this with prayer at the end. One would hope that the couple are aware of the Spirit of God in the midst of them, and that they have opened their lives to the Divine *Thou*. In this sense if there is prayer it is not tacked on as an addendum, but it grows out of the relationship between couple and pastor.

A PREMARITAL COUNSELING EXERCISE

Instructions: Read the following interview critically. In reading keep two areas in mind: (1) the nature of the difficulty the young woman is facing and (2) the counselor's approach to the young woman and his response to her. Certain questions for the reader to consider will be asked at the end of the interview.

The interview was arranged after having had an hour-and-a-half session with this couple. Tom is twenty-one, a college graduate of six months, and is in a graduate program of engineering at the university. Polly is nineteen, a college sophomore, and is currently working and saving money for the wedding. The couple have been going steady for four years, since Polly was a sophomore in high school. Though they have been off and on about the engagement because of Polly's youthfulness, her parents' objections, and Tom's lack of a money-making position, they became engaged last Christmas. Last summer they confronted Polly's parents about their seriousness and won a reluctant agreement that they might become engaged. It is now July, and the couple are talking about a Christmas wedding.

C(*Counselor*): Well, it has been about a month since the three of us sat down.
P(*Polly*): No, I believe it has been about three weeks. I don't know. Time passes awfully quickly. Oh, Mom's going to be home Wednesday.
C: And your Dad in October?
P: Yeah, Dad in October. Mom's bringing my brother and sister back from camp. I'm really looking forward to it. I'm meeting them at the train.

75

C: Are you going to go on your vacation to California?

P: I have to make up my mind pretty soon, or I can't go. (*Pause*) I can't really think of anything that I have in mind to talk about. I'm going to have to have you ask me some questions.

C: Well, as I remember, the reason we thought we might talk was to discuss this fear you have as the wedding gets closer, and what you might do, or by talking to be helped to do, to understand and deal with these feelings.

P: Uh-huh. It's funny—I don't feel that way as much as when I was going to get married in September. Maybe it's just putting it off. I may feel the same way later. But at least I'm able to make a few plans now and I wasn't able to before. I do little things like reading articles (C: uh-huh) which were just impossible before.

C: You blocked on reading an article?

P: Yes, I just couldn't. I would have to quit. It was a strange emotion. I'd start getting very angry and jealous.

C: Feeling angry and jealous, but you didn't know of whom?

P: I'd see this beautiful bride and I'd get jealous.

C: As though this were kind of split off from yourself?

P: Yes. I wasn't jealous of anyone in particular, just the stereotype: "*The bride and groom* usually do this and that." And I'd get this horrible picture of this beautiful and very poised woman which *I'm* not and never have been or hope to be. But I'd think, gee, it would be nice to be like that person.

C: Hmmm. Was this picture a magazine picture or of someone you know?

P: No, it was just sort of glossed over. You know, of THE BRIDE. And she was always extremely beautiful. She was sort of a tall person, and she was . . . blonde. No one I know. (*Polly is short, brunette, and very pretty herself.*)

C: Uh, huh. *Like* someone you know?

P: I don't know any tall blondes, except one of my best friends. But she isn't beautiful. She is sort of icky and neurotic like all of my friends.

C: Oh, hmmm.

P: I think a bride should be beautiful and poised. I don't know what I should do if I were in a situation where I was the center of attention. I'd just panic.

C: This is like other experiences where you were the center of attention and you panicked, huh?

P: Yes. I don't exactly panic. I get sort of mean.

C: Sort of mean?

P: I would like to be the center of attention, but I don't enjoy it. Hmph! That's a paradox. Well, I think I'm getting more at ease about it. At least, I can do some planning and I don't panic when I think of the date. And I can even think sort of what it's going to be like. And that isn't quite as bad.

C: You mean what the experience of the ceremony is like or what being married is like?

P: What the ceremony is like; I think I can imagine what being married is like, and I think I'm going to like that. Although now it has calmed down to just a normal amount of fear; and before I was so scared I just couldn't do anything.

C: Uh-huh. You think it's just the ceremony and it doesn't extend over into marriage itself and the responsibilities?

P: I don't think it extends over into marriage; though I have feelings about marriage, too. I think I would be pretty competent about the practical side of marriage, although my parents don't. They think I would be extremely impractical and incompetent.

C: Both parents feel that way?

P: Oh, yeah. Definitely. I don't. Partly because of my experiences living in the dorm. Gee, I didn't even die. I stayed there six months, and everything went fine. I had the kitchen and the apartment. My folks had been telling me for years I would never learn to cook—my poor husband! And now I have confidence that I will be able to keep house. Although until I had the apartment, I didn't think I would be able to keep house, and I didn't even try.

C: Hmm.

P: When I had the apartment, I knew if I made a mistake cooking, no one was going to get mad at me. I would just throw it out.

C: It wasn't a calamity.

P: I would just have Tom take me out to dinner that night. It wasn't so bad. At home I wouldn't even try. But at the dorm I got all sorts of confidence. I learned how to cook and to keep house and to scrub floors. (C: *uh-huh*) I got to school every day and I didn't fall apart.

C: You were saying you really got a kick out of scrubbing floors.

P: Oh, yeah! It gave me a lot of confidence. And another thing that gave me confidence was my job. My dad had been telling me for years I never would be able to hold a job because I would make a mistake and lose it. Well, I did lose one job, but it wasn't because of a mistake I made. It was

77

because they didn't agree with the approach I made. This was my job at the clinic. 'Course I'm just trying to justify myself because I do feel bad about it. I'm keeping a job now. So as far as practical aspects of marriage go, I might not do too well at first, but at least I could learn how to do it. (*C: Uh-huh*) And that was one thing that really made me wonder. Could I really do it?

C: Your parents didn't build too much confidence in you then?

P: Not about that, I didn't think so. They made me confident about some things, but not about my ability to handle practical details. (*C: Uh-huh*) They would tell me, "You're very sweet and very considerate, but you can't think things through. You can't follow up on things. You're very charming, but you can't get along because you can't cook," and little things like that.

C: Hmm. They sort of complimented you on the one hand and took it away with the other, huh?

P: They really did build up my confidence in some things. They kept telling me I could do a good job in school, and that I had a good imagination. They really did compliment me a lot. They thought that I was sensitive and creative. It wasn't that they were completely ignoring me. (*C: Uh-huh*) Mom can still push up my confidence something wonderful.

C: *She can?*

P: It wasn't that they were just tearing me down. But they didn't have any confidence themselves in my ability to handle practical things.

C: This was really the practical things that go into making a good housewife. (*Pause*)

P: Uh-huh. I want to bring something else up. (*Pause*) Although I feel that I love Tom, I'm not sure of why I do, and I'm not too sure that I do because sometimes I feel that I don't.

QUESTIONS

1. *What are the young woman's problems? Does she understand what the ramifications of the problems are? Is she able to discern the dynamics of each situation or does the counselor have to interpret them to her?*

2. *Has the counselor established rapport sufficiently for the girl to talk openly with him? Does the counselor help her explore the problem sufficiently? Who takes the initiative—counselor or counselee? Were you the counselor, would you consider the couple a good marriage risk?*

VII

Marriage Counseling—Its Nature and Goals

A student pastor is talking to his teacher-advisor about a marriage counseling problem. "The wife came first to me," he said. "She told me that her husband was causing her so much trouble that she could not handle him. He is forty and an ex-service man; he drinks too much, is sexually unresponsive, and cruel in his treatment of the children." The husband told the student a different story. "It seems he feels his twenty-eight-year-old wife has turned her back on him since he returned from the service. Now she takes no pride in keeping the house clean, and he is drinking to get away from all his troubles at home. They've both been to see me privately and now want me to solve their marriage problem. Am I right in seeing them together next time? And if I see them, should I tell them what is wrong? I don't think I know yet what is wrong."

Many of the significant characteristics of marriage counseling are present in this student's report, as are many of its treacheries and shoals. It becomes immediately apparent that marriage counseling is different from personal counseling. What are the differences? First, two people are generally seen, not one; and secondly, the client is the "relationship" between husband and wife, that is, the marriage.[1] This does not presuppose marriage to be a thing in itself apart from the two persons involved. But whenever two persons are engaged in the social-legal relationship called "marriage," certain attitudes, values, role images, and role-behaviors are generated in the relationship. These come into focus in the counseling room.

The couple or individual marriage partner come to the counselor when the interpersonal difficulties between mates are too large for them to

[1] See Clark E. Vincent, *Readings in Marriage Counseling*, p. 1ff. for an exposition of this point of view.

solve alone,[2] and they seek through a third party some adjustment of their problem and a restoration of harmony in their relationship. There are differences of opinion among writers in the field about whether the counselor should be a skilled diagnostician and deal with the unconscious determinants of each personality in the marriage.[3] We are following those who regard marriage counseling as a "helping operation" among comparatively normal people whose problems can be dealt with on an adjustment level and which do not deal with neurotic dispositions of one or both partners. All of this is said while recognizing there are neurotic partners whose interaction makes a "neurotic marriage."[4] The pastor has a responsibility to appraise these and to refer them for psychological treatment. Suffice it to say, the better the minister is at appraising the personalities of those who come for marriage counseling, the better counselor he will become. The more he is aware of the unconscious pressures in himself and in others, the better he will be enabled to accept his own limitations, both personally and professionally. Finally, the more clearly he can help the couple to understand how they perceive themselves and their mates in the marriage roles, the more clearly will the total marriage relationship come into view.

THE GOALS OF MARRIAGE COUNSELING

It is well before one begins counseling a marriage to look at what one's goals are. The unconscious goal of the religiously oriented counselor may be to keep the couple married, to "save the marriage." The writer was once told by a minister that during one year he had saved fifty marriages and in so doing had nearly ruined his own. One is led to doubt that he was of much counsel-help to the persons he saw, though such a "muscular" method surely must have hurt his own marriage. At the risk of being misunderstood, we shall contend that such "messianic" marriage-saving may subtly influence the couple to repress their differences rather than lead them to express them and to work them through. In the long run "plugging up the holes" in marital relationships may lead later to a real "burst in the dikes" of the personalities involved.

[2] Robert Laidlow, in Vincent, *op. cit.,* p. 52.
[3] M. Karpf, "Marriage Counseling and Psychotherapy," *Marriage and Family Living,* XIII (1951), 169.
[4] Victor W. Eisenstein, *Neurotic Interaction in Marriage.*

The goal of marriage counseling is to help the couple involved to work out solutions to their problems to the advantage of each one, both interpersonally and legally.[5] This may mean continuing the marriage, but it also includes the possibility of separation and divorce. The counselor in accordance with basic counseling principles sets the couple in a permissive context where *they* choose whether to stay together or to part company. It should be said that the over-all goal of the religious counselor is to help individuals to "wholeness." By wholeness we mean that integration of individual character which enables the individual to realize himself at all levels of relationship—with nature, society and God. But before the minister does much marriage counseling, he sees some marriages as blocks to wholeness. The counselor does not advise separation, just as he does not advise "staying married." Such advice-giving takes the reins of responsibility out of the couple's hands. Rather he is *for* the individuals, for their right to choose their own destiny under God, and for the possibility of there coming creative solutions out of discreative situations.

From a religious perspective the Protestant minister often feels he is the custodian of values in the community, including the social institution of marriage. He takes Jesus' stricture against divorce[6] quite literally. For him this means holding the line against the rising divorce rate, particularly keeping this *one couple* together. This approach will make of the minister a legal judge who cannot perceive the problems of a marriage clearly, but who can merely arouse the couple's guilt over possible separation. Because every marriage is such a complex network of relationships, no union between husband and wife can be broken lightly. Personalities will be hurt and scarred as a result; this must be accepted. However, the conditions under which husbands and wives can live and maintain some integrity and wholeness vary greatly. What will be stultifying for one wife will not damage another; what one couple can live under will be totally impossible for another. Just as individuals vary in their ability to take stress, so do marriages.

If one maintains that the "wholeness" or salvation of the individual is of a greater value than the maintenance of a social institution when

[5] R. Harper, "Failure in Marriage Counseling," *Marriage and Family Living*, XVII (1955), 362 ff., for an expansion of this point of view.
[6] Matt. 5:31-32.

all values have drained out of it, he will see that for the good of the persons concerned sometimes the marriage must break. Moreover, as religious faith can help the widow adjust to the loss of her mate through death, so it can aid couples to work through loss by separation and help each achieve wholeness, including more fulfilling interpersonal relationships.

Let us now look at the goals of marriage counseling in closer detail. By the nature of the case we are limiting these goals and dealing with such counseling within this narrower scope.

1. *Marriage counseling is limited to current problems in relationships between marriage partners.* This does not mean that emotion is not gathered around the problems and expressed in the counseling. On the contrary such expression and understanding is the main thrust of the counseling. However, the past is not pushed into, nor is personality the focus of discussion.[7] Rather is the counselor concerned with how the partners understand their relationship to each other.

2. *The counselor helps the couple to begin to communicate feelings to one another again.* Emotional communication is most difficult to reestablish once it has been broken. The counselor faces a double-edged task in that he must create an atmosphere of freedom and trust where the marriage partners will not only begin to open up their hearts to him but also to each other. Robert Harper perceptively points out that " . . . as the spouse or client proceeds, with a sense of safety, to express his feelings, he needs to sense that he is being understood and to sense that he is being loved."[8] Love is a multimeaninged word for the care, concern, and esteem which the counselor communicates by word, facial and body expressions, and attitude. But these are the foundation stones to the formation of a helping relationship.

3. *The counselor helps the couple to adjust to certain situations in the marriage which cannot be changed, including each other's character traits.* Franz Alexander, the psychoanalyst, has made the distinction between uncovering (insight) therapy and supportive therapy. Much marriage counseling is of the supportive, sustaining type. No real insight

---

[7] See Dean Johnson, "The Understanding and Use of the Self in Counseling," *Bulletin* of the Menninger Clinic, No. 17 (1953), 29-35 for an opposing point of view.

[8] Robert Harper, "Communication Problems in Marriage and Family Counseling," *Marriage and Family Living,* XX (1958), 110.

into the dynamics of personality is possible or necessary.[9] In supportive counseling the counselor helps the client accept his partner with his limitations. After a certain stage in middle life major personality changes cannot be made and patient understanding and forbearance of the other may be a primary goal. In a similar vein physical handicaps, such as the inability to bear children, may be accepted and dealt with courageously.

4. *The counselor helps the couple to play down personal goals and to work toward ones which are mutually set.* Some disturbed couples who come for help have never accepted marriage as a part of their value system, but try egocentrically to live as though they were still in a single state. The goal is not to submerge each person's individuality and freedom into a "conformist" pattern, but to help the emotionally immature to grow up. The selfish person begins to "play down" his personal goals and to work with the other person in shared goal-setting and goal-seeking. Love grows in such an atmosphere of mutuality, when the other is valued as much or even more than the self.

5. *The counselor aids each partner to understand the other and his role in the marriage, such counseling giving him opportunity to adjust to what the mate and the marriage demand of him.* This is the nub of marriage counseling: the understanding of each others' *role images* and *role relations.* (See Chapter III for definitions.) Let me illustrate: I am a certain kind of husband and expect my wife to be and act a certain way. She sees herself in a certain role in the marriage and also sees me in a certain way. These images and expectations do not coincide but must be clarified, worked through, and adjusted before the marriage is on surer ground. Does this mean the counselee receives no self-understanding through marriage counseling? No, but these goals of personal counseling are derivative and secondary, rather than primary. So long as the relationship between husband and wife is the focus of attention, the primary goals will deal with the adjustment of these two persons to one another. Personal counseling may grow out of marriage counseling, or personal counseling with one partner may center on a disturbed marriage. But marriage counseling as we define it here deals with present maladjustments and misunderstandings between couples as they relate to the

[9] See Regina Flesch, "Treatment Goals and Techniques in Marital Discord," in Vincent, *op. cit.*, pp 223-34.

marriage roles. And it turns on the conversation generated between husband and wife regarding what they expect of one another and how they can either adjust to these expectations or change them.

THE STRUCTURE OF MARRIAGE COUNSELING

One of the major problems the student mentioned at the beginning of the chapter faced was: "Now the couple has come, how should I set up the counseling?" The involvements and ramifications of working with a couple are twice those of counseling on an individual level. Let us examine the possibilities open to the counselor. There are at least four:

1. He can see both marriage partners at separate times.
2. He can see both marriage partners together at the same time.
3. He can see one partner and refer the other to another counselor.
4. He can see only one partner, the other partner being inaccessible for counseling.

Methodologically, some helpers, notably psychiatrists, psychiatric social workers, and lawyers, favor seeing only one partner[10] The focus is the individual and his reaction to and investment in the marriage. Other helpers, in particular educators, marriage counselors, and pastors, favor counseling both partners.[11] For them the focus is the interaction between the couple; and the problem must be faced jointly for help to be received.

There are advantages and disadvantages to both approaches. If the same counselor sees both husband and wife, he is a direct observer to their marital interaction; he perceives the barriers to their communicating with one another; and after both have expressed themselves openly to him he can arrange a joint session in which both may talk to him and to one another. The disadvantages of the "solo" approach are that the counselor is often put in the role of judge or referee; the counselees often expect him to "save" the marriage; and consciously or unconsciously the counselor often takes sides and favors one to the disadvantage of the other.

If the counselor sees only one partner he can empathize—enter into the life experience of the counselee—more completely; he can treat the marriage problems in terms of the person's perceptions of himself and his responsibilities in the marriage; and if there are joint sessions, the

---

[10] See Skidmore, *et al., op. cit.*
[11] M. Robert Gomberg, in Vincent, *op. cit.*, p. 306.

counselor can be his "advocate" in a wholehearted way. The disadvantages of this approach are that distortions creep into the counselee's conversation which the counselor naïvely accepts; the counselor cannot "see" the marriage except through the client's eyes; communication with the other counselor, if there be one, may break down, and the marriage may not be helped; if the other partner is seen, the counseling is more than personal counseling. The minister, because of the unavailability of another counselor, may be forced to see both partners, and have to follow through with them. However, if the conflict is severe, he may want to refer one partner to another counselor even at a distance.[12] If two pastors in a community have marriage counseling training and experience, they can often instigate a cross-referral plan for difficult marriage counseling.

A MARRIAGE COUNSELING CASE

John and Helen Wood came to see the pastor one raw February night. She was a small, retiring girl with a small childlike face which belied her twenty-six years. John was a small-statured, dark-haired, handsome man of twenty-eight, who had worked since high school as a salesman. They were married seven years ago and have two children, John, now two, and Mary, just six months. The counselor talked first to her, and in slow halting fashion she pieced out the problem. She said she had been unfaithful to John. She knew this had hurt him, but she felt anxious and lonely having him away on the road. In his absence, she had had an affair with her employer at work.

It happened this way. John traveled for his company one week out of two. Last November, following the birth of her daughter, she had become depressed, and with John's encouragement sought part time employment modeling clothing in a department store. After a while George, her employer, began asking her out to dinner. Out of loneliness and distress over her marriage she let him make love to her. They had been intimate only three times, she said, but the last time they were together, John had returned home early on the plane. When he came up

---

[12] In the Marriage Council of Philadelphia, Emily H. Mudd follows the practice of having one counselor see both partners unless the conflict is severe. See Vincent, *op. cit.,* p. 302.

the drive of their suburban home, he noticed the car gone. The baby-sitter told him Helen had gone out with a man. When she returned, her hair tousled and clothing wrinkled, he cross-examined her until she broke down and admitted being out with George. He then went to George's apartment and made a scene in front of George and his wife, and told Helen never to see him again. They decided then that both should see a marriage counselor and came to their pastor.

Helen then gave some of her family background. She said that she is the youngest of three children. Her sister is happily married. Her brother, however, has been in-and-out of mental hospitals for the past five years. Her father is an alcoholic, but she has always felt closer to him than to her mother. She met John when she was seventeen, and he was her only boy friend. They were married when she was nineteen and he twenty-one. During early marriage they wandered about the country spending their time in the West. After six years of unsettled living Helen decided to leave him and to come back to her home town. He followed her six months later and found a job as a salesman near his home.

John in his private sessions displayed a mixture of the salesman's brashness and a retiring sensitivity. He said the affair had left him numb, and that it hit him hardest when he learned that his wife had had sexual relations with George. He said that he still loved her though he felt that he will probably always throw this affair in her face, and that it will probably dissolve their marriage. He realized that previously he had roamed around the country and had not given his wife a steady secure home. He had gotten into debt from installment buying of automobiles and from expensive living in the West, and finally he had to send her home. He said that at this period their marriage had nearly broken up. She had told him that if he did not come back home, she would get a divorce. Since getting back and securing the present position, he had felt more settled until the present difficulty. While he talked, he acted like a hurt boy and failed to see his own guilt in the matter.

A counseling structure was worked out so that the counselor would see husband and wife at first alone, and when they had worked through the problem sufficiently, he would see them together. Helen presented a very dependent picture to the counselor. She was guilty over the promiscuous relations, but she did not feel wrong in running out on her husband after the way he had treated her. In their early marriage he had traveled over the country in various jobs and expected her to pick up and move at a moment's notice. In California he had had at least three affairs with older women and had boasted of them openly in her presence. She had looked for gentleness, openness, and fairness in John as she had found it in her father, but it was not there. As she expressed her resentment of John's treatment, she began to see that she was searching for something in her lover, George, an older man, which she had not found so far in her marriage.

John presented a curious streak through the early part of the counseling. He appeared to want to hear more and more about the affair, first from Helen; then he went to George to hear it from his side; finally, he dated George's wife to hear it from her. He asked Helen to see George again and to end the affair. Then he hired a taxi to go to their rendezvous, asking the taxi driver to go into the restaurant to spy upon them and to report their doings back to him. He tortured himself with visions of Helen in George's arms while he was away on selling tours. And his curiosity extended to telling Helen that he had had sexual relations with George's wife in order to see her reaction to this exploit. With the counselor he failed to see his "double-standard" morality or his pattern of neglect toward Helen and the children. He reacted to George, however, as someone who threatened his manhood, much as a small child reacts to his father's domination.

With the support of the counselor Helen began to assert some independence toward John. At first she resented John's continuing to harp about the affair after it was over. And she began to understand that John was expecting of her a childlike devotion rather than the love of a wife, just as she was expecting that he "baby" her as her father had. About this time she had a dream in which the city was in flames and she was running from place to place looking in cellars to find her father, and when she found him he could not speak. Following the nightmare she sent her husband looking through every "skid-row" in the city for her father, until John traced him to within seven days of his disappearance. The counselor did not interpret the dream, though the similarity in the loss of her father and the loss of her lover appears fairly clear.

Interestingly enough, this experience had two results: John at first felt closer to his wife, as though he could do something for her in searching for her father; on the other hand, it made him feel inadequate for her, and he began an argument in which, this time, she fought back. They both became so angry that they left the house for several hours. When they returned, they sat down and talked as they had not talked for months. He promised not to go over the affair again. She insisted that if he would spend more time with her and the children on weekends, she would not leave him again. As a result he stopped fantasying that she was running around while he was on sales tours. He began to trust her again.

As spring arrived, Helen became more expansive. She enjoyed being out alone in the warmth of the sun, hanging up the clothes. She reported that she enjoyed the children for themselves. She also developed some independence in being able to stand up to John's mother and sister and to stand by John in his selection of beds for the children. As Helen grew in independence, John had real difficulty in accepting her. He continued to want the counselor's judgment as to who was right and who was wrong in the extra-marital affair. On one of the trips he made a goodly number of sales and came back to the counselor saying he wanted to terminate; the counseling kept him too stirred up. Helen and John concluded with a joint session. Here they both agreed they were better able to talk things over between them. However, it appeared from John's standpoint that the affair had not been forgiven but merely dropped for the time being. They left together to buy the beds which they decided upon for the children, rather a symbol of their independence and companionship.

It was the counselor's conclusion that the marriage is still on a tentative basis, although it has weathered this crisis. Helen has grown some in independence and in understanding her need to break from unrealistic expectations regarding John and her need to function as a person with rights in the marriage.

THE FLOW OF EARLY MARRIAGE COUNSELING

The first year of married life is climactic for the couple, and in 40 per cent of the cases studied, the marriage ends in separation or divorce. Yet it is the most hopeful period so far as marriage counseling is concerned.[13] If the couple is aware that help is available and that difficulties can be talked through and adjustments made with the counselor's aid, there is no need for the early marriage to break. In the following section the difficulties in early marriage are cited. However, it is also applicable when any couple seek help early and the problems have not caused a serious rupture in the marriage. Certain methods will be spelled out now, with the case providing us with illustrative material.

Identification of the Problem

The primary task for the counselor and the couple together is to locate the problem. The counselor must bring to this certain understandings of marriage; but he cannot identify the problem until the couple have unloaded their strong feelings and resentments and given their "side" of things. They "know" their marriage much better than the counselor, though the counselor may have talked with hundreds of couples. Here *they* are "experts."

Each partner begins, therefore, to identify the problem. It is a commonly accepted counseling principle that the presenting problem—adultery in this case—is symptomatic of more basic difficulties. The same is true when the person blames the in-laws, feels that money is mismanaged, or points to a nagging wife as the trouble spot. These troubles are like a fever in the body; they are symptoms of more basic interpersonal difficulties. The couple moves with the counselor to put their finger on what is rubbing them "sore" in their marriage relationship. One acts spitefully, as this young woman did, by having an affair; the other reacts as the husband did by staying out late and drinking. Back of their hurting each other are more basic breakdowns. They are no longer communicating effectively; nor is there real understanding of what each expects of the marriage and of each other as marriage partner.

Perceiving Breakdown of Communication

The couple has sought out a helper because they no longer are able to talk through conflict areas. Words are no longer used to tell the other person something about oneself or how the other looks to one. Rather words are used as strong instruments of power or hatred or vengeance.

[13] Robert Foster, *Marriage and Family Relationships* (New York: The Macmillan Company, 1950), p. 107. See cases studied of early marriage.

As in this case when the husband becomes loud and tries to talk the wife down; the wife withdraws in silence, and goes about for days with no more than a mumbled "yes" or "no."

Silence became a wall between the couple. "The only time we talk to one another is to fight," said the couple. The husband assumes the office of district attorney and gives his wife the third degree until she tells him all about the affair. She complains that she could forget about the other man if he would only stop throwing it in her face. He recognizes that he must continue to hurt her with his "talk about the other man" because he has been hurt so badly.

In the private interviews with one partner the counselor enables him to talk "freely" about the sources of irritation in the marriage relationship. The person has been unable to do this with his partner because every statement was met with a countercharge, with spiteful behavior, or with icy silence. It is the opening again of the blocked communication process that will eventually enable the couple to talk to one another. The joint session may be the place for this. (We shall go into the joint interview in detail in the next chapter.) Suffice it to say that what marriage counseling provides the person is the opportunity to communicate his feelings openly to a sensitive human being, who makes the opportunity possible for the person to communicate these feelings to his partner with some hope of being understood.

Perceiving the Breakdown of Role Behavior

Since marriage is a social relationship, it is composed of a network of expectations, hopes, rights, and duties which cluster around the husband role and wife role.[14] Difficulties arise between spouses when there is a disparity between each one's perception of his role and that of his mate, and when, often unconsciously, he behaves in an opposite manner to what his mate expects of him.

This is most obvious in the case of Helen and John. He functioned as "breadwinner" but felt this gave him the right to dominate Helen. He thought of himself as very unselfish; she saw him as selfish and cruel in his attitudes toward her. She expected the kindness and gentleness in a husband she had received from her father and sought it out with an

[14] See A. R. Manger, "Role Theory and Marriage Counseling," *Social Forces*, XXXV (1957), 200-209.

older man when John did not give it to her. He saw her as one who should "be" there when he came home; she "ran out" of his role expectations to have a good time.

These become even more apparent in our cultural period when role definitions of husband and wife are shifting. He thinks of himself as "breadwinner" and expects his wife to be a typical "hausfrau." She has continued to work and therefore has taken over some of the breadwinner role; she expects him to share this role with her, but also to help with the housework on week ends. He rebels at this and escapes to the golf course. A simple adjustment of getting hubby to help with the house cleaning is not enough. Because as the wife talks on, she reveals that she looks to her husband as a "tower of strength" and feels insecure in the business world. Moreover, underneath he wants a companion at golf and feels his wife should be more emancipated from the kitchen. Counseling should move them from the symptomatic statement to the communication of mutual role understandings and behaviors and how these compare: husband's with wife's and wife's with husband's.

The Counselor's Role

It is a difficult thing to allow a third party into the intimacies of one's marriage. This is one reason for the reluctance of some to seek a marriage counselor. Need one say it should make the counselor particularly sensitive to tread softly in the initial stages of contact with the couple or person. And it should give him the awareness that the members of the marriage may see him as a "third party" threatening the marriage.[15] He may become a part of a "competitive triad," being used by one as a lever to make the other "come to tow."

The counselor must begin, therefore, as in personal counseling by offering a safe and trustworthy relationship with either one or both partners to the marriage. He allows the person to talk out his symptomatic problems with their accompanying feelings until he comes to what appears to be his attitudes and feelings about the relationship. In the case of John and Helen back of the adultery were irresponsible attitudes and attempts to hurt the other on both sides. It was not until the second and third interviews that these attitudes became apparent to the counselees.

[15] See Lionel Lane, "The Entrance and Exit of the Marriage Counselor," *Marriage and Family Living*, XVII (1955), 59.

The counselor "observes" the marriage, particularly in the joint sessions. This means he must act as "participant-observer" in the triad. He helps the couple set up lines of communication and then sits back and watches the interaction (often fireworks!). He reflects, "What kind of persons am I dealing with? And what is going on between them?"

He helps each to understand what he is doing to disturb the harmony between them and to accept the responsibility for his actions and to deal with the guilt incurred by those actions. For example, John had "run around" during the earlier years of their marriage and felt little guilt consciously. But when Helen did the same thing, he projected his own guilt on Helen and thus tried to avoid his own responsibility for the breach in the marriage. In this instance John never accepted this responsibility for his own part in the difficulty; to admit this would have been to lose too much "face." The counselor aids each partner to understand what the other expects of him in terms of role behavior, and to square this with his own self-concept. A husband has a certain concept of himself and of his role in the marriage; so does a wife. But when these do not jibe, the marriage relationship is in jeopardy. Helen, when she began to develop independence, felt herself to be a grown woman and wanted to be treated like one. John, however, continued to treat her like a child. On the other hand he needed some recognition of his dependency feelings, and when Helen did not recognize them, he sought refuge with the other man's wife. The counseling involved clarifying these ambiguities in their expectations of one another as husband and wife. Then the partner could accept or reject them, or modify his self-concept to take the partner's role expectations into account. This latter was reached to a limited extent in the case presented.

Most important, the counselor maintains an emotionally balanced, objective, and non-threatened perspective throughout the counselee's expression of the feelings, complaints, and ideas for adjustment. This is most difficult in counseling both parties. The counselor may feel rather naturally drawn to one partner. But if he sides with this partner even unconsciously, he will lose the other. Uneven scheduling of appointments, accepting a fee from one rather than another, or judgment of one's client's behavior, even to himself—these are some ways of losing objectivity. If he is threatened by the intense expression of feelings either in private or joint session, he may disqualify himself from being of real help as a catalyst in the relationship. Acceptance of the counselee, as well as recognizing he is going through stormy waters in one of the most important relationships of his life, should be a primary attitude of the counselor. He cannot play God and by omnipotent powers glue this couple back together again.[16] He knows the reins of decision are in the hands of the couple involved. He is *for* them, that is, he feels they can make the right decision themselves after they know all the factors involved and what changes they want, if any, in the relationship. But he is there representing stability, understanding, and faith in them and in what the marriage of two spirits might become. In this way he is a "servant of God," a channel through whom the blocks to creativity, understanding, and love may be removed.

But every counselor is a human being, too; therefore, he must recognize there are some marriages he simply cannot help.[17] And it is folly to remain with the couple when they could better function with another counselor, even a psychiatrist or a lawyer. Here the minister with a "messiah" complex is most sorely tried. If he continues this way overlong with couples, he may need to examine his own projections in counseling, yes, even his own marriage. We shall deal with these problems at greater length in future chapters.

We have been concerned in this chapter with the nature of marriage counseling, its goals, and its structure and flow, with a case study as an orienting center. Now it behooves us to examine in closer detail what is involved in the reconciliation process between husband and wife when the communication processes and role behavior have broken down completely. This takes us beyond early marriage counseling to counseling with the "later-marrieds." The primary process is the same, but the problems and personal ramifications will engage the counselor in greater complexities of relationship and nuances of counseling.

[16] M. Karpf. "One very good therapist . . . prayed each morning that he may conquer the temptation to play God, and prayed each evening for forgiveness for having succumbed to the temptation," "Some Guiding Principles in Marriage Counseling," *Marriage and Family Living*, XIII (1951), 51.

[17] See Harper, *op. cit.*, p. 111.

VIII

Estrangement and Reconciliation

When does a marriage go bad? Certainly not at the first fight, for often couples have some kind of fracas on the honeymoon. If a man and woman have not had a serious difference of opinion before, they are liable to be frightened for their marriage. But their attraction for one another bridges this rift and they are together again. Neither is a hassle over their respective rights within a marriage deleterious in its effects on the couple. This kind of argument can be of problem-solving sort, with each knowing better where he stands after it is over. The couple goes through a kind of disillusioning process in the early months of marriage which prepares them for steady growth. Some couples may think their marriage is going bad at this period and come to the counselor with the melancholy news, "We're falling out of love, John and I." One is reminded of the father's comment to his little cherub in one of James Thurber's cartoons, "That's right," he says, "We're all disenchanted." No, this is not when a marriage goes bad; it may simply be a sign of growth in the marriage. It is only when through a combination of interpersonal differences and circumstances a partner is prompted to think, and then say, and finally to act out the threat of leaving the other that a marriage is in difficulty. It is the experience of most marriage counselors that the average couple waits too long to get help with their marriage. The rift in the marriage is wide before either will accept the fact of failure and seek a third party. The threat to see a lawyer may be the precipitating cause; this drives the other to a counselor. Or it may be severe quarreling to the point of violence or the discovery of one's mate in a clandestine affair. The couple is severely estranged, so that the problems of reestablishing communication and co-operation in the marriage are difficult. If only they would seek help sooner, one thinks.

We turn now to the more severely estranged couples as candidates for counseling. These are not couples who seek and get help in the early period of their marriage. These are they who allow kindling to be added daily to the fires of anger and resentment which burn between them until they realize that the love that formerly drew them together has been consumed. This is by nature of things more difficult counseling, but reconciliation is possible for some of these couples! And the fact that one of them has sought you out is a small indication that they want to make up rather than separate. One does not enter the counseling determined to glue the couple together; but once it is clear to you that they want to follow the steps of reconciliation, this is your guiding principle.

THE NATURE OF ESTRANGEMENT

Marriage is a risk even when the couple have known each other from childhood. It is an attempt to bridge the gap between the solitariness of me and the solitariness of you. It is born of basic needs on several levels of personality—from the biological need for sexual union to the psychological need for intimacy to the spiritual need to care intensely about another human being's welfare. When such basic need systems become interrelated, it is natural that there will be both attraction and repulsion. The one I love I also hate at times. And I feel this conflict of inner feelings when he does not understand me or refuses "to let me in" to his solitary self. In other words my hatred is expressed when my love for my mate is frustrated, or when he fails to meet my needs for intimacy, or for companionship, or for sexual union.

To be "estranged" means that two who have been intimate have become strangers again. For the process of growth in love to be possible means that the possibility of deterioration of love is also imminent. Just as the skills of painting and music need cultivation, so too does the art of love. When that art is neglected, the couple finds that they are unable to "care" properly about the other person, that the psychic attraction that once drew them to each other's company is dwindling, and that this is beginning to show itself in their sexual relationship.

Before an actual divorce is planned or even thought of, a couple is involved in an "emotional divorce." [1] This means that they cease com-

[1] Jean Despert, *Children of Divorce* (New York: Doubleday & Company, Inc., 1953). This is her phrase.

municating to one another at anything other than a superficial or practical level. If they talk, it may be in the nature of destructive quarrels, those not of a problem-solving kind, but quarrels which aim at the weaknesses in the other's personality and character and destroy feelings of mutuality. If they keep quiet, it is not a creative silence but a leaving of the other's presence. "I felt he walked out on me even though he sat in the living room watching TV," said an estranged wife. When hostility and resentment become the dominant pattern of the relationship, these feelings need not be verbally expressed. They can be "acted out" by one or both partners in an adulterous affair, or in drinking to excess, or in abuse or irresponsibility to the children or the spouse. Often this is unconscious, and the erring partner is unaware of what is driving him and of how much this behavior is damaging the marriage.

What does the marriage counselor look for in the estranged partners' relationship? His primary responsibility here is analysis of the marriage and diagnosis of the disturbance between the couple. The counselor perceives these matters even though he does not reveal them to the couple at the time of his perception. Such procedure has often ruined a counseling session for the overeager beginner, no matter how much it did for his ego.

The primary thing he looks for is the nature of the role relationship between husband and wife. Six people at least are involved, as has been indicated in the previous chapters:

Figure 4

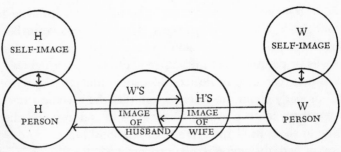

The blurring of roles can take place at any level. For instance, John sees himself as an ideal provider and his wife as a social counterpart, one whose parties help him in his business. Mary, however, thinks of John more as a father to her children, to whom she is devoted, and this house-wife's role prevents her from being the hostess John desires. These disturbances in role relationship, even though unexpressed, may be the key to the estrangement going on between John and Mary.

Another thing the counselor looks for is emotional immaturity on the part of one or both. Mary may be growing to a more mature level in her new capacity as mother to their children; John wanting the center of the stage as in earlier years, resents the children's intrusion on their social life. Or Mary may develop in the marriage until the time she moves away from her mother or loses her in death. Then she becomes wheedling, demanding, and childish. Immaturity in marriage often means the inability to give up an egocentric way of life and to share the demands and responsibilities that go with adulthood. One may be legally "married" and emotionally "single."

The counselor may then want to investigate how each partner is fulfilling the other's needs. The relationship ideally is one of interdependence—in the sexual area, each have erotic needs which the other is able to satisfy. However, as the couple grows in their knowledge of one another, they become better able to complement one another sexually and interpersonally. The physical union becomes charged with meanings: at times to express animal passion, at other times pride in the other's accomplishments, at times security from the world, at times spiritual ecstasy in a vital religious sense. But sexual intercourse, too, can be a hostile club to drive a couple apart as it is used or withheld from the other.

So, too, with interpersonal needs the couple can become more knowledgeable of what each wants from the other in terms of companionship. These needs are harmonized, so that the quiet times at home which satisfy one do not outweigh the social events away from the home which satisfy the other. When selfishness predominates, the other's interpersonal needs do not matter; each person becomes an individual and runs to the bridge club or bowling alley without concern for the other, oftentimes even without consulting him.

The value needs and religious needs of the other may be glossed over with little sensitivity. Mary feels that she should be a part of the League of Women Voters to participate in community betterment; John thinks this activity superfluous. Or John wants to attend church faithfully every Sunday; Mary would rather sleep and get up late one day a week. The meaning of one's faith or practice of his religion is often the most secret; and a couple may share every other area of their lives but this. Because their most intimate thoughts and feelings are not shared, they become estranged and are no longer intimate.

Finally, a marriage relationship may be the product of a neurotic interaction. That is to say, unconscious components operate to influence the choice of mate and the conflicts which follow. Bela Mittelmann gives four examples of neurotic partnership:

1. An aggressive, sadistic partner marries a dependent, submissive, masochistic person. The one hurts and humiliates the other who passively endures the pain. Each satisfies the other's neurotic need.

2. An emotionally detached person marries a partner who has an intense need for affection. Difficulty arises when the detached person's fears are aroused by his partner's demands for affection and he becomes more isolated, this causing the dependent one to feel rejected.

3. Two persons who desire to dominate may marry and find themselves in an endless battle, attacking the other or defending oneself. Each has dependency needs which prevent him from getting out of the union.

4. The helpless partner depends on a "saviour" type of mate for help, the saviour needing someone to help. The demands for help are greater than any human can fulfill and difficulty soon arises in the marriage.[2]

Dr. Ruth Fox adds a fifth type of marriage to this group:

5. The alcoholic-alcoholic spouse. Studies show that the alcoholic's wife, for example, is not responsible for his drinking but is one of the reasons for his continuing to drink to excess. Her ego ideal is of a powerful woman, so she marries a weak and dependent male. She must feel superior and keep her husband inferior. When her husband becomes obstinate, she no longer has a "baby" on her hands; and the marriage is in difficulty.[3]

In these neurotic marriages each partner fulfills a complementary pattern and obtains a measure of satisfaction and safety through meeting

[2] "Analysis of Reciprocal Neurotic Patterns in Family Relationships" in Victor W. Eisenstein, *Neurotic Interaction in Marriage*, pp. 82-84.
[3] Ruth Fox, "The Alcoholic Spouse," in Victor Eisenstein, *Neurotic Interaction in Marriage*, p. 159.

neurotic needs or having them met. However, each expects too much of the other, and resentments are aroused when, for instance, the bottomless pit of dependency needs is not filled. This makes the neurotic feel rejected and he begins the cycle of anxiety and guilt, again bringing him around to the old infantile hurts and feelings of helplessness which are the core of his neurosis. These patterns can even be intensified to the point that one finds two psychotics involved in a marriage. This is what the French call *folie á deux,* two people involved in each other's psychosis.

Needless to say, the minister cannot deal directly with problems which are so deep-seated and involved. However, nothing exempts him from having couples with problems of this proportion come to his door. He can with training and experience learn to "spot" neurotics whose sickness is making the marriage sick. And he can do his best service to the couple by making a psychiatric referral. The marriage will not be helped usually until one or both partners obtain psychotherapy.

A CASE OF RECONCILIATION

Below there follows a case study in which the goal of counseling was to reconcile an estranged couple. The reader should examine it as he has examined the previous case studies and interviews: first, to appraise where the difficulty lies in the marriage relationship; and second, to discern what approach the counselor takes with the couple to work through the difficulty. Following this, he can look more understandingly at the principles and methods of reconciliation-counseling.

John Jackson called for an appointment on referral from his wife Mary's physician. Both husband and wife came to see the counselor, and after he had explained the counseling procedure, he saw Mrs. Jackson alone.

She began her talk with the counselor by explaining that she had been in the hospital recently for one day for female surgery, and was under sedatives at the present and felt very tense. From leading questions to gain background material the counselor then learned Mary was forty-six, had come from a Midwestern farm, and had two brothers and two sisters. She also revealed that this marriage was her second, her first husband having left her for another woman after a marriage of fifteen years. At that time Mary was suffering from a confining illness and was hospitalized. She added that she and John have been married for six years, and that she had no children by either marriage.

She laid their present marital difficulty to Mr. Jackson's temper. With restraint she told of her trouble when she returned from her most recent stay in the hospital: First, she suspected that John ran around while she was hospitalized; at least, he did not stand by her during the operation. At home he would not fix any meals for her and went out to a restaurant, leaving her alone. Finally, she called her brother, telling him of the trouble and getting him to fix her a meal. Seeing how upset his sister was, Mary's brother took her to a doctor, who gave her tranquilizers. Meanwhile, John stayed away from home for two days, and when he returned, he whipped the dog in a blind rage.

Mary then told of another argument she and John had had the week end before this first counseling session. She had again called her brother, who again took her to the doctor. This time the doctor suggested that the Jacksons see a marriage counselor. Her conversation turned again to her present health. She reported that she did not feel that she had gone through the change of life, although her menstrual cycle was upset. She was tense from her work, a job she did at home. But the main source of difficulty, in her opinion, was that her husband let her down when he would not care for her while she was sick. "What can I expect in my old age if he acts like this now?" she asked the counselor.

The counselor then saw Mary's husband John, a short, heavy-set man of forty-four years. He worked as a watchman on the swing shift at a factory. In revealing his background John said he came from a family of five children and grew up having to care for his blind mother. When he had returned from the service, he had had sole care and responsibility for her. He found it necessary to place her in one rest home after another when she became too difficult for the personnel at each. She died shortly after his marriage to Mary.

John then told how he met his wife at a dance. She invited him home and fixed him something to eat. From this gesture as well as Mary's personable way, John said he thought Mary was the one whom he wanted to marry and with whom he would settle down. After four months of courtship they were married, each being about forty at the time. John sold his house downtown and bought a house in the suburbs. He stated that he liked this life, though he did not like his wife to be friendly with the neighbors or for people to borrow things from him.

He reported that because Mary was deaf, she did not drive well. Consequently, he did not allow her to shop alone, but went with her, driving her to all of her appointments. He further added that he thought perhaps her difficulty was a result of the change of life and her disappointment over not having children.

As for their recent arguments he said that at the time of her hospitalization he went to see Mary but did not stay at the ward during her operation. But he emphatically stated that he did not run around on her as she had implied. When she came home, she had cursed and nagged him. Then, when her brother came over, she ran him down, and her criticism upset him so that he left the house.

At the second counseling session Mrs. Jackson no longer was receiving medication and appeared a lot less tense. She sat down and spoke again of the "awful week" after she returned from the hospital. She explained this was not the kind of marriage she wanted. John's actions made her feel as she had felt when she was in the hospital ten years ago and her former husband had run around and left her. She could not get over the fact that John would treat her this way during an illness. The counselor brought up the long illness of John's mother and suggested that he might have been acting toward his wife as though she were his mother. Mary could see that not getting meals for him made him feel that way. Since she was able to prepare his meals, he was at least not so surly. She then complained of his moods of pouting and gave this example: John would come home from work and inspect the house, as if it were not clean. Then she would not get a civil word from him. If the house were all right, John would gradually loosen up. She again told the counselor that she did not like having someone so temperamental around the house.

Mary brought up the subject of friends. "He has driven them all away," she said. She told of his insulting her in front of her friends. Then the counselor inquired about the Jacksons' church attendance, and Mary said that they had not attended church since their move to the suburbs, her poor hearing being the reason. She pulled a copy of *Unity* magazine from her pocketbook and told how much this meant to her. She pointed to a passage on love and admitted she could not understand it. The counselor asked if she found that she could not love at present with so much hate in her. She nodded in assent.

At the next session John came expecting to say little, but once he began talking, he found he had a great deal to say. He indicated that his main problem with Mary was her tension. When she was tense, he was tense and the result was usually an argument. They had had a small fracas the past week over the fact that she had forgotten to tabulate a rental account. John said he went to the renter during the week end and neither knew·whether the rent had been paid. On the way home the Jacksons had argued about this and continued to do so at home. Mary became so upset that she vomited as a result. John then told the counselor that he felt it was bad to argue so much. He talked shyly about their sexual relations and said when Mary had complained a few years ago that such intimacies hurt her, he had given it up. He felt that as she had grown old before he had and did not want sexual relations, this was understandable. John emphasized that he would not run around but would just give this side of things up. When the counselor spoke of the possibility of sexual relations after forty, John said he had heard about it, but was not insistent on it.

The counselor asked John to tell his side of things about the incident following Mary's return from the hospital. He appeared to want to evade the issue but justified himself by saying he would help around the house when Mary worked along with him; however, it was asking too much to want him to cook for her. When the counselor raised the question of recreation, John replied that all they ever did was go out to dinner and then go for rides in the car. He added that they danced only at company parties. This might be something they could continue, he agreed. Regarding Mary's work, John had suggested she quit working in a factory and do the job at home. He agreed that the job made her feel tense, but he did not want her to quit doing it.

At the end of the hour the counselor arranged a joint session as a means of reconciling the Jacksons' differences. It was his evaluation that there were many values in the marriage, though neither husband nor wife had learned to communicate their real wishes to each other nor had arranged for means of settling differences between them.

There followed a two-hour reconciling session the next week in which both John and Mary were asked to tell what they thought was wrong with the marriage. Mary indicated she thought the main trouble was his loss of temper. "He blows up so I can't talk to him. He does not want to take care of me when I am sick," she stated. John said he thought the trouble was her tension. "She gets tense and makes me tense and then I blow up at her. This fighting is not good and we both should stop it." The area of tensions was talked over and they noted that both had created situations so that they wanted to fight rather than solve their problems. Their buying at the grocery store became a focus of discussion. They both had gone shopping but before they had gotten home, they had fought over what they had bought, about his driving, or how much they had spent. The counselor spoke of the different modes of shopping which couples employ: the wife going alone, the husband going alone, or sometimes doing it together. Mary indicated she would like to try shopping alone, and John reluctantly agreed to this. He spoke of her deafness as the reason for his not allowing her to drive. She had not known this before and was hurt. They talked further, however, about getting clearance with the insurance company so that he would feel easier about her driving alone.

The second area of reconciliation concerned the time each had out alone. He had not allowed her to have friends. On the other hand, when he went out with friends from work, she had had him paged on the loud-speaker at the restaurant. They agreed they both should have time out alone. He agreed that she should have perhaps one afternoon a week out with a girl friend to go to a matinee or to shop; she agreed that he could have a comparable time out with his male friends. With the counselor they began to see the adjustment necessary in marriage, particularly in late marriages. They understood that they had either to adjust or be separated.

The pattern of their relationship was clarified as follows: John felt imposed on for doing things that she wanted of him, namely, shopping, cleaning, or cooking when she was ill. He was a person with little patience and the demands of his wife drove him to lose his temper and to feelings of disgust. Mary, on the other hand, felt deprived. She married John when one marriage had failed and expected him to perform up to her expectations. He had not allowed her to function as a whole person and this made her angry. She picked on him until he lost his temper and then she felt more deprived. The counselor discussed with

103

John how he might do all he felt he could and without losing his temper tell her when she demanded too much. The counselor asked Mary how she might accommodate herself to John as he was and live with him that way. As the session concluded, both seemed to have the wind out of their sails. The counselor asked them, however, to try out these accommodations for two weeks and then to come back for another joint session.

At the second joint session it was apparent that the couple had made progress in their adaptation to one another. She had spent a morning with her cousin shopping, and felt much happier with this additional freedom. He said that she had not been nagging him and that he felt less tension; therefore, he had not blown up with her. They had had only one small difference and this concerned a visit to a neighbor's home to swap antique furniture. He felt that they had received the worst part of the bargain and feared she would tell the other woman the way he felt. When she assured him that she had not broken his confidence, he seemed to accept it and to be less fearful of her gossiping.

The couple spent a good part of the session talking about matters of trust and distrust. He appeared never to have developed the ability to trust people. The marriage itself was a big step for him in trusting another human being, and he had had periods when he did not trust his wife at all. She had had a feeling of not being able to bank on him since the hospital incident. Although that was a month ago, she brought it up again as an example of her loss of confidence in him. He reiterated that if she were ill, he would call the best physicians and get her to the best hospital, but that he was unable to give her individual attention.

The counselor asked who the boss of the family was. John indicated he wanted that responsibility shared. He said that they had discussed this when they were married and had decided she should handle the books, but that he wanted some share in shopping for groceries, clothing, and furniture. She indicated, however, that in her running of the business at home she, too, wanted the freedom to do as she pleased without his cross-examining her every evening. Both Mary and John showed considerable insight during this session. At one time she blurted out that they seemed to be entirely different personalities and therefore unable to understand how the other person felt about things. He recognized at one point that she seemed to be trying to change him. He said this was impossible, that he was the kind of person he was, and for her to try to change him now was asking too much.

At the close of the counseling the counselor summarized: They appeared to be getting along considerably better than they were a month ago, but though this particular crisis was over, they were going to experience considerable adjustment now which they had not faced up to at the start of their marriage. The fact that they each wanted companionship from each other, and would be considerably unhappier if they parted gave some foundation to their marriage. However, to be happy together they needed to see the other person as he was and to accept and understand him as he was without trying to change him. Change at that period in their lives was too difficult and too much to expect. However, understanding and acceptance would work toward making their marriage considerably happier and their life together one of mutual satisfaction. They said that they were both going to church the following Sunday where a good public address system would allow her to hear the service. He did not appear to desist from this, but was willing to make some adjustments socially if it would help the marriage.

As they left the counselor shook hands with them and said if they ever got into difficulties again to let him know. She, in particular, seemed happy to know that there was a port in a storm and that they need not wait so long next time to get help. The counselor's appraisal was that this was a reconciliation between two middle-aged people with strong personality differences. The fundamental problems had not been solved, but some accommodation had been made by the couple so that they had weathered this crisis, and perhaps had some insight as to how to weather the next one. The counselor expected to see them again if they had another difficult period.

GROUND RULES IN ESTRANGEMENT CASES

It is well in estrangement cases for the counselor and counselees to establish some ground rules by which they plan to operate in the sessions. The counselor has no legal procedure or law to enforce these rules; this is a "gentleman's agreement." The only power is the persuasion of each person's conscience to "play fair" and to give the other person the same treatment he wants to receive. Put in simple form these rules look something like this:

1. Both husband and wife agree to counsel regarding the marriage and agree on the counselor. If one partner refuses counseling, this weakens the possibilities of doing much to strengthen the marriage at the outset. Too, the couples should decide whether they shall see one counselor or go to separate counselors and then remain by this decision.

2. Both husband and wife agree to delay their final decision regarding the marriage, allowing time during the counseling so that they see all the factors involved in staying together or separating.

3. If they both decide to reconcile within the period of counseling, they will not revoke their decision until all possibilities have been exhausted to re-establish the marriage.

4. Both husband and wife agree to keep the expression of feelings, particularly of a negative character, within the counseling session. To carry home hostilities and keep on fighting serves no purpose outside the counseling room. This is a difficult ground rule to keep in the heat of discussion.

5. The counselor agrees to keep the confidences of each partner within the counseling room. He does not tattle to the other partner nor to anyone else about the session.

6. The counselor does not promise miracles; he does promise to be as objective and understanding a helper as he can to the parties he sees.

7. The counselor makes it plain to the husband and/or wife that the decisions to be made are their responsibility and not his. This *rule* may need to be stated at several points during the counseling itself.

8. Finally, regarding appointments, the counselor follows the practice of seeing first one partner alone, and then the other alone, until the problem is in the open; then he sees them both together in a double session to do what is possible in making necessary adjustments in the marriage relationship.

THE PROCESS OF RECONCILIATION

The counselor who first begins working with a feuding couple may develop a deeper appreciation for labor arbitration and international diplomacy. He may openly confront for the first time the force of hostility and the intensity of resentment which drive a wedge between two people. How to resolve these deep feelings will require all his astuteness and patience. Moreover, he will find that each situation is in many respects different from any other he has read about or worked with. Thus, the process described below can only set down guidelines and cannot be expected to be a detailed map for the counselor to follow. Such guidelines may be of some help, however, as they are applied to the counseling case given above or as the minister looks at his own case write-up from their perspective.

The primary function of the early sessions with husband and wife is to allow the expression of deep-seated resentments and hostilities. (This is to presuppose that husband and wife both see the same counselor.) Both members of the marriage need to talk over their "gripes" and "beefs" about the other alone with the counselor. John and Mary have been in heated arguments during the last month. Previously, they appeared able to argue and to come out somewhere, and to resolve their differences of opinion. But now the argument is out of hand; John has blown up and said some mean things about Mary; and Mary has countered by refusing sexual relations and threatening to go home to mother.

The counselor helps the couple to drain off the deeper feelings of hostility by accepting them without arguing as to the rightness or wrongness of the provocation. The basis for their feelings is interpersonal. "What does this action mean to you?" the counselor asks. "What does it mean to your mate?" When they are able to get behind the action to the motive, they can begin to see the reasons for the conflict. It can be situational: Mary is overtired from her Christmas job and subject to flare-ups. Or it can be conflict of interests: John wants to join the country club for business purposes; Mary wants to become more deeply involved in the church for religious reasons. Or it may be the result of role ambiguities and misunderstandings: John would like a more "feminine" wife, while Mary enjoys a dominant position, particularly with regard to the finances of the home. Any of these conflicts can be dealt with directly without recourse to analyzing the personalities of John and Mary.

The goal of these sessions is to move toward the joint session where the couple can quarrel constructively again. The presence of a third party who has the best interests of each at heart is disarming. Exaggerations are out of place; the emotions have subsided around the issues and the couple face their problems with some desire and motive for solving them. They can argue, but it is from step to step in some kind of progression. The counselor is not afraid of feelings being expressed at this time, but if feelings run high in the joint session, he may want to arrange more individual sessions. This way, the talking out of these feelings is worked on immediately so that a further joint session is more productive.

A cooling-off period may be helpful to the couple who is embittered and disaffected with one another. As one wife said, "The trouble with our marriage is that there is no surprise left. After ten years I don't raise an issue because I know almost automatically what his response will be. I'm sure I don't know him completely but I don't seem able to get through to him at any new point." A vacation from the marriage might be helpful to the people who are deadlocked in order to get away temporarily from the situation. The hours spent each week with the counselor may be all that is necessary to gain perspective. But it has been the writer's experience while counseling with deeply resentful couples that a period at the club, or a short trip to relatives, or even a separate vacation provides the necessary time to cool off and regain emotional equilibrium enough to continue counseling. The counselor may have some reservations about this kind of move lest it be the opening of the door to permanent separation. However, so long as the person or persons agree to come back to the counselor to talk about the relationship, the marriage is not broken.

Realistic confrontation of the other person is another phase of the reconciling process. The partner through the disharmony in their marriage has heard the other person wrongly, seen him as a blurred image, perceived him in a distorted way. Let us look at this phase from the standpoint of *marital roles* again. The husband has certain "real" attributes: he is quiet, hard-working, a bit unsocial, but a sound provider for the home. His wife, however, has certain expectations of him of an "ideal" sort: she wants him to be an outgoing, sociable participant in the party world. One can diagram this relationship in this way:

Figure 5

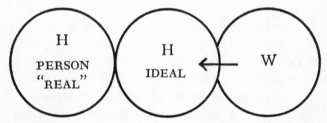

The wife can be seen to be related unrealistically to her husband through a role distortion. The counselor helps the husband to understand the wife's expectations of him; and he also helps the wife to understand the realistic possibilities of the husband as against her expectations. This may involve a disillusioning process on the part of the wife as well as adjustment on the part of the husband until the husband's role relationship is perceived by both in nearly identical terms. This means that

Figure 6

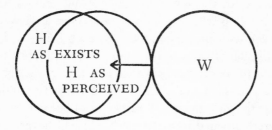

each accepts the other as he is, with both his assets and his liabilities, rather than operating in terms of a fantasied picture of the other. "Prince Charming" is now my *John,* even in work clothes washing the car. Mary is loved for who she is, even when in curlers and dressing gown. This kind of acceptance of the other person lays the groundwork for forgiveness as it is worked out in later counseling.

<u>*A working plan for the marriage*</u> may now be established. It is not possible to plunge into talks about budget or sexual relations or the use of leisure time until the preliminary spadework has been done. The counselor and his counselees will continually be sidetracked by negative feelings which have come from one or the other's default at these points. How, for instance, can a budget be worked on if Mary continually is reminded of John's extravagances and her deprivations as a result? However, where the negative feelings have been expressed, the tempers have cooled, and the couple have started productive problem-solving within the counseling sessions, a joint session can be arranged in which the key issues can be discussed. It is at this point Judge Louis Burke draws up a reconciliation agreement which is discussed by the couple and signed as a contract.[4] This kind of legal document is out of the counselor's field;

[4] See Louis Burke, *With This Ring* (New York: McGraw-Hill Book Co., Inc., 1958), Appendix.

however, the discussion of the issues should eventuate in some agreement.

Just as premarital counseling centers at one point on a budget, reconciliation may bring the couple around a table with a counselor to hammer out a workable financial plan. So, too, with the physical side of marriage; each has expressed his desires or fears to the counselor. They now seek to harmonize their desires and to work out their fears in the presence of an understanding third person. Common interests and activities may assume the center of the stage, as the husband decides to give up his twice-a-week bowling with the boys to bowl once a week with his wife and once a week with the office group. So each issue—in-laws, personal appearance, division of work responsibility, respecting privacy, the use of alcohol—comes up with some possibility of a working agreement to be arranged. The counselor understands and conveys the understanding to the couple that the agreement will not be ideal but will be a compromise which they are motivated to make work. He will never cease to be surprised at how long some couples live together without reaching such an agreement.

Along about this time *the courtship period begins again* quite naturally. When reconciliation actually starts operating between two people, each is spontaneously motivated to "win" the other again. The love previously obscured by hostile feelings comes to the fore and seeks expression. Now, it surely can't be like two teenagers falling in love again, you say. No, but observations of couples at this stage will teach the counselor the possibilities that human personality has under favorable conditions of growing toward another again. The counseling procedure should have supplied those favorable conditions. The reconciling process is not a mechanical step-by-step model, but a growth into increasing awareness of the other person, of who he or she really is, and what they contribute to the marriage. Appreciation of the other's values is inwardly perceived, and first one, then the other begins to show it.

The graces and bonuses of marriage are reinstated. How much these mean to a marriage! But when couples begin to fight they are like luxuries, expendable. The counselor may help the husband in a supportive way, as he decides to take his wife out for dinner, or to remember her birthday. Or he may support the wife as she seeks to make overtures to her husband about reinstating sexual relations. The husband actually woos his wife, and she responds encouragingly.

Gibson Winter writes that a couple must actually decide to enter a covenant of intimacy. Involved is the decision to listen to the other person, to be personally present; and the decision to stand together in the relationship, to stand by the other person during illness or crisis without assurance of reward.[5] Such decisions can come during reconciliation-counseling, when the couple begin to move toward each other and to see the marriage as a valuable thing to be conserved and worked for.

Religious resources are recognized and used in the closing phases of counseling. Some readers may have questioned the absence of such resources up to this point. How is this counseling any different from what a social worker or psychologist might do? This is a good question to which the answer might be that it is not different at all in method. The only difference is in the role of the counselor and in those resources which he has to offer which come from religion and the church. The couple sought him out because he was a minister as well as a counselor, and this perception underlies the total relationship as was indicated in Chapter VII. However, to bring in prayer or Bible reading too soon in the counseling may block the expression of feelings, particularly those of a negative character. One counselor on a reconciliation board made a practice at a certain point in the hour's proceedings to ask the couple to bow with him while he prayed. Others on the board reported that the reaction was not always an attitude of reverence on the part of the couple.

The point is that once the process of forgiveness is under way, the couple can better recognize the meanings and force of religion. The power of forgiveness is greater than either or both of them; they are grasped by it. They feel the undergirding support of God as they accept their share of guilt and reach out in tentative exploration toward the other person. After a joint session where such positive acceptance of each other is expressed and the couple affirms their relationship again, prayer becomes a rededication and benediction. For the couple to attend worship services together again is now a positive motivation and not a legalistic requirement. They "begin again" out of the freshness of their interest in one another and their realization of the curing, healing powers which have flowed into their lives. The minister-counselor draws these insights

[5] Gibson Winter, *Love and Conflict* (New York: Doubleday & Company, Inc. 1958), p. 111.

into awareness when he prays with the couple. If the couple prays, they recognize what God means to them through the reconciling process.

A NOTE ON THE COURTS AND RECONCILIATION

Mention has been made of Judge Louis Burke's procedure in California. It should be noted that the legal profession in general looks with favor upon reconciliation as a desirable process between estranged couples and that various procedures are being worked out in relation to the courts. Says Judge Paul Alexander of Ohio, "Thoughtful members of the legal profession in virtually every part of this country have been increasingly appalled at the unspeakable ineptitude and downright disastrousness of our old fashioned legalistic way of handling family cases." [6]

The means of working out marriage counseling in relation to the court (domestic relations or civil court) have been many. However, they can be divided into three main approaches:

1. The "friend of the court" (example: Michigan) in which a person is assigned to instruct the couple with regard to their duties during the trial and after the decree. This is not counseling, but guidance with regard to obeying court orders in relation to alimony, custody of children, etc.

2. Compulsory counseling, in which the couple is required to see a judge, social worker, or panel of reconcilers assigned to the court (example: California.) Divorce proceedings are suspended while the possibility of reconciliation is worked out. Judge Burke reports success in 43 per cent of the cases in his court, with 75 per cent of those reconciled reported living together after one year.

3. A combination of mandatory investigation-report to the judge and attorneys and voluntary short-term counseling (example: Ohio). In this last, according to Ralph Bridgman,[7] there is a neater distinction between the judicial and counseling function as the referrals are made to pastors and social-case-work agencies for continuing guidance and counseling.

[6] From an address to the Assembly of Social Scientists, 1954, and quoted by Ralph Bridgman, *Pastoral Psychology*, October, 1958, p. 25.

[7] See two articles by Ralph Bridgman: "Marital Discord," *Pastoral Psychology*, September, 1958, pp. 16-24, "Divorce and Reconciliation," *Pastoral Psychology*, October, 1958, pp. 25-32.

It would be hoped that pastors might be trained in marriage counseling to the point where they could conscientiously accept such referrals. Moreover, the socially alert minister, in a state where the reconciliation procedures are in need of rethinking and reform, can make a contribution in working with others to bring the law into better accord with reconciliation counseling.

IX

Divorce and Post-Divorce

Some marriages fail and are dissolved; the minister may well recognize
this fact. To preach against divorce does not stem the tide any more
than standing along a shore shouting at the waves keeps them from
breaking at one's feet. After a certain stage is reached, reconciliation
becomes impossible between some couples. To take the investigations
and therapeutic experience of psychiatrists, social workers, and psychologists seriously is to recognize that where physical or mental injury
of a child or youth or adult is involved, divorce is not only possible but
desirable. If one follows the principle that man is not made for marriage
but marriage for man, he can counsel for the best situation for both
husband and wife, rather than try to enforce legalistic principles. Then,
perhaps as a clergyman he can be of real help to the couple who come
to that poignant moment when they decide to separate and through the
courts bring about a dissolution of their marriage bonds. There will be
psychological and spiritual hurt in any divorce action, but sometimes for
the couple it is the lesser of two evils.

WHY DO THEY DIVORCE?

The clergyman should be interested in the question of why couples
get divorces. To counsel effectively, these underlying reasons and mo-
tives need to be uncovered. Then, too, the pastor can do better preventative work with couples' marriages if he knows what provokes serious
ruptures in their relationships. Let us get a broad perspective at the
beginning.

Several years ago, Professor Lewis M. Terman and his associates
listed nearly sixty grievances which husbands and wives have about each

other which led to serious trouble.[1] M. R. C. Astley found four roots to marital stress, namely: immaturity of one or both partners; character problems which involve distortions of personal values; neuroses and psychoses with their attendant effects on the partner; and situational reactions as a business reverse or prolonged separation.[2] Evelyn Duvall, on the other hand, narrows the causes of divorce to two, namely: a serious breakdown in character which cannot be remedied, and a basic incompatibility in which one is going in an opposite direction to another in terms of interests and values.[3] F. A. Magoun is the most direct of all: he finds incompatibility to be the root cause of divorce. "All else," he says, "cruelty, adultery, drunkenness—is merely rebellion against the frustration of incompatibility itself. Divorce is the result, not the cause of failure." [4]

Such a brief survey points out that there is no basic cause, but that many causes move the individuals to that point when they not only leave one another's presence, but their company as well. If the counseling minister has left the reins of responsibility with the couple, he accepts their decision with equanimity and helps to hold them steady, personally and in terms of their religious faith, while the steps are being taken which dissolve the marriage. He recognizes that the reasons for failure to reconcile may have been his own lack of skill and perception. But more often it is that the couple is inaccessible to counseling: They already had made up their minds to separate or they did not work hard enough to adjust their differences. A messiah complex will push the minister into clamping his own solution on the couple, or openly rejecting them if they decide for divorce. The first divorce action the counseling pastor works through will test him severely at the point of his basic assumptions and tolerances.

THE DISSOLVING OF A MARRIAGE

If the minister is honest with himself, he will perceive how much the community, including the church, has shaped his conception of divorce.

[1] *Psychological Factors in Marital Happiness* (New York: McGraw-Hill Book Co., Inc., 1938).
[2] "Fidelity and Infidelity" in Emily Mudd and Aron Krich, *Man and Wife*, pp. 85-90.
[3] In Stewart, *op. cit.*, p. 1 ff.
[4] *Love and Marriage*, Revised Edition (New York: Harper & Bros., 1956), p. 171.

According to sociologists, all family systems have some kind of "escape hatch" built into them, and these include annulment, separation, and divorce.[5] Marital stability is valued within the family system and the church has taken a position as conserver of marriage.

Let us examine, for purpose of clarification, the Roman Catholic position over against the Protestant position as enlightened by the teachings of Jesus concerning divorce.

The Roman Catholic position is simple and clear. Marriage is a sacrament of the Church and as such is a permanent institution from which believers have no recourse. "The canon law never permits the dissolution of a marriage between persons when both were baptized or if it has been physically consummated, nor does it allow the dissolution of the marriage of the unbaptized except in the unusual instance of the Pauline Privilege or the privilege of faith." The Pauline Privilege refers to 1 Cor. 7:2 and states when one member is converted to Catholicism and the other is not converted and does not wish to cohabit, the marriage is dissolved. The privilege of faith is broader in application referring to the right of a Catholic married to a nonbeliever to contract a new marriage with a Catholic where such marriage would result in favor of the faith, provided the former marriage is dissolved by pontifical authority. The other exceptions are (1) annulment when a marriage is proved invalid and (2) dispensation from a nonconsummated marriage by the pope when there is just cause (danger of scandal, proof of impotence, proof of contagious disease, and an invalid marriage being some of the grounds).[6]

The Protestant position is not a uniform one with respect to divorce, but ranges from absolute denial on the part of the orthodox groups to a completely liberal attitude on the part of liberal groups. It is most difficult to appeal to the Bible for justification of one's position. In the passages in which Jesus dealt with the matter, it is possible to come out for or against divorce. Let us look at the matter from the spirit of Jesus' teaching.[7] In a truly reforming way Jesus swept aside some laws (oaths), made radical changes in others (the sabbath and the rites of purification),

[5] See William J. Goode, *After Divorce*.

[6] Brandon Brown, "Divorce," *The Catholic Encyclopedia*, Vol. 18, Supplement 2. See also Mihanovich, Tebuepp, and Thomas, *A Guide to Catholic Marriage* (Milwaukee: The Bruce Publishing Co., 1955), pp. 148-149.

[7] See Matt. 5:31-32; Mark 10:2-12; Luke 16:18.

and attempted to demonstrate how the law of love superceded and fulfilled the Mosaic law (murder, retaliation, divorce, and adultery). Speaking against the background of current rabbinical debate, he lifted the
matter of marriage to the level of a sacramental act instituted by God
and a life-binding commitment. His disciples were to live in the Kingdom
in a relationship of self-giving and faithfulness, particularly in their
marriages and families. This meant marriage was permanent and sacred.

However, Jesus was not legalistic, and despite some of the churches'
stands he made human integrity and spiritual values of greater importance than regulations. Institutions, like the sabbath, are made for man
and not man for the institution. His sympathy for the adulterer, his
emphasis on forgiveness, and the possibility of a second chance would
make it appear he would recognize the necessity of divorce. There are
instances when a man and a woman are damaging each other's personalities terribly and ruining the chances of their children for a normal life.
Then divorce seems to be the only possibility. Henry Bowman makes this
into a central principle: divorce is possible when it is appropriate for
human welfare. As he says, "A Christian marriage is not preserved by
form or force, by law or doctrine, but only by the capacity of the couple
through love to establish and sustain a spiritual unity." [8]

The Methodist Church represents a middle ground among Protestant
churches in its attitude toward divorce and remarriage. Like other free
churches, it repudiated the dogma of the sacramental character of marriage and opened the way for divorce and for the regulation of marriage
legally within the civil court rather than the ecclesiastical court. As the
mores of the community have changed with regard to acceptance of
divorce, so has the *Discipline of The Methodist Church* been revised
in its statement. A study of the *Discipline* from the early part of the
twentieth century to the present would show a liberalization of attitudes
and church rubrics. The *Discipline* for 1960 states:

> The time has come when every person planning marriage should have the
> opportunity for skilled and careful counseling by ministers or staff workers
> who are prepared in this field. If this is to be done, pastors must be trained
> to guide young people through premarital and postmarital counseling. . . .
> It is important that Protestant youth discuss . . . [mixed marriage] with

[8] *A Christian Interpretation of Marriage* (Philadelphia: Westminster Press, 1959),
p. 75.

their ministers before it is too late. Ministers are urged to discuss with both youth and parents the likelihood of failure in mixed marriages. . . .

We believe that planned parenthood practiced in Christian conscience fulfills rather than violates the will of God. . . .

As ministers, we are obligated to aid by counsel, persons who have experienced broken marriage, and to guide them so that they may make satisfactory adjustments.

. . . .

In view of the seriousness with which the Scriptures and the Church regard divorce, a minister may solemnize the marriage of a divorced person only when he has satisfied himself by careful counseling that: (*a*) the divorced person is sufficiently aware of the factors leading to the failure of the previous marriage, (*b*) the divorced person is sincerely preparing to make the proposed marriage truly Christian, and (*c*) sufficient time has elapsed for adequate preparation and counseling.[9]

The difficulty today is that with the liberalization of laws regarding the procurement of divorce and with more couples seeking relief through the courts, the community does not yet have a standard operating procedure toward divorce or the divorcee.[10] There is not yet a culturally approved way of acting toward this "escape hatch" to marriage. The divorcé caught in the legal imputation of guilt by court proceedings (which cannot grant a divorce without imputing such guilt) is a "maverick" in most communities. And the church, reputed to be a champion of the weak and fallen, finds itself often in the Pharisaical position of scorning this person. This pitiable letter from the Forties, I am sure, still finds its mark. A woman wrote:

In the sudden alarm over increasing divorces, I wonder if ministers realize how they are offending divorcées in the pews. I come from a deeply religious family. I have taught young people in church schools and worked in churches all my life. My husband, a minister, left me when our children were babies. Now Sunday after Sunday, I am told about the sin of divorce. I am employed in a law office and know that divorce is perfectly legal yet my church calls it

[9] *Doctrines and Discipline of The Methodist Church* (Nashville, Tenn.; The Methodist Publishing House, 1960), paragraphs 2021 and 356, in part. Used by permission.

[10] See Goode, *op. cit.*, p. 11.

a sin. . . . Is there not a better way of combating divorce than by maligning innocent victims? [11]

RESPONSIBILITY OF THE MINISTER-COUNSELOR

The minister who counsels with a couple with marital difficulty should not aim at reconciliation every time. He should allow the couple to make a decision for or against the marriage in the light of the counseling process and whether or not the conflicts can be resolved to the best interests of both husband and wife. In fact, this is the basic purpose of early counseling with a couple in deadlock—to decide for continuing the marriage or for divorce. As Roswell Johnson says, the decision should not be suppressed, avoided, or delayed unduly.

The purpose of a good divorce process is to make a wise decision—i.e.—to decide for a divorce if such a course promotes the welfare of those concerned, or to deny it if the divorce would work more harm than benefit . . . the process should accomplish its purpose with a minimum of harm.[12]

Let us suppose that the couple has made this decision at the end of a counseling session, as in the case study below. The minister's next responsibility is to see that the husband and wife both obtain legal counsel. The minister is not a lawyer, though he should be acquainted with the marriage, divorce, and family laws of his state. Caution is recommended, however, that legal advice not be given by the minister lest he be subject to charges by one or both spouses. This is beyond his area of competence and he needs to recognize this at the outset. As George Thorman points out, "State laws vary so greatly that only a competent lawyer can guide the person seeking the divorce through the maze of legal procedure. Rules of evidence, waiting periods, custody of children, settlement of property—all add to the complexity of the legal aspects of divorce." [13]

Some of the legal aspects of the dissolving of marriage we can state:

1. *Annulment* is the legal process of declaring that a marriage has not been properly constituted. When force or duress has been used in establishing the marriage or when one or both members are below legal

---

[11] *The Christian Century*, Vol. 63 (1946), 872.

[12] "Suppressed, Delayed, Damaging and Avoided Divorce," *The Law and Contemporary Problems*, XVIII (1953), 72.

[13] George Thorman, in Stewart, *op. cit.*, pp. 156-157.

age, the marriage can be dissolved in this way. Intoxication, consanguinity, feeblemindedness or insanity, prior marriage, and in some states interracial marriage are also grounds for annulment.

2. *Desertion,* often called "the poor man's divorce," exists when one member of the marriage leaves the other with or without his knowledge. The courts can be resorted to in order to bring the deserting member back or to force him to support the wife or child. However, for many of the poor legal aid is too expensive and welfare help is the only recourse.

3. *Separation (separatio a mensa et thoro)* is the state where the couple no longer lives together, but neither is allowed to remarry, and the husband is responsible for the maintenance and support of the wife and children. This may be a preliminary step in interlocutory divorce decrees, or it may be a relatively permanent situation as in the case of Roman Catholics.

4. *Divorce action* is the legal process in which the couple engages actually to dissolve the marriage. The action may be either criminal action or civil action. The former applies to charges of assault and battery, neglect, desertion, or contributing to the delinquency of a minor. The latter applies to petitions to dissolve the marriage, actions for support and alimony, and for custody and right of visitation and/or companionship with the children.

Many in the legal profession recognize the anachronisms of contemporary divorce law. Attorney Edward Sherman in private conversation[14] stated that the civil action is a contest in which the truth is supposed to come out by pitting two people against one another in a ring with the judge as referee. Rather than being remedial, the court action adds fuel to the fires of hostility between the couple when Jane Smith vs. Joe Smith come to court with their lawyers. As conferences and discussions have gone on about the faults of the legal system, the consensus has been that

divorce litigation is the one striking exception in the whole field of our law to the method that the defendant is trying to prevent the plaintiff from succeeding and that this real contest will bring out the true facts and the best legal construction of those facts.[15]

[14] January 30, 1958, in Denver, Colorado.
[15] Paul Sayre, "Divorce for the Unworthy," *The Law and Contemporary Problems,* XVIII (1953), 26-27.

The grounds for divorce vary from state to state, from New York with only one to many states with thirteen and more. The usual grounds are adultery, physical and mental cruelty, drunkenness, drug addiction, desertion, abandonment, imprisonment for a felony, impotence, and indignities to the person. A divorce was granted by Judge Joseph E. Cook in Denver in 1957 when a woman gave her husband a choice between her or the chickens he kept in the house, and he replied, "I'll take the chickens." The lawyers usually find the grounds that would be least objectionable and decide who shall sue; then the couple can enter a contract which is known as the separation agreement. The court merely rules on the technicalities of the divorce, so that very little of the real marriage difficulty gets into the court. The procedure may be over in minutes, particularly when the divorce is not contested. And it gives one pause to realize that 90 per cent of all divorce actions are uncontested.

One final word needs to be said regarding the minister's immunity in court action. In nearly all the 50 states of the United States this is written into statute: the seal of the confessional cannot be broken in court. The clergyman would find it to his advantage to check the statutes of his own state in this regard, particularly if he counsels couples who come to the courts for divorce. He may be asked to testify as to the good character of his counselee if the latter feels the divorce action is going against him. However strong his sentiments, by the nature of his office he needs to respect the seal of the confessional. While his testimony might be beneficial at one point, it could be damaging at another. It is well therefore to keep outside the legal action. The legal counsel is the one to find corroborating witnesses, and he should do this outside the counseling sphere.

DIVORCE COUNSELING

The first step in divorce counseling we have already indicated: that is, to guide the couple making a decision to divorce. As a part of this the counselor needs to point out the emotional cost of divorce, particularly as the husband and/or wife verbalize these feelings.

There is a considerable loss of self-esteem. The man has invested considerable time, money, and effort in building a home and in getting his wife and children financially established. To lose this is to lose a considerable part of himself. The wife, perhaps more than her husband, has her feelings of success as a person bound up in whether she succeeds as a wife and a mother. When divorce is imminent, she suffers considerable loss of esteem in her own eyes. Along with this is the loss of status in the eyes of friends. Though divorce is being increasingly recognized as a social matter, to become divorced means that one loses friends who have been formed mutually by both husband and wife. Too, one loses friends who do not approve of the divorce action itself—this is inevitable.

There will be difficulties with relatives on both sides, particularly if custody of children is involved. The grandparents have not had a falling out, and may not understand the inability to see the children as frequently. If the divorce action is contested, brothers and sisters may line up behind the partner in what looks like a clan fight. Misunderstandings of the family are multiplied as the separation actually takes place.

The couple will undergo a drastic change in personal habits, in plans, and in their whole style of life. Quite obviously there will be a change in their sexual and affectional expressions, though in leading up to divorce they have probably accommodated themselves to this. But the habits of work and play, of vocation and avocation change as the two now become single again. The husband, if in a public profession, may have to secure another job; the wife may have to start work again. The plans for retirement are quashed; the children's education may now take a different turn.

Most important to face is the pain of loneliness and separation. If the husband takes a room apart before the divorce, or if the wife goes to live with relatives, these feelings are experienced and expressed in the counseling at this point. The counselor helps the person to verbalize them and to experience them fully rather than to deny them by projection or frenzied activity. Some individuals get very active in church work at this period and the minister should be aware of the "denying" side of this behavior. The fundamental problem here as it is after the divorce is to accept the fact that one is single again.

After the divorce the pastor owes it to the couple or to one party at least to continue the counseling process. The person may have serious religious qualms regarding the divorce and he comes to see the pastor to talk these over. He married with the full intent of staying with his spouse " 'til death do us part," and now feels guilty in breaking this vow before

God. The pastoral counselor does not reassure at this point, but accepts these feelings and helps him to verbalize additional feelings.

The primary feelings center in the loss the person has suffered in the departure of his mate. Counseling after divorce is very similar to grief work which the pastor does after the death of a loved one. A marriage has died, and both parties react to this loss as though they were bereaved. John feels relieved that the stress of argument and the strain of conflict is over, but he also feels empty, defeated, and completely alone. Mary, on the other hand, suffers intense feelings of hostility about John and beneath her bitterness is guilt at her failure to measure up as a wife. The pastor allows John to relive the past episodes with Mary and to reconstruct how they were resolved, until as in grief work, he can lay them aside and close the door on this phase of his life. Mary, on the other hand, needs to accept her own responsibility for the split-up. The pastor helps her to see how she has a share in the guilt and in order to forgive she, too, must be forgiven. Since John has gone, the forgiveness is mediated through the pastor's acceptance and through Mary's awareness of the forgiveness of God.

Religious qualms are not genuinely faced until this period though they may be raised earlier. Prayer, either silent or verbalized, is appreciated at this point. The pastor may move into the church sanctuary at the end of a session in his office. The person can sit in the pew or kneel at the altar with the pastor as the forgiveness of God is acknowledged in his life. The author favors the Protestant pastor's standing, kneeling, or sitting beside the parishioner in this process. He is not a mediator type of priest, but one who has experienced God's forgiveness and continually stands in need of its renewal just as the parishioner does. His counseling role has underlined this through the weeks in the face-to-face relationship. It is not now contraindicted in this symbolic act of prayer.

Other needs may be expressed by John or Mary in their community or church relations after divorce. Mary, for instance, finds difficulty in taking up with her women's group members. Some of the women disapprove of what she has done; others feel embarrassed by her presence. She finds it impossible now to attend occasions where couples predominate. A "grass widow" is not a safe person around one's husband, wives feel. And she feels odd when couples center their conversation in children and homes and family matters. The facts of the matter are, sociologists tell us, there is no clearly defined role for the divorcée. She does not know what is expected of her and society treats her ambiguously.

The counseling minister can surely make Mary's road somewhat smoother. She needs to face the financial problems involved in living on alimony and child support—certainly there is a slimmer budget than before. Obtaining a new job and making adjustments for care of the children need to be negotiated. The counselor is warned against strictly "action counseling" here—getting the job or providing the child care. However, he can support the parishioner emotionally while these adjustments are being made and perhaps provide references with regard to employment and care of children.

Further, the counselor finds that the divorced couple has difficulty in forming new friends. Bill, even six months after the divorce, is living an isolated existence. He fears getting emotionally involved again with women since he has suffered so severely as a result of this broken marriage. The hesitation has more to commend it than a sudden marriage on the "rebound." But isolation has in it the seeds of mental illness. Bill needs leading out to the point where he begins to form new friendships with men *and* women. He is not held in suspicion as a divorcé as Mary is; but he may unduly restrict himself because of his fears about marriage. If he is young, his sexual needs may cause him difficulty. They are no longer adequately met and he may get erotically involved in a relationship with a woman whom he has no intention of marrying. To continue counseling during this period can be of immense help to him.

The pastor may be just the steadying influence to keep the person from escaping his plight to a large city or place where he is completely unknown.[16] Though the Protestant church is not yet this kind of "fellowship of the forgiven," it is to be hoped and planned for that there will be groups within the church where the divorced as well as the widowed and the unmarried will find acceptance and a place of responsibility.[17]

The children of divorce represent a unique and pitiable group.[18] As has been indicated, divorce may not be the worst outcome for them. To live in a family where daily conflict and interpersonal tension keep

[16] Bossard and Dillon discovered that this is just what divorced women do. See *American Journal of Sociology*, XL (1935), pp. 503-507.
[17] See Chapter XIV.
[18] Despert, *op. cit.*

mother and father at each other's throats or frozen in noncommunication may be more damaging emotionally than living without one parent. When divorce is imminent, if not before, the counseling minister needs to be aware of the children. He knows that couples who want to stay together "for the children's sake" may be doing them great damage. So, too, is he conscious that the children may be tugged and pulled as to their loyalties to "mommy" or "daddy" in the marital conflict.

In the counseling which leads the couple to decide for divorce, they may discuss the best alternative for the child. He may live in complete custody of the mother or of the father; he may live alternately with the mother and the father; he may live with neither but with relatives, the grandparents for instance. Or he may live with one parent and a step-parent in the case of remarriage. Or he may be placed by the welfare authorities in a foster home. Before the divorce action these alternatives can be responsibly discussed; but at the time a lawyer is secured, custody is made a part of the legal separation contract, and the parents must abide by the court action.

The counselor, if he sees the child, helps him to work through his feelings about the separation. The writer's experience has been that these feelings are often repressed, but once the child's confidence is secured, they come out quite readily. He often feels abandoned; mother or daddy have decided to leave me behind. He also feels angry; he has lost his respect for and trust in the adult world. "I hate them," he says. He may interiorize this anger and try to hurt himself; an accident in which he falls from a tree and breaks his arm may indicate anger and a desire for mother to treat him like her baby again. He may be exceedingly anxious and not eat or sleep properly during the crisis of breaking up the home. Particularly if one parent tries to use the child's loyalty as a weapon against the other, the child who loves them both feels the ambivalence inside him and it literally tears him apart. Work with children does not differ basically from work with adults, but as we shall discuss in the following chapters, it may require some special training and experience before one is capable of helping a child in any basic way with his feelings. However, if the pastor is acquainted with the child through church school or a church group, he may have an entree that it would take another professional worker several sessions to establish. Certainly with

150,000 to 200,000 children affected every year by divorce, someone should be counseling to help them make adequate adjustments.[19]

The remarriage of the divorcée brings up the final problems involved in divorce counseling. Two strands of our discussion came together at this point: the church's general disapproval of remarriage (the Catholic Church forbids it unless the spouse has died; some Protestant churches allow it only for the innocent party), and the counselor's attempt to help the divorcée form new relationships with potential marriage partners. The facts as they exist in mid-century American society point to an increasing number of remarriages. Professor M. F. Nimkoff's investigations of remarriage discover that "better than six out of seven of those divorced in recent decades are remarrying, which is greater than the proportion in earlier times . . . studies in the United States show that in subsequent marriages, divorced persons, especially women, usually make better adjustments than they did in the first marriage." [20] Rather than condemning or condoning the divorcé's past behavior, the counseling pastor helps him to face the future relationships he makes with those of the opposite sex with more insight and understanding, in order to learn what he can contribute to the marriage role and what he can expect from it. Remarriages are made with less "stardust in the eyes" and more realism. Certainly there should be physical attraction and idealism as to what marriage can mean for each one involved. But fantasy is separated from reality in the counseling before remarriage. And particularly if the person looked for some "ideal" in his first marriage, he is made aware of these tendencies as they appear in the counseling discussions with the minister before this marriage. The "Gospel of the Second Chance" should certainly operate at this point. Without sentimentality or glossing over principles, the counseling minister can move beyond the forgiving aspect of counseling to the new situation where a maturing individual will "try again" with utter seriousness to form a lasting relationship with another human being.

The Divorcé's Anonymous[21] group should be called to the attention

---

[19] K. Davis, *The Annals of the American Academy of Political and Social Science*, (1950), 272, pp. 9-22.

[20] "The Family in the U.S.," *Marriage and Family Living* XVI (1954), 396.

[21] Write to *Divorcé's Anonymous* for the group in your city or town. Headquarters: P.O. Box 1342, Chicago 80, Illinois.

of the counseling minister as a resource like Alcoholics Anonymous and Recovery. It can be of supportive help of a group counseling sort for divorcees. The group helps these individuals to adjust to their new estate through weekly meetings with other divorcees. Divorcé's Anonymous holds the following creed:

1. Divorce is not a solution.
2. Marriage is a holy and desirable estate.
3. Development of future generations of physically, mentally, and emotionally sound persons depends upon the health and soundness of marriage and the family.
4. There is a spiritual power greater than man whose help is essential.
5. A willingness is needed to help others to a deeper understanding and better adjustment to the married life.

We shall discuss group counseling procedures for couples in difficulty in a later chapter. However, it seems appropriate that this resource be mentioned here for those couples who have already divorced and are in need of the support and aid of group therapy.

A DIVORCE COUNSELING CASE

Instructions: Make an appraisal of the difficulties between the following couple. As in the premarital case, keep the two areas in mind: (1) the interpersonal relationships between the man and his wife and (2) the counselor's approach to the couple and his response to them. Again, certain questions will be discussed at the end of the interview along these two lines.

Lonnie and Lorraine Brown, ages forty-five and forty-four respectively, were referred to the counselor by their pastor. He reported that their marriage was on the rocks after some twenty-two years. They had one married daughter, Violet, age twenty-one. Lonnie came from a farm family, being an only son with two sisters. He had had one year in an engineering school but did not finish because of the marriage. He had worked the bulk of his life for a mid-western state in the treasury department. He had left his job and come to his present location after he and his wife had reconciled through the offices of a lawyer. At the time of the interview he worked for a bank.

Lorraine was orphaned at an early age and lived with aunts and uncles during her childhood. Finally, when she was sixteen, a favorite aunt offered her a home until she was married. Following the marriage she became pregnant almost immediately. Violet was born by breach delivery and was wanted at first by neither parent. During the interview Lorraine complained about Lonnie's drinking to excess, his refusal to allow her money to spend from their joint savings account, and his refusal to discuss their problems.

Lonnie complained that she was continually ill. She nagged at him to take her out, to go to dinner or to concerts, and he had rather stay at home. She did not want to sleep with him; in fact, it had been nearly a year and a half since they had had sexual relations.

The counselor structured the interviews so that he would see each of them twice separately and then be able to arrange a joint interview with them both. In the ensuing two interviews with Lorraine, she portrayed herself as one who had suffered much during the marriage, having done things which her husband should have done. She accused him of excessive drinking, penuriousness, and a lack of romance in their marriage. When he came in, he stressed that he wanted a wife who would do the housework and who would help him in his business by going to parties and mixing with his bosses and their wives. Because of her illness and inability to go out or do things around the house, he felt she had been failing him.

Lonnie and Lorraine had separated twice previously: first, when Violet was born, and secondly, three years before the interview when she had gotten fed up, feeling he did not give her enough love or emotional support. When they had reconciled, the stipulations had been: that they move to this state and start life anew; that they establish a joint bank account; that they do things together; and that she obtain a position so that she would not have so much time on her hands. They had carried out the letter of the law, but the difficuties had returned.

At the joint interview discussion focused on what they would do on their vacation. He wanted to go to a national park, obtain a cabin, fish, and relax. She declared that she would not do housework in a cabin or stay in the wilds; she wanted some time to relax herself. In the early part of the interview, much hostility was vented. She had the following role expectation: "I want you to do things with me, be a bold defender and provider, who provides me with all the love I never had." He presented this role expectation: "I want you to be a good *hausfrau*, to go to parties with me as a beautiful socialite, to help me with my career as an executive." They now understood the dreams each had of the other, and were rebelling against these expectations. Lonnie would not wait on her or take her on trips; Lorraine would not go to bed with him and by her illness would excuse herself from going to parties with him. The session ended in an impasse, the counselor refusing to make the decision of where they should go on vacation or how.

The counselor next saw Lonnie alone. He wanted help with the decision of going on his vacation alone. He was concerned that this would mean he could not go back to Lorraine. As a result of the interview he decided to go to the national park alone.

Lorraine came in, ostensibly cheerful but extremely broken up by the fact that the joint session had not been a success for her. She was resentful that her husband had paid the fees for the sessions, and she took some of this resentment out against the counselor by breaking a promise which she had made two evenings before. The counselor had asked that neither should leave the other until more counseling had taken place. She, however, had told her daughter Violet that she could no longer live with Lonnie but would have to leave him. She cried when the broken promise was pointed out to her, saying that Lonnie had broken her and that she did not have the strength to stay with him. She said she wanted to talk again, but that she was at the point of seeing a lawyer.

The next interview she appeared less defensive and talked about her feeling toward mothers. She disliked Lonnie's dependency upon his mother, financially and otherwise. She disliked the fact that his mother had loaned him money on a house which he had never repaid and that she had given him a car. She was angry and jealous at Lonnie's dependency. She also said the counselor reminded her of an earlier minister who counseled her to return when she left Lonnie and she had felt it her duty to stand by this promise. The counselor clarified his relationship to her at this point, pointing out that he did not necessarily want her to stay with her husband but to talk through the difficulties until an intelligent decision could be made.

Lonnie returned from the vacation tanned and relaxed. Underneath he was depressed, however, saying he had not been able to talk with Lorraine since he returned. The battleground now appeared to be the savings account book. He would not relinquish this to her because he feared she would leave him and take the money. On the other hand, he was deflated because his wife had paid the rent on their apartment and was attempting to rebel at his management of the finances.

The second joint interview was held two weeks after the first one. Neither Lonnie nor Lorraine communicated much with each other as the beginning. When asked if they might review how to do things differently, Lonnie suggested he would be willing to review the distribution of finances, including putting the savings book on the table. Lorraine said she would be willing to review the distribution of jobs, though she did not want to be called a "housewife" by Lonnie. They talked these things over and got to the point of asking one another. "Do you love me?" Lorraine said she had no feeling at all for him. This hurt him and he went back to his old grievances, particularly his resentment at her inability to play the part of the executive's wife. She spoke of having to suffer at a spring office party because of her illness and because Lonnie would not take her home. When they came to the point of decision, he said, "Well, if you do not love me, I guess we'd better split up." She would not argue against this but said she would see a lawyer. The counselor left the door open for them to return to see him.

Lorraine returned a week later with a great feeling of relief at having removed herself from the tension of living with Lonnie. She talked over again the accusations he had made against her and appealed to the counselor for his moral judgment. The counselor refused to judge but rather attempted to support her through this period of emotional separation. The second session she talked more about herself and her relationship with her daughter. She related to the counselor, as she had to the former minister, her desire for guidance in her spiritual life. She had never had a father and had strong needs for strength which her husband had not provided. She then went on a two weeks' vacation during which she had a complete check-up at an allergy clinic and was put on a new diet and asked to quit smoking and to find a new job away from dust. She showed worries over her financial life, and when asked about the divorce, she showed signs of putting it off. She looked into the matter of her husband's drinking, even going to a favorite tavern and surprising him so badly that he quickly gulped his drink and left the premises.

Two months later, Lorraine came back to the counselor for two more sessions. Her daughter had been having difficulties, according to the referring pastor. It seems Violet was doing similar things to her husband as Lorraine had done to Lonnie: nagging, neglecting the home, and showing hostility to her mother-in-law. The pastor had seen them for several interviews and wondered how much Lorraine was contributing to the daughter's behavior. Lorraine appeared to be trying to win the daughter to her side of things and to get the daughter to reject Lonnie. The incident of the baptism of Violet's child become a focus of discussion. The difficulty of inviting Lonnie to a baptism party was discussed, with Lorraine finally deciding not to. At the end of this session she broke down and cried, saying she was really angry, mostly at herself for living with this man so long and not having anything to show for it.

The divorce became final in March of the following year after a six months' waiting period, but not without much litigation over property. Lorraine and Lonnie still attend the same church though at different hours. Lonnie adjusted to the separation rather quickly and began dating an attractive middle-aged lady. A two years' follow-up revealed that both had remarried: Lonnie to a reserved, quiet and well-dressed woman much like his idealized image of his wife; Lorraine to a tall, solicitous, giving man, again like her idealized image of a husband. They both reported that they were very happy in the second marriage.

QUESTIONS

1. *Analyze the interpersonal difficulties between Lonnie and Lorraine. What does the matter appear to be in their role expectations and role behavior? Why did they live together so long without breaking permanently? Why did they break their relationship at this juncture in their lives?*
2. *What role does the marriage counselor play in this series of interviews? Do you feel he could have reconciled the couple by doing something differently? What does the counselor appear to do following the separation of the couple? Is his role different at this point than it has been previously? How is it different, if it is?*

X

Family Counseling—Its Nature and Goals

A FAMILY COUNSELING CASE

Jerry and Alice Jones came to the pastor in late May to talk over difficulty they were having in their marriage. They were concerned about whether to divorce or not, since their marriage appeared to be on the rocks. Jerry was a small youthful looking man, aged thirty-six, rather retiring, and reluctant to talk about the difficulty. Alice was thirty, small and pretty, with many "little girl" mannerisms. They had been married ten years and had two children: Jim, nine, and Janice, three and a half, having lost a baby between these two births.

They had come to the Midwest from the East. Jerry had preceded the family in order to find work, and had brought Jim along with him. He finally had located a hardware store he wanted to buy, and with his mother's assistance had been able to put a down payment on it. Alice and Janice had remained in the East with her folks. She had obtained a job as a secretary in order to provide a living until Jerry got established. The period apart—some nine months—had been very difficult for her in that she was lonely and felt like a child again with her parents. After she was able to sell their old house, she and Janice had moved to the Midwest town to settle with Jerry and Jim in a garage apartment.

Almost immediately, Alice had discovered that Jerry was having an affair with Lola, an old girl friend of war days. Jerry had known Lola when he was stationed in this town in 1945, and had fallen in love with her before he knew Alice. The romance was ill-starred from the beginning, for Lola had revealed to him that she was already married to a soldier overseas and that she could not leave him since she was to bear his baby. Though Jerry and Lola felt they loved each other, they had parted feeling their relationship had better end.

Jerry had wanted to get established in the Midwest in order to see Lola again. He had begun seeing her as soon as he had arrived; in fact, he had located a store very near to her home. When Alice discovered all this, she became insanely jealous. Jerry claimed he had had no sexual relations with Lola; however, he had managed to see her every day and had spent considerable time on the telephone talking to her. When the couple came for counseling, Jerry's mother was living with them. Since she knew about Lola, she was continually keeping the issue inflamed and consequently driving Jerry and Alice apart. This was the first crisis to which the couple addressed themselves. However, the situation soon developed into family counseling since the mother-in-law and the children were involved in the case.

The last of July another crisis was generated. The landlord of Jerry and Alice's apartment, a friend of Lola's family, discovered the affair and spilled the beans to Lola's brother at their lodge. Gossip developed in the community about Jerry and Lola and began to affect Jerry's hardware business. Children in the neighborhood began to tease Jim and Janice about their daddy. In talking this over with the counselor, Jerry decided to go directly to Lola's brother and deny any intimacies with her. Alice decided on her own to go to Lola for a showdown. When she did, Lola was very hurt at the accusations, and assured Alice that she and Jerry were just friends and that they never could be anything else. Following this incident Jerry and Alice did not get along any better, however. Though they did not argue openly in the presence of the counselor, they were not able to communicate their wishes or thoughts to the other at home. Toward the end of August in a joint session, they decided to see a lawyer and begin action for divorce. Alice was crushed by her failure to hold Jerry, but she agreed reluctantly if she could keep the children.

Before school started another crisis ensued. Jim became involved with two older boys in the neighborhood in a homosexual incident. Jerry and Alice were shocked by this and brought charges against the two boys in juvenile court. They did not want to prosecute but wanted merely to give the boys a "scare" so that they would know such behavior could not be tolerated in their community. The crisis caused Jerry to forestall any divorce action and the couple terminated their interviews with the counselor with their marriage in a state of suspension.

It should be pointed out at this juncture that the crisis with the family threw the father and mother closer together and made the father realize he was neglecting his boy, and perhaps keeping him in a neighborhood where he might get into further trouble. The romance with Lola had blinded him to his family responsibilities, which he was now seeing with eyes wide open. Though the counselor did not see the couple face to face, he did learn by telephone that Jerry had to give up the hardware store in bankruptcy proceedings. They had found it impossible to make a business go in this section of town. The business reverse forced Jerry to move his family to another section of town, away from Lola and the boys which gave Jim the trouble.

Jerry, however, found no work in the city, and at Christmas time he and Alice decided that they would have to give up their efforts to establish themselves in the city and move back to their parents' home in the East. They packed their belongings, and having put them on a moving van, the family began driving East. When they got into the next state, they encountered a snowstorm which forced them to stop in a little town. There they stopped, too, to reconsider their actions and they decided that they were being hasty and should go back to the city from which they came and try again. They turned around, went back to the city, and then called the movers—blocked in a neighboring city by the snowstorm—telling them to return their belongings. The following week Alice secured a position as a secretary in a downtown business office. The first of January Jerry was able to secure a position as a salesman for a national company. When he took the two weeks' training course, he received the highest mark in the class which built up his confidence.

One year later, in talking with the counselor Jerry indicated that he and Alice were now closer together than they had been for years. Following their return they had taken a week-end holiday together. There they had talked over their difficulties and made some new resolves about ways in which they wanted to work together as a family. Jim is now doing excellent work in a new school away from the old neighborhood where he had to take the kidding of other boys about his father and Lola.

Janice is now flowering in nursery school without the tensions which her mother made her feel because of the difficulties between her and Jerry. What began as divorce counseling can be looked on as family counseling because of the family context in which it was worked out. The counselor saw only father and mother, but the problems with the other woman, the mother-in-law, and the children widened the context to the entire family.

THE GROUP APPROACH TO FAMILY COUNSELING

When the counselor deals with a family, he recognizes that he is confronted with an intricate system of loyalties and responsibilities, of needs and relationships. If the intertwining of expectations and duties represented in marriage appear difficult to unravel, the complexities of role structures in the family are that much more so. However, the conceptualization of the family as a role system will help the counselor understand what is happening in a family as well as offer some help in confronting family problems.

Family counseling is defined as counseling with one or more members of a kinship group where children are involved.[1] The children do not have to be seen by the counselor because husband and wife relations are always affected by the presence of children and vice versa. Other names for family counseling are "parental counseling" and "child guidance"; in the former the parents may be seen alone; in the latter the child may be counseled apart from his parents.

Clinical evidence from practicing case workers, psychologists, and psychiatrists establishes the fact that the family should be treated as a unit.[2] When something goes wrong in the family, it is almost impossible to counsel with one member apart from the other members because the difficulty lies not simply with one emotionally distressed person. It lies between the members themselves: in the splits, barriers, and feelings of isolation generated between them.

[1] A marriage and family counselor should have a basic knowledge of the institution of the American family. The variety of patterns of family living depending on age, ethnic group, social strata and locale will make a big difference in the counseling material elicited.

[2] Nathan Ackerman, *The Psychodynamics of Family Life.*

A brief explanation of the role structure of the family of four in our case study may illuminate this point:

Figure 7

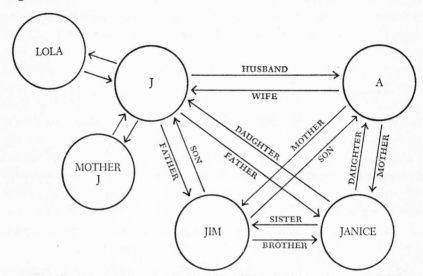

Jerry and Alice relate to each other in the roles of husband and wife. Jerry fulfills the role of breadwinner and provider of the home, and Alice the role of homemaker and assistant at the hardware store. However, in addition, Jerry is father to each child as Alice is mother. Each child fulfills the role of son and daughter respectively. They are by the nature of their age dependent on their parents for the necessities of existence and for nurture. The family system works for the Jones family so long as each understands his role or place in the system, accepts it, and does his best to accomplish his duty for the functioning of the family. When one member fails to do his part, as Jerry did when he began staying away from the family to spend time with Lola, the family system is threatened. It is not simply that Alice feels her husband is deserting her but that the children are losing the support both economic and emotional of a father. Jerry's mother was a similar threat; that is, she attempted to take over some of Jerry's breadwinning role in her financing of his business, and to function as a kind of severe conscience to drive Jerry further away from the home by her nagging. The results were felt not only by Jerry and Alice but by Jim and Janice in the tension created by the adults in the family.

The role structure is further complicated by the fact that each member of the family operates in terms of an accepted role and an ideal role. Alice expected Jerry to be a certain kind of father, to spend more time with Jim as he was growing up. Jerry escaped this duty and gratified some of his emotional needs for security with Lola. In a similar way Jerry expected Alice to be more mature in her attitudes as a wife and a mother; whereas in reality she was dependent and needed to lean upon him. Jim and little Janice also had certain expectations of their parents which in reality were not being fulfilled. The children felt the tension between their parents and were puzzled as to why certain eruptions of anger on their mother's part spilled over onto them. "Why don't you keep your room picked up? Why don't you practice your cornet?" asked Alice of Jim. He never seemed to be able to do the right thing when mother was upset.

CRISES WITHIN THE FAMILY

"Crises," says Reuben Hill, "are those situations which create a sharpened insecurity or which block the usual pattern of action or call for new ones." [3] These may be from outside the family, as the crises generated by war or depression. The father must leave for service in the armed forces, or he is out of work as a result of a national recession—these crises invade the family from outside the system. The Jones's bout with unemployment as a result of losing the hardware store is another example. The other kind of crisis springs from within the family itself and is a result of disturbances in interpersonal relationships and role behavior. The difficulty the Joneses had with Lola and with Jerry's mother are instances of this intrafamily crisis.

Other kinds of family troubles can usually be traced to crises outside or inside the family system: Financial problems may result from the death of the provider or from the profligate spending habits of a family member or both. Illness of one of the family members may be thought of as an invasion from outside the family; on the other hand, if it is a mental illness or a disease of psychosomatic origins, it may be exacerbated

[5] *Ibid.*, pp. 110-11. Used by permission.

by the tensions in the family. So, too, with a child's delinquency: the parents may see it as the outcome of his association with bad companions. However, parental tensions, as operated in the Jones family, can be a contributing factor to deviancy, or at least to the child's being in a state of anxiety where such deviation is a release of emotional tension. The causation is always multiple for him; and the crisis, though originating in events outside the home, has repercussions in the family itself.

Whether a family can meet a crisis or not is measured by two factors: (1) their level of integration, and (2) their adaptability and flexibility in solving problems. In the family *integrity* is synonomous with the *character* of the individual person. This integrity is a product of the harmonious working together of the various family members at their respective roles. *Adaptability* and *flexibility* are the family's *intelligence*. Whether the individuals within a family can solve the problems brought about by a crisis is determined by their ability to adapt themselves to new situations and to assume different roles if circumstances call for it.[4] The crisis which brought the Jones family to the very bottom financially and forced them to start out for their parents' home also solidified them to the place where they began to work together on their problems and to redistribute role obligations. Alice returned to work and became the breadwinner so Jerry could go to school and start out on a new vocational career.

The acute illness of the breadwinner is another example of a family's level of integration and adaptability. For instance, the mother and eldest son might have to go to work to earn enough for the family's livelihood and for the new medical expenses. Older sister might be required to take over some housekeeping functions that mother surrendered. And even baby brother now might help by setting the table, a job which heretofore he has shirked.

Some families are "crisis-prone," says Hill. He means that like the accident-prone individual, they appear to be in a chronic state of crisis. The truth of the matter is that this family may suffer no more difficulty than any other; however, their level of integration and flexibility is low so that they are not adequate to meet the crisis. Alcoholism in one or both parents, neuroticism, mental deficiency or mental illness of family members may be the reason for the lack of integrity of the family. What-

---

[4] Koos, *op. cit.*

ever the inherent reason, a hardship is perceived as a crisis, and it makes a shambles of family organization.

Koos points out that in the recovery of the family from the crisis a certain curve can be plotted thus:[5]

Figure 8

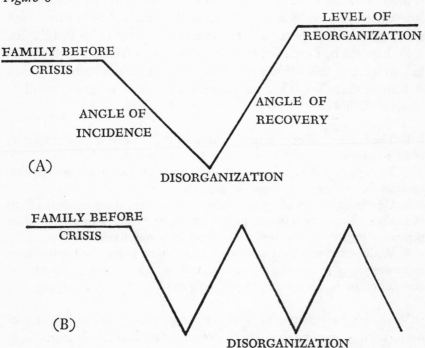

The crisis hits the family as it did the Joneses. They are completely disorganized, so much so that they feel like children who must return to their parents. But when they take stock of things, they begin to work again on their problems, and their family life is reorganized and they begin a climb of recovery. The new level on which they are operating, without the threat of such problems as the "other woman," the mother-in-law, or the bad companions is at a somewhat higher level than before the crisis was precipitated. In the last graph (B) an example is given of a weakly organized family who encounters a second and third

[5] *Ibid.,* pp. 110-11. Used by permission.

hardship and is unable to solve its problems at all. Prolonged crisis can bring a family to the point of "losing any feeling for one another." The duties once performed automatically soon become so hollow that physical illness, delinquency or desertion may cause the break up of the family. Koos discovered among lower-class families that the end result of failure to meet crisis was a loss of authority of the family. The children, particularly adolescents, no longer are drawn to the figures of their parents but seek their relationships outside the family in the street gangs and cliques.

Perhaps the best means of evaluating whether a family is successful or fails in meeting crises is to place them on a continuum such as Nathan Ackerman describes. This classification runs from most successful to complete failures:

1. The family confronts, accurately defines and achieves a realistic solution of its problems.
2. Though unable to achieve a realistic solution, the family nevertheless contains the problem and controls its noxious effects.
3. Unable to find an effective solution or to contain the destructive effects of conflict, the family responds to the tension of failure with an acting-out pattern of impulsive, ill-judged, self-defeating, harmful behavior. . . .
4. With persistent failure at the preceding three levels, the family shows increasing signs of emotional disintegration, which in some circumstances may culminate in disorganization of family ties.[5]

With this background of family systems and the crises which may overtake them in mind, let us now look at the goals of family counseling.

THE GOALS OF FAMILY COUNSELING

It is obvious upon reflection that family counseling involves one in more complex goals than individual counseling. In working with an individual, the counselor helps him to formulate goals, commensurate with his own self-realization within a certain community. When one deals with a family, however, he is involved in mutual interactions of individuals in a system. The individuals are seen as persons, to be sure, but the family system in its shifting, dynamic, ever-moving state is also

[5] Ackerman, *op. cit.*, pp. 99-100.

the subject of counseling. The goals, therefore, are largely interpersonal ones, and the counselor treats the "family" rather than individuals alone.

In such counseling the counselor and clients arrive at goals which are mutually acceptable to each member. The primary goal would be to establish a family system which functions for the mutual benefit of all concerned. The varieties of such organization are endless. However, the ingredients which make up such a system have some common feature in middle-class American families. In the first place, each member of the family should be aware of his role and the other member's complementary role, and he should accept this or modify it for each member's benefit. In the Jones family, the crux of their problem was confusion at this point. When Jerry and Alice became clear as to what each expected of the other in terms of their operation as husband, father, wife, and mother, they could begin to see their way ahead in the crisis they faced.

Then, the family unit has to become the source of satisfaction for the needs of each family member. This means not simply the elemental needs of food, clothing, and shelter, but security needs as well. For the Joneses the need-satisfactions became ambiguous, not only to Jerry who went to Lola's home for security satisfactions, but to young Jim as well, who in his confusion had fallen in with a "bad crowd." The centripetal forces in their family driving them apart had become stronger than the centrifugal forces pulling them together. Only when this process had reversed itself through their conscious problem-solving activity, were the members capable of finding such satisfactions within the family.

A part of the decision is the finding of a common definition of the good of the family and an acceptance of this "good" as prior to the individual "good" of the family members. This does not mean a surrender on the part of the mother of her natural rights so that the children's goods may be realized. This often is interpreted as the Christian way of solving family problems. On the other hand, it does not mean each member continues to consider his own goods as an individual with no consideration of the family's good. This, too, leads to anarchy. However, each member accommodates his goods to live within a family where each member "counts for one." So the children's goods are important to Jerry and Alice as they decide to move to a new neighborhood. But so must their own ideas and goals be considered. Alice's obtaining a job helps her in her own maturity, even as it helps the family through a financial crisis. And

141

though Janice does not see as much of her mother or receive as much care as before, the good of the family requires accommodation on her part, too.

Moreover, the family must gain a sense of direction and some feeling that they are moving in that direction at least to a small degree. These goals are for many families materialistic in nature in terms of buying a home, a new car, or a boat. However, as soon as children are born and their care and education comes into the picture, goals of a more social nature become formulated. One sees in the case of the Joneses the sense of direction "acted out" quite dramatically. When they moved to a different section of town, they attempted to get away from their crisis, only to have it compounded by the loss of employment. The beginning of an exodus back East betrayed their lack of purpose and encroaching feelings of dependency upon their parents. But the resolution to go back and try again re-established a sense of direction and gave them a feeling of moving slowly toward the goal of an autonomous life as a family. It has solidified them somewhat, though the cracks in their family structure are still apparent from the previous crises.

The minister will want to go beyond the secular counselor in his desire to have the family find and operate within a faith and system of values. This cannot, however, be foisted on the family by the minister. In their crisis period, the value of activity often cannot be understood. Things have gone awry; relationships are upset; there appears to be no sense of direction observable anywhere. Families may drop out of church activity and worship while they are going through this crisis period, and the minister should understand this. But once a sense of direction and integrity begins to be re-established, the members of the family can sort out their values into some kind of system. Their faith in each other returns, and so, too, does their faith in God and in a religious way of life. In other words religion for them is not offered as a panacea, but rather religion is a central part of the attitude of the minister—his trust in individuals and belief in family life as worth working for. And when the crisis is weathered, these values and attitudes can be verbalized by the family members and seen for what they are and can be instated in their family system.

Similarity should be apparent to the reader between the pastor and the social worker. The case worker and pastor both call in the home and attempt to understand the family background of problems. They both represent an institution, the case worker being from a social agency, the minister from the church. Too, they both restrict the level of their counseling to the level of family problems. Neither is trained to do "depth work" in personality and so operate with the conscious material presented by family members. But as Ackerman and others point out, even the psychotherapist could better understand family problems if he visited homes when the tensions arise.

Differences between the two workers are also apparent. In the pastor's case he does not ordinarily take a family history but relies on background which he has of the family from membership records and other church contacts. He must also work with the family within the church organization and does not have the independent status of the social worker. He sees the husband at men's club, the wife at women's society, the children at church school, and all at morning service. Then, too, the minister represents a certain scale of values and life orientation, which the social worker *may* not. Some social workers may partake a bit of this "religious role" if they work with a denominational agency, but usually not in quite the same way the minister does.

COUNSELOR, A THIRD FORCE

The entrance of the family counselor into the family system is like the break-through of a third force into a deadlocked battle. It is difficult for middle-class families to allow this to happen. To admit a need for help is somehow to come down in the status ladder. Lower-class families get help from welfare agencies with some feelings of lowering themselves, but after they do it several times, they wall these feelings off and they are no longer consciously felt. But a middle-class family gets help only when sickness or death occurs. If the social illness of delinquency or desertion strikes, the culture has planned no avenues to seek for help. So that when the family counselor is called, it is *"in extremis"* and with considerable reluctance.

He enters as a "third force" to help modify family relationships. It is difficult for one member not to consider him an "intruder." He must allay a lot of suspicion before he can establish the working relationship possible for counseling to proceed. His outside "influence" is beneficial only when it is accepted and unblocks the creative problem-solving abilities of each member. In parent-child problems, authority problems are involved which make this difficult again. To be a "beneficent" third force, the counselor must be aware not only of his own attitudes and evaluations toward family troubles, but be particularly aware of displacements, transferences, and identifications with authority which each family member brings to him upon his entrance into the home.

Family counseling is at the heart of the pastor's work in the parish. Whether he wants to be or not, he is a family counselor. It behooves him to understand what he is about when he undertakes it, as well as how to proceed in the actual case. In the following chapter we move to the next step of structuring and counseling the concrete family problem.

XI

Family Counseling—Its Structure and Flow

THE STRUCTURE OF FAMILY COUNSELING

Midway between personal counseling and group counseling stands family counseling. The counselor no longer sees things from the point of view of one individual; yet he is not involved with a group as a group leader is. Rather he finds the focus of treatment to be at least three people: mother, father, and child. If more than one child is involved, or if more than one generation of parents (married couple and in-laws, for example) is involved, the counselor may see more than three people. The center of the counseling, however, is the family unit. Just as marriage counseling finds the object of treatment to be the "marriage," the relationship between husband and wife, so family counseling finds the object of treatment to be the "family," the bonds that exist between parents and children.

Since the family is the source of the disturbance, it is important for the counselor or counselors to see each party involved. Some good is derived by personal counseling with a mother; however, as we shall see below, for the relationship to be altered between a mother and child, both should be seen. No doubt, the father, too, is a contributing cause to the difficulty, so ideally he should be seen also. These four possibilities are open then to the family counselor:

1. See one parent alone; usually this is the mother.
2. See the child alone. In an adolescent problem the counselor may begin with the youth.
3. See both parents. In an instance of difficulty over the disciplining of a young child, this may be the form of the counseling.
4. See the entire family group. For the best results with family difficulties, this practice is recommended.

145

The structure of interviewing varies, as it does in marriage counseling, between one counselor or several being involved with the family. The same counselor may see all parties if the difficulty exists between a mother and her child, or if the parents are working out an adoption procedure, or if the problem is that of pregnancy before marriage. Here, the problem is so closely interrelated between the two people that one counselor can best give it his attention and help the parties to some workable solution. However, when hostility and seemingly irreconcilable conflict exists between family members, two counselors may be in order. Examples are when a father and mother are in dire disagreement about the welfare of a child, or when an adolescent and his parents are involved in struggles over authority. Better to have two people work in this situation, consult with one another, and finally set up joint interviews, than to be caught in internecine warfare and lose the confidence of both parties.

The minister may find that he has no other option than to see all family members because of his relationship to them through the church. He may profitably see them all in the first interview. However, it behooves him then to determine how many parties he may profitably see and whom he should refer. In the case study below, the counselor found it best, because of the nature of the counseling situation, to refer the boy.

The minister is at a distinct advantage if he chooses to work with all family members. Like the social worker he can visit the family in their home and through "participant-observation" of their behavior with their "manners down," he can understand what the trouble is. Furthermore, he can see how each member acts to other members and what their reaction is to their roles as understood in the family. Nathan Ackerman, a psychotherapist, feels this is so important that he recommends that psychotherapists make a visit to homes of patients with which they are working. Only in the family setting can they be realistically understood, he says.[1]

A CASE STUDY OF A REJECTING MOTHER

Mrs. Lucy Brown came to the pastor to discuss the difficulty she was having with her son Bobby, age twelve. She said he consistently refused

[1] Ackerman, *op. cit.*, p. 129.

to obey her and because of his negative attitudes was failing his grade in school. She was thirty-five and a former teacher of music. Her husband Bill was thirty-seven, an engineer in an aviation company. The boy had been sullen, resentful, and secretive since the age of seven. At that time he developed intense sibling rivalry with his sister Jane, now nine. She consistently got good grades, was pretty, and idolized by her parents. Mrs. Brown said both children were bed-wetters.

Mrs. Brown spent the first interview relating an incident in which Bobby wanted to go to a movie with his little friend Charles, two years his junior. This threw her into a rage because he wanted to make friends with this younger boy, and she slapped him. She was in tears about her behavior and wondered why she could not control him even when she hit him. She told of his interest in guns, warships, cannons, and the escape of prisoners from jail, with no insight as to what it meant.

From the second interview on, Mrs. Brown realized that much of the problem was her own inadequacies and insecurities, and if she could get straightened out, she could help Bobby. She then related her story to the counselor, slowly and tearfully. She said that she was an adopted child, born illegitimately to a young girl who had made an alliance with the town banker. She had been adopted by an older couple—her father, a carpenter who was rather submissive, leaving decisions to her mother, a woman who was very systematic in her actions but very cool in her emotions. She said as she grew up she learned to play the piano, but her mother wanted her to excel in everything. She had had to practice three hours a day; if she brought home anything but A's on her report card, her mother would spank her. Lucy was upset by her mother, but she never expressed any anger except once when she kicked her and got spanked in turn.

In college Lucy went with a young man from a neighboring male college. Nothing ever came of it until she had sexual relations with another man, Bill, and became pregnant by him. Bill and her college friend appeared to pass her back and forth between them until finally Bill assumed responsibility for her. She then had an abortion and they were married. During Lucy and Bill's last year in college they lived together but engaged in no sexual relations for fear of another pregnancy. Bill began with an airplane company and worked himself up to his present position as an engineer. Bill's parents were much wealthier than hers, and, particularly when the children went to visit them, they made her feel like a failure. A crisis arose that she reported during the third session. It concerned Bobby's desire to visit his grandparents in New York City. After talking it through, she decided to let him go. Without him around she felt no tension that week. But when he returned and she discovered grandma had bought Bobby a new suit, she became jealous and very resentful again.

The counselor suggested at this time that she read Dorothy Baruch's *New Ways in Discipline* as a help in understanding her own way of discipline. She related to the counselor as a bad girl, who expected to be spanked, to a father. But on the other hand, it became apparent she wanted to receive acceptance from him and to begin to develop her own potentialities. She came back after reading the book, realizing that she was paddling Bobby to relieve her own tensions. She recognized, too, that she was compulsively clean, that she had high standards for herself, and therefore expected the children to be clean and attain "success." At the suggestion of the counselor she began to make inquiries about getting Bobby to a child guidance center, that he might also get counseling. She resolved, too, to stop, look, and listen before flying off the handle.

The third month her conversation centered about entering a Mrs. America contest and the desire she had for some kind of status. One day she came in with a smile on her face saying that for the past week she had been "Mrs. Witch." She had flown off the handle at Bobby's bringing home a low report card. She had let Bill handle the situation, however, and he did this not by talking to him but by sending him to bed. The second incident was the arrival of the Mrs. America judges who caught her down on her hands and knees in shorts cleaning a dirty house. She said, "I put a clean house ahead of my kids." She cried over her jealousy of other company wives who have new houses and fine clothes and furs. These women appear at ease while she feels ill at ease socially.

The fourth month the counselor consulted with a psychiatrist about the case. He suggested that Lucy was suffering from unforgiven guilt. The abortion, her feelings of being unworthy and unaccepted in her own home, her feelings of being an unworthy mother and wife, all made her extremely anxious and tense and she took these feelings out upon Bobby. She recognized that she was not accepting him, but she felt extremely put upon in that she was unable to develop her musical career. It was the psychiatrist's opinion that Bobby should receive psychiatric help and that following the practice of child guidance services a social worker should see Mrs. Brown.

The pastor continued to see her for the next six weeks, however. During this period she began to feel and express love for Bobby. She recognized that he needed attention, that many of the things that he was doing were demands for her attention. In comforting him after a fight with his sister, she recognized that she did love him and that she wanted him to grow up into a fine manhood. Bobby began to go to a child guidance center but would tell Lucy nothing about what happened. Meanwhile she and Bill began to work together on discipline problems. One example of how they stood together was their refusing to buy Bobby a new baseball after he lost his old one. Lucy felt stronger when Bill helped her with Bobby's training. A final crisis dealt with her fear of a new pregnancy. She had not wanted any more children since she was occupied so with Bobby. She attempted a home treatment of gin and sugar, but discovered with a sigh of relief that the doctor could find no pregnancy.

At the last counseling session, she reported a successful dinner party in which even the division superintendent's wife had complimented her. She had accepted the fact that Bobby had failed his year in school. The principal of the school had called and asked to see Bill, her husband, and Bill went to talk to him concerning the fact of Bobby's not being mature enough to enter junior high school. Bill returned and told Lucy he knew it was not all her fault, that they were both to blame in their treatment of their son. She realized that Bobby should not be punished but that he needed love and support from his parents in these growing years.

In conclusion it should be said that Lucy Brown had come a long way. She understood better why she had been tense and had felt herself a failure. She saw the value of letting up her pressure on Bobby. However, Bobby's failure in school still needed working through. The fact that Bill stood by her at that time and that he now realized his responsibility toward Bobby was a step ahead. She stated that she would call the pastor if she needed more counseling next fall. But she left the office with a radiant smile on her face and much more self-acceptance. She now felt she had the ability to make her way as a woman, wife, and a mother.

FLOW OF FAMILY COUNSELING

The Initial Interview

Using the case of Lucy Brown as an example of family counseling, the reader is asked to look at the dynamics involved. This case is an instance of the counselor seeing one member of the family, the boy being referred to a child guidance center for help. The school was particularly aware of the boy's emotional difficulty and they brought this to the mother's attention. When Lucy came to see the pastoral counselor, she was already motivated to get help although she did not know what kind. The initial interview served as a means of appraisal of the problem, as it does in marriage counseling and in personal counseling.[2]

The counselor asks himself as the counselee unfolds his problem: is this difficulty from outside the family or inside the family? If it is outside the family, what in particular is provoking the problem—is it the loss of a job, illness, the absence of one or both parents from the home, the failure of the mother to conceive a child, or a questionable neighborhood providing a source of "bad companions" for the child? If the problem comes from outside the family, is this properly within my jurisdiction as a minister? Or should the family be referred to an agency or institution within the community? In case of referral it is obvious the clergyman needs to know the social agencies and institutions in his area and to have some understanding of their function and the way a referral is handled. In a large city a directory of social agencies is usually available and the minister can familiarize himself with the agencies when he first arrives at a new parish. In rural areas or in small towns the social worker assigned to social security welfare at the county seat can be an excellent contact-person to help with referrals.[3]

If the problem is within the family, the minister needs carefully to ascertain the resources—emotional, intellectual, financial, and spiritual—of the family. He needs to determine whether he and/or his staff have the time and training to handle the problem most effectively. Some questions to ask himself are: Is this basically a personality problem of one or more members of the family? That is, does anyone need psychiatric

---

[2] Client-centered counselors will not diagnose. However, in the context of the family we are suggesting appraisal of the family's difficulty as a legitimate procedure.

[3] See Wayne Oates, *Where to Go For Help* (Philadelphia: Westminster Press, 1958).

help in the group? In the instance of the Brown family Bobby definitely needed psychiatric help. Then, does the family have the necessary integrity and adaptability to meet the problem? This is where the home visit may be set up in order to observe what the resources of the family actually are. The counselor determines whether the children are being severely damaged by staying in the home during a crisis. Had they better be "placed" in a relative's home or a foster home temporarily? If so, is agency help needed to do this? In Bobby's case his weekly visits to the child guidance center were sufficient, along with periodic trips alone to the grandparents to relieve the pressure at home.

The most basic question the minister faces is: Is this a problem to which this family can normally adjust with conscious level, supportive counseling, or will radical treatment be necessary? He needs to recognize that as a counseling minister he can handle the former; the latter will most likely have to be referred.

Succeeding Interviews

Once the minister has decided that this problem is within his province and ability, and that the family appears to be capable of handling the problem, he begins counseling the member or members of the family. The pastor commits himself to the family for the duration of the crisis or until the resources of the family appear capable of meeting the problem. This means he does not "give up" on them but sees them individually and collectively until things are "going right again." This needs to be said because if anything can frustrate the counselor and make him want to quit, it is family counseling! There are so many nuances of relationship that can stir a family up and such multiple reactions to situations that some counselors think family unity and harmony are gifts, even mystery, and grace. They are much more than the adding of two parents' intentions plus two children's responses. The counselor, particularly in his home visit, must become aware of the interaction between family members: How do father and mother react to one another? How do parents and children get along? What about brother and sister—do they have sources of tension between themselves? Although the counselor did not visit the Brown home in the case above, the disturbances between parents and children were the focus of the counseling. The rejection Lucy felt came from the fact of her own illegitimacy and being treated as "different" by her own mother. Her own feelings of rejection she foisted on her own children, particularly Bobby. The poor boy could not do anything right and finally set out to prove to his parents he was worthless by failing his grade. The bedwetting both he and Jane engaged in was a symptom of the tension in the home.

In looking at a disturbance in a home like this, the counselor is particularly aware of the sense of failure each family member is suffering. The mother is aware of failing as a mother, a most basic feeling to understand, to face, and to work through. With Lucy Brown, for instance, this was central, for she felt her own mother had failed her in putting her up for adoption. Her stepmother, too, had failed by her rigidity and inability to give her love and acceptance. Add to this her own failure to receive her first child and the guilt this engendered, and it is easier to understand Lucy's inability to accept this demanding, restless boy. Mr. Brown, too, felt a sense of failure as a father. He had taken Lucy "on the rebound" and felt sorely distressed by their first year of marriage. Nevertheless, Bobby was his son and he should provide for him. However, he ran away from Bobby's problems leaving them for Lucy to cope with. The boy tried to get attention from his father, but Mr. Brown was too occupied with getting ahead in his business to devote enough attention to the lad. Bobby felt a sense of failure as a son. He got the adoration and attention from his grandparents without the demands upon him to produce. Lucy said to him by her attitudes: "Produce in school or you won't be loved." This drove the boy to further failure by the psychological "principle of self-fulfilling prophecy" [4] If the best is demanded and the worst is expected, the child will fulfill the worst expectations.

Regarding the role of motherhood, the counselor may well inquire of the counselee why she wanted to become a mother. The incidence of mothers who did not want the child in the first place is high. The child either was conceived before marriage, was conceived by accident, or even if planned, arrived to disrupt the mother's career or social plans. Other mothers may have deeply desired the child but found the demands put upon her too great to bear. She is not deriving pleasure from motherhood or finding a sense of fulfillment in the role. The conception of a child "to save a marriage" brings further complications into the picture.

[4] See Robert Merton, *Social Theory and Social Structure* (Chicago: The Free Press of Glencoe, Illinois, 1949).

Rather than saving the marriage, a child may further expose a couple to their incompatibilities and bring out further immaturities. The role of mother is an adult role which if accepted and affirmed by a woman is a measure of her maturity and emotional growth. In a sense she was created for this role and the conceiving and bearing of a child helps her fulfill herself. To fail here is to undermine a very central part of her personality.

Not in quite the same way, the father may sense that he has failed. The father's self picture is made up more of his role in his vocation and in the community. Fatherhood is more peripheral to him. However, within the close kinship system as practiced in America, the man derives great satisfaction from his wife and family. If things are not right at home, he has little haven from the world of business and community activity. In Bill Brown's instance, this is particularly apparent. He could not understand why Bobby was acting like he was. Did he not spend good money to send him to camp, only to have him lose or "mess up" all of his equipment? "Why couldn't the boy behave when his father was with him?" It made him wonder if perhaps he—Bill Brown—had taken a misstep sometime in the past. The father is the one who teaches the boy the male role; and if the father falls down here, the boy is confused and angry. When the mother gets frustrated with no husband to help her with the teaching and disciplining task, she blames not only the father, but the boy overmuch. The father then rejects both wife and children by spending more time at business and at the golf club. The cycle has been established. In counseling the minister helps mother, father, and child to perceive what is happening between them. What is making them reject the child, for example? And what misunderstandings of each other and rejection of role responsibilities are making them fractionated rather than integrated in family living?

When children four and above are involved, the counselor owes it to them either to counsel them himself or to see to it that they obtain therapeutic help. The role of the child counselor is threefold: he acts first as an auxiliary parent while the real parents are getting help; second, he acts as teacher, guiding the child in his encounter with and assimilation of new experience; third, he acts as therapist, allowing the child the expression and understanding of feelings centering in conflicts with the parents. Although I would not recommend the untrained minister to

153

enter this highly complex field, I would suggest that many ministers with the aptitude could get training and engage in child counseling. Play therapy is an area in which the young child can engage and gain considerable help.[5] The child tends to communicate his feelings through his body and motor activity. Play becomes the means through which the child talks with the therapist. His play pattern can thus give the counselor a vivid understanding of child-parent relationships, and further allow the child to drain off hostilities until he can accept the adults on a different basis. In such instances the therapist draws at least two limits to the expression of hostility: the child cannot destroy property or hurt the counselor. In every other regard, however, the child has freedom. Often this "freedom with limits" becomes the basis on which the child can trust the adult world again. His difficulty has not been too little discipline or too severe discipline. His trouble has rather been not knowing where he stood, as in Bobby Brown's case, when parents switched from one extreme to another in inconsistent handling of him.

In parent-child relationships the clergyman may be called in at particular crisis periods to offer counsel. When the first child is born, a couple may encounter difficulty making the transition. Formerly they were simply husband and wife. Now they are father and mother. The man, in particular, if he has been jealous or insecure with his wife, may react to baby as though to a rival. Things are not the same and never will be the same with this child now in the home. In this crisis the minister is already present in his pastoral role; he should be perceptive of incipient difficulty. When the child goes to school for the first time, there is another crisis period. He is no longer a baby, but a developing child. If the mother has difficulty accepting this transition, wanting to keep the apron strings tied tight, the transition may presage trouble. Even more is this so at the onset of adolescence. The mother has neglected to inform her daughter about the menstrual cycle, but expected her to discover this truth herself. Now the daughter, not finding a place to confide in her mother, is doing things behind her mother's back. The mother is upset because her daughter is no longer acting as an obedient child. She is not facing the daughter's physiological change and the resultant needs and tensions in her. Counseling may be asked for at this point. Finally,

[5] See Dorothy Baruch, *One Little Boy* (New York: Julian Press, Inc., 1952), for an illustration of play therapy.

154

when the youth faces marriage, the parents may undergo a crisis. We have spent considerable time on premarital counseling with the couple facing marriage. Few people recognize the parents' real distress upon giving up a son or daughter. Jokes are made about it, but it is a serious matter to the parents. Counseling, perhaps only of a comradely sort, may be extended to parents at this time. With some parents the pastor may encounter a reaction close to grief at this emotional loss. Since the clergyman is close to the family at these particular periods, he should be sensitive to parents' needs to talk to an understanding person during the crisis.

The counselor helps the various members find their goals and values centering in the family. This does not mean a "chummy togetherness" enforced from the outside. Rather it means the various family members tackling their problems from within the "inside" of the family. This may involve a couple's considering the adoption of a child;[6] a family's reworking its budget in the light of adolescent needs and contributions in point of earnings; a family council centering around the educational, vocational, or marriage plans of the children; or a joint session of family with the counselor working through relationships with in-laws.

Let us take the latter as an example. In-laws can soon become "outlaws" when parents hold faulty attitudes toward a married child or vice versa. Phillip Roche says the stereotype of the "mother-in-law" in our culture is the counterpart of the witch in fact and fancy.[7] The son displaces the feelings of hostility he held toward his mother to the mother-in-law. He is too dependent yet upon his real mother as the wife is upon her father. This leads to difficulty on the part of the young couple. The situation is aggravated when the unhappy parents project their own misery on their married child and find it difficult to give up their authority over them. A source of tension may be the disciplining of the first child. Two styles of discipline usually emerge. One is lenient, the other harsher. The older generation may compete for the loyalty of the child and "spoil" the child by giving in to him. Or they may be oversevere, causing the child to become confused. It is to be hoped that both sets of

---

[6] See *So You Want to Adopt a Baby*, Public Affairs Pamphlet 173. Also *To Those Denied a Child*, Planned Parenthood Pamphlet 501. Write Madison Avenue, New York 22, New York.

[7] See P. Roche, "Early Life Experience and Marriage," Mudd and Krich, *op. cit.*

grandparents will be welcome to the attentions of the grandchild, but in the event the conflict is driving a wedge between parents and child, they may have to be told politely what the parents desire. In the final analysis the grandparents have raised their children; they should allow the new generation the freedom to make their own mistakes. The pastor may have to intercede in some instances to help the grandparents understand this.

The counselor may be called in to intrafamily conflicts to help the members work out acute differences. Particularly is this so in the parent-adolescent difficulties when the young person is working out his new feelings of independence to the distress of mother or father who wants to keep him a dependent child. As a youth worker the minister may see and talk to the youth first. If he counsels with him, he soon becomes aware of the fact that he is cast in the role of "auxiliary parent." "Why can't my father see things this way?" wails the boy. The temptation, of course, is to take the side of the boy against the parent. However, genuine family counseling does not take place until the counselor has seen both parents and tried to understand their position and attitudes, and then tried to get all three together for joint counseling. The writer has consulted with a minister who worked all year with an adolescent girl, only to see the counseling fail because the parents refused to recognize the problem and agree to talk about it.

The adolescent has tremendous conflicts over the new urgency of his sexual drives and the hostility and conflict with parents and other authorities associated with these drives. Ackerman suggests along with weekly counseling the adolescent be involved in weekly group therapy as a supplement.[8] The important factor to recognize is that the adolescent needs to gain self-esteem and to do it not at cross-purposes to his parents or society but within a framework of family values. The revolt can be channeled without its causing such dire interpersonal hurt and the rupture of family relationships.

In Lucy Brown's case her revolt centered in the sexual area. Her struggles with her mother drove her to "act out" her hostility in an affair with Bill. Some psychoanalysts[9] point out that where the mother has borne an illegitimate child, the daughter identifies with her to the

[8] Ackerman, *op. cit.*, pp. 289-95.
[9] Helene Deutsch, *The Psychology of Women.*

extent that she must do the same thing. Or the mother may reject the daughter so that she feels devalued to the point where she will "act out" in the sexual area to further devalue herself. For the minister to understand the unwed mother, he needs to put his judgmental attitudes aside, and enter into her frame of reference and see what is moving her in these directions. A psychodynamic point of view will help him understand her motivations. These he cannot interpret as a counselor, but he can help the adolescent girl and her mother come to some kind of reconciliation. This is at the heart of "relationship-counseling" and gets the minister involved with the family in more than a passive bystander role.

The family may come to the minister and desire him to "give the unborn child a name" or to put Lucy "back on the right path." Both coercions must be avoided. To marry a couple, unsuited for one another with nothing between them but an unborn child is surely unsound. So, too, is to lecture a girl or a boy when they are "caught" in such an interpersonal dilemma. The decision is the couple's—whether to marry or not. So, too, is the lesson, to be learned from the experience, theirs to talk through and to understand. The minister is a representative of a religious community, but this is neither puritanical nor rigid in saying that the couple must follow one way. To bring children into an environment where they are wanted may mean the baby is given up for adoption. To perform weddings based on mature love and self-direction may mean this couple decides not to marry but to wait. Larry and Cora's case in the early chapter showed that when some couples wait, they marry eventually, but on a more realistic and mature basis. (This was the eventual outcome of the case: Larry and Cora married a year later and now have three healthy children; Priscilla married another man after the annulment.)

The final phase of family counseling is the counselor's helping the group to find and operate within a growing faith and sense of values. Forgiveness may be a scarcely understood process until a family has had a serious rupture and needs to find their way back into each other's graces again. Gibson Winter says:

Parents can build a whole new dimension of life for children by confessing their injustices and asking forgiveness. These experiences help a child to see forgiveness as part of the fabric of every human relationship. Children learn that parents are also subject to a rightness which they cannot determine. They also learn that transgression of that rightness is not the end of a relationship. In fact, they learn that transgressions can be the opportunities for deeper relationship than personal.[10]

Just as the latter periods of reconciliation can lead a couple to a heightened awareness of the forgiveness of God, so, too, can the latter portion of family counseling. A family to whom prayer has been just a ritual or for whom it has lost all meaning, find a depth-experience which has not only shaken them but centered them down to new realities. God is the focal point of their family life; prayer is a way of life in which the reality of God is acknowledged. Faith in each other and in the structure of their lives becomes grounded in that reality. The counseling minister does not intrude his theology or his experience into the emerging religious situation. Often he can only stand back and let the family express for itself what their "new faith" is, and how it supports and undergirds now what was formerly a pretty shaky foundation.

That many families will not approach this last experience is readily acknowledged. The minister becomes increasingly aware that the more family counseling he does additional resources are needed. He does not have time enough for all the problems he knows exist. He feels like Peter with not enough fingers to repair holes in the dikes of family life. In the remaining chapters we shall turn our attention directly to this problem looking at: group counseling as a resource; the marriage counseling center as a professional counseling structure; and family life education as a long term approach to the problem. The minister need not feel alone in his concern for marriage. He has many allies and many ancillary supports for his counseling.

A FAMILY COUNSELING FORM

Here follows a form which the pastor may use in his counseling with families. Although the pastor does not take a social history, as the social worker does in his work with families, he does need some basic information to use for guidelines in his counseling with the different family members. Rather than structuring the interview to answer these ques-

[10] Winter, *op cit.*, p. 128.

tions, the pastor may be aware of these areas before the interview and afterwards reconstruct the conversation with the form before him. In that way he can avoid the probing question, and yet, he can discover certain basic information for his record of the family.

1. Interview with Primary Family Member[11]
   A. What is the presenting problem?
   B. What are the background facts concerning family, i.e.: physical setting, social and cultural setting, religious setting? (The pastor may add information here from membership records and pastoral contacts.)
   C. How has the family adapted itself to the community?
   D. How has the family met external threats, i.e.: disease, economic reverses, war, etc.?
   E. How is the family organized internally? What is the membership role structure, i.e.: father, mother, sister, brother, mother-in-law, etc.?
   F. How is the family functioning at present, i.e.: health of marriage, reaction to parenthood, parent-child relationships, sibling relationships?
2. Home Visit
   The home visit by the pastor is used to observe family interaction directly and to obtain any of the above information as well as to speak to any family members not previously interviewed.
3. Evaluation of Family Situation by Counselor and/or Staff
4. Prognosis and Disposition of Family Problem

A CHILD COUNSELING FORM

If the counselor sees a child alone in an interview or in a play therapy situation, he may use the following form to register his counseling impressions.

1. Organization of the child's personality at present.
2. Character of child's environment, physical and interpersonal.
3. Child's relation to mother, father, siblings.
4. Evaluation of child's problem.
5. Treatment of child, suggested and/or undertaken.
6. Referral and disposition of child's problem.

[11] Adapted from Ackerman, *op. cit.*, pp. 138, 143.

XII

Group Marriage Counseling

Get a group of young couples together, and they usually sit as couples and want to discuss problems which they are facing as couples. Get a group of mid-marrieds together, and soon there are two groups formed— the women at one end of the room and the men at the other. Have you ever observed this phenomena and wondered what has made the difference? Why does one group want to talk as couples and the other group as "stags," even though in a mixed setting?

One reason is that in early marriage husbands and wives are alive to one another and to the adjustments required in marriage. Later on they have become familiar to each other or at least have adopted temporary stopgap solutions and blocked out certain areas from discussion. It is more exciting then to scout out members of one's own sex and act as a single person again. For many men and women the division of the sexes into men's clubs and women's circles feeds this escapist tendency in mid-life.

What we shall propose in this chapter is that the church with its program and personnel entertain the use of group counseling for the care and treatment of marriage and family problems.[1] The advantages are: (1) More marriage problems can be treated at the incipient stages. (2) Couples with problems about which they hesitate to seek individual counseling may safely come to a group where less of the "spotlight" is on them. (3) The pastor can with his limited time and energy counsel more couples in groups over a year. (4) Couples with common problems can

[1] Robert Leslie in his Ph.D. dissertation *Group Therapy as a Method for Church Work,* Boston University, 1948, has developed at an early date a group therapy approach to counseling in the church. His articles in *Journal of Pastoral Care* since have explicated his position.

face them with others who have suggestions and emotional support to help them "turn a corner" in their lives.

Group counseling is a comparatively new process, and its application to couples with marriage problems is even more recent.[2] The brief description in this chapter should enable the reader to see the advantages of working with couples in the capacity of group counseling leader. What is suggested, however, is that the reader experience group counseling as a group member—either as an individual or with his wife in a couples' group—before he attempts to carry out group counseling himself. It has been pointed out before that as one progresses from the one-to-one relationship in personal counseling to the multiple relationship of marriage and family counseling, the dynamics become more complex and more difficult to understand and handle. This is even more in evidence when working with ten persons in a group as a group leader. To be "on top" of the interaction while serving as a catalytic agent requires experience, knowledge, and maturity. To "tinker" with individuals' marriages without knowing what one is doing can do great damage—even more in a group situation than in the private conference room because controls are not as possible and one cannot concentrate attention as well on one person.

THEORY OF GROUP COUNSELING

Group counseling is defined by Gaskill and Mudd as "a dynamic relationship between a counselor and the members of a group, involving presentation and discussion of subjects about which the counselor has special knowledge, which is of general and specific concern to the group and around which emotions may be brought out and attitudes developed and changed."[3] Specifically applied to marriage, such groups could include premaritals, young marrieds, or mid-marrieds, organized around the discussion of problems particularly faced at their cycle of marriage.

Group counseling differs from group psychotherapy, as practiced by Jacob Moreno and his associates and the psychoanalytic schools. Group psychotherapy is a long-term process supervised by a psychotherapist

[2] See L. Levine and J. Boadsky, "Group Pre-Marital Counseling," *Mental Hygiene*, XXXII (1949), pp. 577-587. See also Skidmore, *et al., op. cit.*, pp. 295-96.

[3] E. Gaskill and E. Mudd, "A Decade of Group Counseling," *Social Case Work*, May, 1950, p. 194.

generally in which unconscious conflicts and feelings are dealt with by both the group and the leader. The leader tends to act like a "father figure" and the members as children in the family with sibling rivalry, reactions to parental authorities, and childhood difficulties unearthed and analyzed in the group. Group psychotherapy is more directive, particularly as practiced by Moreno and the sociodramatists, the group leader taking a very active part in the process. Group counseling, on the other hand, deals with largely present-day problems between members in the group through the discussion method. The leader is a group co-ordinator and clarifier (not a father figure) who uses client-centered and permissive approaches allowing the group members to work on one another's problems. For example, in dealing with problems of handling of money, feelings are brought out and after open ventilation, solutions are discussed and sometimes accepted by couples on a trial basis.

Group counseling differs from the average discussion group in that the problems presented for discussion are personal problems, coming out of the experiences of group members. The learning which individual members undergo is not in the realm of fact and theory but in the area of feelings, attitudes, and behavior. In a married group these learnings would be in relationship to the marriage roles as understood by both partners. The problems too difficult to be solved by individuals or couples are faced with a group geared to problem-solving. When individuals work through such experiences they learn methods of problem-solving which they can carry over into the behavior in their marriages and with their families.

The minister-counselor is particularly concerned about his role as a group leader. It should be pointed out that he functions differently in this kind of group than in any other groups he leads. More than likely the members of the group will expect him to function in an autocratic, "expert" fashion, providing the final answers, unsnarling discussions, even rewarding and punishing participants in the discussion. It is well at the start to recognize the "stereotype" of strong leader which many of the group foist on the minister. He is part Moses, part Solomon, even part Jesus, depending on the members' needs. A great deal of his job at the beginning will be to orient the group both by his words and his actions as to how he will function as a "democratic leader." It is well for the minister to have worked out his difficulties with assuming the leadership role before he begins group counseling. Otherwise, he will surely find he is placing his own troubles on the group.

In group counseling the leader may start out in a fairly familiar way, presenting material for discussion. For example, it may be a common problem faced by young marrieds, a situation for role-playing, or a problem play. The members are asked to apply the subject to their own situation, express their feelings about the problem or the main character of the play. Thus, from the start the problems become highly personalized and charged with subjective meaning. The leader provides an emotional climate which is non-judgmental, accepting, and reality-seeking. He does this by throwing the floor open to any topic, by refusing to judge issues from a moralistic viewpoint, by providing members an intelligent ear for their ideas and orienting the discussion to the reality of the group itself. Moreover, the leader helps clarify emotional situations between members—with a married group, it would be between couples —so that they may see the way they interact with another and so that feelings of love and hate can be recognized. In particular, the leader's job is to work himself out of the leadership role to the extent that the leadership function moves from member to member as insight is gained and as capacity for problem-solving emerges within the group.[4] The leader may retain his titular role, but he feels less need for structure as group members see him as less an authority, and as each is able to suggest his problems for discussion and others help him to clarify, understand, and work out his problems.

ROLE-PLAYING

An adjunct to group counseling is role-playing which may grow out of the session in an unstructured way, or be the primary focus of discussion from the beginning of a session.

Role-playing is a comparatively new educational technique. Helen Driver defines it as "any kind of action in which a person attempts to portray the character, attitude, feeling, and action of another person." [5] This kind of "acting out" process is a variation of Jacob Moreno's tech-

[4] See Launor Carter, "Recording and Evaluating the Performance of Individuals as Members of Small Groups," Hare, *et al.*, *Small Groups*, p. 497.

[5] Helen Driver, *Multiple Counseling* (Madison, Wisconsin: Monona Publications, 1954), p. 109.

nique of sociodrama, in which the players and audience deal with the interactions of people in fulfilling a specified social role.[6]

Structured role-playing may be established through the use of a written drama in which a family situation is portrayed. The presentation of the play by several members reading the respective parts is much as a first reading of a play. Some examples are those written by the American Theater Wing, such as *What Did I Do?* (child-parent discipline problem) *Random Target* (the need of the child to express hostility) and *According to Size* (child-parent dependency problems).[7] The players usually enjoy getting into the particular roles and may identify to such an extent that they can correctly spell out the characters' feelings in the play. Such a person can help bring the discussion to the level of real feeling.

The unstructured role-playing situation evolves when a problem is faced by an individual or couple in the group which can better be acted out than discussed. The leader can ask them if the person would define the problem so that a play can be worked out. Then the characters are cast, and observers are "warmed up" concerning the situation. Then the problem is acted out with the leader cutting the play at an appropriate spot. This usually happens after no more than ten minutes of "acting." The group is free to discuss and analyze the situation and behavior of the actors and observers. Following the discussion the group may want to make plans for further testing the insights and practicing new behavior in another social context.[8]

The group leader may want to designate an "alter ego" or double for the main actors in the role-playing. This person speaks the "asides" (what the character is thinking) while the actors talk in a socially acceptable way. With married couples, for example, a husband and wife can act out their difficulties in handling a budget while the doubles tell them how they feel below the surface, and furthermore bring these feelings into the group's awareness where they may become the topic of discussion.

---

[6] See J. Moreno, *Who Shall Survive?* (Washington, D. C.: Nervous and Mental Disease Publication, 1934).

[7] May be obtained from Human Relations Aids, 1790 Broadway, New York 19 New York.

[8] See Grace Levit and Helen Jennings, "Learning Through Role Playing," *How to Use Role Playing* (Chicago: Adult Education Association, 1955).

Role-playing has the advantage of sparking interest in a group and uncovering problems, after the group is comfortable enough in one another's presence to join such open discussion. Caution should be expressed, however, so that the leader does not overuse this one technique, or that he not push the group into problems of a depth which he as a counselor cannot handle. In a structured group one may spend a full hour with a community play and its discussion. In an unstructured group fifteen or twenty minutes may be all the time spent in role-playing and discussing a specific problem. A leader who is sensitive to the dynamics of the group will know just how and when to introduce role-playing as a technique.

CASE STUDY: FIRST GROUP MEETING OF FIVE COUPLES

Time: One hour and a half.

Place: A couple's apartment

Couples: Ellie and Dick; Sherm and Mary; Pam and Keith; Violet and Brad; Stu and Ruth; Leader and his wife Anne.

Leader: You folks know how this started. I've talked to most of you. This group has no structure, except that its focus is marriage—your own marriages, and it can begin anywhere. You can talk about your own way of meeting or how your courtship worked out, and how you got married. Or you can throw that to the winds, and begin wherever you would like to begin. The only structure is the ending of it. Whenever we've gone an hour or an hour and fifteen minutes, we'll quit. It's up to you. I don't know all of you too well, and we'll be glad to share our marriage . . . over the years. (*Laughter*)

Brad: Who talks the most, the men or the women?

Ellie: It all depends who's answering the question. (*Laughter*)

Leader: Well, if you want some empirical research, we could do that over a number of meetings. (*Laughter*)

Ellie: I don't think we know each other too well either.

Leader: Do you want to start, Ellie? (*Laughter*)

Ellie: Oh, all right. I'm a school teacher. I graduated in '58 and this is my second year teaching. I'll let Dick tell how we got acquainted. We've been married since Christmas. My dad's a preacher and I've moved around hither and yon. Someday I'd like to quit teaching and, uh, go back to school or, uh, keep house. My folks live in —— right now. Better let Dick speak now and defend himself.

Dick: You've said nothing I could disagree with so far.

Leader: She's going to let you talk now, Dick. (*Laughter*)

Dick: We met when her folks pastored my home church. We first met when she was a senior and I was a junior in high school, and we became acquainted at a church camp. We had known each other before that, but this was when all the stuff started. (*Laughter*) And it's been going on ever since. We went together about five years . . . and then we got married.

Mary: How long were you engaged?

Dick: About eight months . . . no, ten months.

Sherm: She's been taking a poll. She has everyone all tabulated.

Leader: Here's a gal doing some research. (*Laughter*)

Ellie: For one year of that time I was at college and Dick was still in high school.

Sherm: Well, here's where I butt in. I was born in —— and I spent my early years in eastern United States because my father moved every two months. He's a geologist. He worked in the field in those days so that I went to the first three grades in seven or eight states.

Mary: That's where the trouble all began. (*Laughter*)

Sherm: We moved here when I was in junior high, and I went to high school all in one place, and that was pretty nice. I went to the University and that's where I met Mary, when I was a sophomore, wasn't it?

Mary: Don't you remember you were a freshman?

Sherm: Majored in philosophy after switching majors many times. I think I met Mary at some fraternity blast. Went out three or four times and didn't see each other for eight months. Then we took up again.

Mary: He lost interest.

Sherm: Pretty bored. (*Laughter*) I started going to a student group and met her again. . . . You couldn't get away from her in that group. This is the way it was. We went with each other and got engaged and were engaged about a year and a half.

Mary: Was it that long? It didn't seem . . .

Sherm: (*Interrupting*) Got married two and a half years ago. Got married December 22.

Ellie: Another Christmas wedding.

Sherm: There's only one problem though. Everyone gives you the same present for Christmas and your anniversary. (*Laughter*) (*To Mary*) Got anything to add?

Mary: Well . . . my major is music education, and I taught school in ——
and this lasted two years. And this year I'm taking a vacation and sub-
stitute teaching.

Sherm: I might add I'm going to be a college teacher of philosophy.

Dick: Amen, brother!

Pam: (*To the group*) Should I defend us? (*Her husband had not arrived
as yet, being on another appointment.*) Well, Keith and I are both from
——. We kind of grew up together. We met at college and we met at
church. He's one of three brothers—I'll not mention the other two.
He's a music major and can teach music. I was born in —— and since
my father was in "Y" work we traveled around and finally landed
in ——. Well, I graduated and now am working at —— as a secretary.
Keith and I went together but not very long actually. I've known him
quite a while and somehow we kept running into one another around
church, and then he came to seminary and came home vacation time.
We got engaged and we were married the next summer. Two months
tomorrow, and we're expecting to start a family early next summer. I
think that's us.

Brad: I talk too much. I'm going to let her talk.

Violet: Well, I'm teaching this year. I worked at school last year and met
many of you. We have four children, so our family is well started. Brad
takes care of the children except when he's in school. That's all, I guess.

Brad: Come, come. Tell them about your background.

Violet: I majored in education, taught school all the time I was in college,
and for two and a half years was a D.R.E. All set up in a beautiful
church until I met him. (*Laughter*) Met at a church conference through
mutual friends. He was a student at college, and I had graduated from
college and he was a freshman. And he's been in school ever since we've
been married.

Brad: Well, uh, I've had a previous marriage before I met Vi. I farmed—I'm
getting ahead of my story—I was in the service for two years and farmed
for eight. And finally tragedy hit my life. That's changed the course of
quite a few things. But instead of wasting away, I decided to go to college
and so I did. When I first went, they told me I'd never see the senior
year. I was too much like a hick and had too many hayseeds in my hair.
(*Laughs*) So it was my freshman year when I was at conference with
my friend who is now my brother-in-law that I first ran into Vi. She
had gone to college when my first brother-in-law was there but I had to
go across the state to meet her. My friend was standing there, and I
was casting an eye at Vi and he said, "Yes, Brad, why don't you do some-

thing about it?" (*Laughter*) And that's the way it all started. (*Laughs*)

Leader: Did it just take that week?

Violet: Two days. (*Laughter*) I didn't think I'd ever see him again. I mean, boy, has he ever got a line. (*Laughter*) So I went back to the church and the first day the minister came in and said, "The fellow you were seen with at the conference, you could have him if you want him!" (*Laughter*) I'd just started two sessions of church school and it was my program, and I had recruited many teachers. I really felt obligated to the church. And the minister said, "Any time you feel you want to get married, feel free to."

Brad: He was a good talker.

Violet: I thought nothing would come of it, but it did; he called me up and he wrote a letter which was a miracle. He came across the state several times. We met in June and were married in November.

Brad: We were married on the anniversary of my grandfather's second marriage. Just a coincidence.

Violet: I married Brad and got two little girls all on the same day, and now we have two little boys of our own.

Girls: Ohhhh! Ahhh!

Violet: Everything's going along real fine.

Anne: My name's Anne, I was interested (*to Sherm*) in your growing up in the East. *Sherm:* Where? *Anne:* In central ———

Sherm: I was in ——— (another state). Excuse me.

Anne: Honestly, the way you traveled around I don't blame you.

Sherm: I think we lived near ———. I was only in kindergarten so I don't . . .

Anne: You went to a number of schools. I started out in a one room school and went six grades and then grammar school, high school and the University.

Brad: You sound about as ancient as I do.

Anne: About as what? Ancient you say. (*Laughter*)

Violet: He went to the first grade in a horse and buggy. (*Laughter*)

Anne: Then I was lucky to have a year in the West to do student work in this college. Then I came back to seminary in New York and that's where I met my husband. We met at a philosophy class at the university.

Leader: On the way back.

Brad: I just wonder who that "prof" was.

Anne: (*Names him*) We were engaged about a year and a half. We were engaged in May and married a year the following August. Oh, I'll let you tell where all we lived.

Leader: You worked that year . . .

Anne: . . . That intermediate year, I worked as a D.R.E. and the minister I worked for married us, so it was with his blessing, too. Well, we have three children—a boy eight, a girl five, and a boy four.

Stu: Do you want to add your bit now?

Leader: Let's see, she was talking about where all we've lived. I'm from ——, grew up in the southeastern part of the state and went to school at —— college and seminary at ——, and met Anne at —— following seminary, and our first church was at —— on Long Island.

Ellie: My dad's first church was at —— on the north shore.

Leader: Well, this is on the south shore. We went to the university in —— where I did student work for three years. Then I finished my graduate work at —— and held a church at the time. One child was born during student work days and two small ones in that graduate period. Following that, we moved to —— where I had a double job as pastor of a church and chaplain of a mental hospital, and from there we moved out here. We figured once we had lived in eight homes. It's horrible! We haven't moved since we have settled here—two years and we hope many more. (*Pause*) You'll probably hear more about our courtship later. Anne had gone to the university during the war and men were not too plentiful, and for that reason she was spared (*Laughter*) from having found someone. And then she came to seminary where there was an abundance of men, so as a result I had an awful lot of competition to beat down. And we had a real hectic year. . . .

Anne: I think you had a more hectic year than I. (*Laughter*)

Leader: But she dated some men who are now theologians at other seminaries.

Anne: At least once. (*Laughter*) (*Pause*)

Leader: Stu.

Stu: Ruth, why don't you start off. I usually talk too much.

Ruth: Well, I was born in Japan in quite a big city. My father was a business-man, and I went to school until senior high and got into a mission school and went to college. In my junior summer—I had been going to International Christian work camp every summer—and my third year I tried to get into Okinawa but some kind of delay occurred and I had to stay an extra week in a different camp. And Stu was there in the army. (*Stu laughs.*) I didn't think of anything in particular, so many things were going on. (*Laughter*) Nothing happened to me anyway, and in July he saw me, and then next January he didn't say anything about marriage. He just talked about future plans. (*Laughter*) He didn't ask me to marry him; just talked about things we could do in the future.

(*Laughter*) Finally we got married in March the following year. We knew each other about a year and a half. Friends ask me how I married Stu, and rather than tell the long story I say I didn't know any English but to say "Yes." (*Laughter*)

Stu: Well, I was born way out in ———. The nearest town was ———, and the next nearest ———, and the next —— which is on the map. My folks had been farmers for several generations, and pretty well isolated. Mother was born in —— valley and knew little of the outside world. During the war years my father came to —— for advancement to get out of backward ways, and later moved to ———. My father's an itinerant preacher and still preaches from time to time. Also, he developed a sales business which is pretty good. They don't place too much emphasis on money. I've done some interesting things, I think. When I was out of high school, I hitchhiked to Mexico on $125 (*Girls: Oooh!*) which was a great experience, and I got a lot of publicity out of it which I enjoyed. I went back to college and stayed two years, and got tired of college and so I got a job in the "Y" in ———. I was drafted in four months and finally went to Japan and was in the Signal Corps. And I participated in this work camp and when we married we went the other way around the world and finally got here.

(*Knock! Knock!*)

Keith: Hello.

Ellie: Defend yourself. Pam began without you.

Leader: We've been telling about how we met, the courtship, and what it led to. *Keith:* Marriage. (*Laughter*)

Leader: We've heard her side of it. *Keith:* (*Silence*)

Ruth: I was in ———— and I was having some problems. I didn't know about Stu. But I didn't think seriously of marriage, leaving my family and all.

Dick: Everyone is still there then?

Ruth: Yes, everybody: my brothers, sisters and parents.

Stu: I think we were quite fortunate. In many interracial, international marriages, one of the parents objects. But in our case her parents were very accepting, very Americanized in fact. My parents accept Ruth very well, in fact, my mother said when I left, if I fell in love with a Japanese girl that was quite all right, so . . .

Keith: You followed her suggestion.

Ruth: When I asked my father about marriage, he said he wanted me to have one more year of college, but he didn't object.

Stu: Though in her family her mother was the counselor. We spent one interesting evening discussing if there was any mental illness in my family. (*Laughter*)

Keith: A real Western technique.

(*Interruption for phone call*)

Keith: What kind of thing are we saying before I go committing myself?

Pam: Where were you born, where did you grow up, where did you go to school, what your major was, how you met, why you met?

Keith: Why you met?

Pam: A good question.

Keith: Well, I was born and raised in ——, went to school there, went to the University and majored in many subjects, graduated in music education.

Leader: There is another music educator here. (*Nodding to Mary*)

Keith: Uh, I've known Pam for some time. I don't know where I met her, to be honest.

Pam: Probably at church.

Keith: Known her for sometime. There's a little age difference there, so Pam was always a little girl. I came to seminary and I don't know what happened. She must have grown up. (*Laughter*)

Anne: This is when you went home at Christmas vacation? You met again?

Keith: I'd been writing letters, and I don't know whether she was encouraging things by the way she was writing letters. I kind of suspect it. (*Laughter*) Hello! What else am I supposed to be telling? I'm at a distinct disadvantage because I don't know what we're letting forth.

Leader: That's good. How did you get engaged?

Keith: Did you ask me or did I ask you?

Pam: That has been some question. I think the theory is that you asked me.

Leader: This was at Christmas time, did you say?

Keith: Yes, I was home for a month. That was either long enough time or too long, I don't know. She caught me at a very weak moment. I was about to go back to school and be away for three more months. And I thought, well, what the heck!

Pam: I like that!

Keith: I probably went home with some idea of doing something like that. So I hopped into my little car. But of course I wasn't sure and I don't know when I became sure, but I did. (*Pause*)

Leader: How's your research, Mary? (*Laughter*)

Sherm: Mary is doing some research on engagement.

Mary: Well, I think most of them from about half a year to a year.

Sherm: She's been taking a Gallup Poll.

Mary: I was talking to someone the other day who got engaged after about a week and they got married very soon after the engagement. And (*Laughter*) . . .

Ellie: Well, they would have had all their fights after they got married that we had before we got married. (*Laughter*)

Leader: But you, Mary and Sherm, and Anne and I are the longest—one and a half years.

This represents the first forty-five minutes of an hour-and-a-half session. The second half of the period the group went back to compare their engagements with those of their parents. Since most of their parents had become married during the depression, they discovered their parents had been engaged longer, had been more concerned about money—though Stu reported that his father had married with one dollar in his pocket and he had given that to the preacher. Their parents generally had finished their education and were engaged in a trade or profession before they married. The group gave evidence of favoring the shorter engagement and they had resorted to various arrangements so that they might marry in college: the wives working, holding student charges or part-time work on the part of husbands, and the husbands caring for the children and doing housework as part of their role responsibility. The leader reported that when he went to seminary, only fifteen per cent of the students were married (1943); today studies show over sixty-five per cent, and in this seminary seventy-five per cent. The group agreed next time to meet in Stu and Ruth's apartment because of the imminence of their baby's birth. They left with real evidence of fellow feeling, and it can be imagined that what went on in the group was the topic for conversation for six couples that night before bed.

Observations of leader and his wife:

1. Much tension was relieved through laughter as reserve was broken down in talking about personal matters before the group.

2. The first exchange, reported here, dealt mainly with details on a superficial level. When they dealt with their parents, they began to speak of more personal things more easily.

3. Individuals looked for identification features with one another as each reported: the same wedding anniversaries, coming from similar parts of the country, going to similar schools, being from the city or from the country. The leader encouraged this, as did his wife.

4. The two heterogenous couples—Brad, married again after having lost his first wife, and Vi, and Stu and Ruth, who had made a marriage across cultures—spoke more on the first time around, and broke the ice for the other couples to talk about more personal things. They sensed their difference from others and wanted to explain this.

5. The leader and his wife held out to the group personal knowledge about themselves, in other words, did not hold themselves aloof from the group, and the group realized that the process would be as costly to them as it would to each student. The leader is also a teacher in the seminary which the men attend, and so has to overcome some feelings of aloofness which are part of his role. His wife tends to help do this with her approach to the group.

6. No husband-wife interaction was interpreted in this first session, though the reader will no doubt be aware of some attitudes on the parts of couples toward one another and their relationship to the marriage. The opportunity to role play and perform sociodrama was brought up by the leader, and the group appeared to be intensely interested in this.

THE STRUCTURE AND FLOW OF GROUP MARRIAGE COUNSELING

With the above group meeting as a guide we can now look more specifically at the matter of setting up a group and how the group functions during the period of its life. In beginning a marriage counseling group, the leader needs to select the members carefully from couples who want to work out common problems. The couples should be close in age or have been married about the same number of years. The common problems can be, for example: (1) preparation for marriage (2) preparation for parenthood (3) understanding adolescents (4) adjusting to a childless home at middle age. The couples should be varied to the extent that varying experiences and backgrounds can be brought to bear on the problem. For example, an interracial couple can bring a different perspective to problems which other couples who married after a high school romance could not know. A subtle balance between homogeneity and heterogeneity needs to be sought.

The leader should interview the couples before the group begins, in order to determine their interest in the group and the extent of their interpersonal difficulties. Some of the couples should continue in marriage counseling during the group process because their problems are too much to be handled by the group alone. If possible, the leader should secure an experienced person—perhaps his wife—to serve as recorder-observer for the group. If a psychologically trained person were to do this, the leader and recorder should spend an hour or so each week interpreting for each other what is going on in the group (See Methods of Observation which recorder-observer can use at end of chapter.) With the members' permission a tape recording of the session may be made for study between sessions.

Regarding the structure of the session itself, the leader should provide the basic framework for the group. That is, he should limit the number of members to ten persons or five couples. A group with two couples is enough, however, for basic interaction. The number of meetings can be arranged for from ten to fifteen times, if possible. It is better to have a stopping point prearranged; otherwise, the group may dwindle in numbers and die from disinterest. The group members need to commit themselves to this block of time, and only in an emergency absent themselves from a meeting. Such commitment heightens interest and seriousness about counseling work. The group should meet in a private room where they will not be interrupted. A circle of chairs with no head encourages the best discussion. Timewise, the meeting should be limited from an hour to an hour and a half. Tempers tire and flare up and problem-solving abilities wane if discussion is longer than ninety minutes.

The method of discussion can be varied among:

1. A structured discussion, i. e., on the track over a common marriage or family problem, as "managing finances."

2. Unstructured flow of conversation around several problems. This appears to be a "bull session" except for the fact that the problems are not theoretical but are present within the group.

3. Structured role-playing in which a play is brought in by the leader or group committee. The community plays which lend themselves to this use were discussed in the section on role-playing.

4. Unstructured role-playing in which a spontaneous situation develops in the group when leader and members decide to role play.

The flow of group marriage counseling is as varied, as multifarious as the flow of a river. It is not just that the individuals differ within the group, but each person interacts differently with every other person in the group. Here is a dominant wife who has "henpecked" her husband, but she interacts with a strong male in the group in rather a subdued way. Her husband sees another side of her and also the possibilities of his becoming strong with her at home. As pointed out by Mudd, Stone, Karpf, and Nelson:

Patterns of behavior as they emerge within the group are typical of patterns of behavior group members exhibit outside of the group . . . through assuming a role of responsibility toward others, egos become strengthened. Because of the support given each other by group members, resistances are worked through more quickly than in individual counseling. The support which is given and received and the strengthened ego both motivate and facilitate modification of behavior. Briefly, the group approximates a real life situation where clients can immediately reality-test the emotional reactions involved in their interpersonal relations.[9]

Dominance-submission patterns between spouses can particularly become evident in group counseling, as mentioned above. The leader can observe dominance by observing who talked the most and who won most of the decisions. The tendency in a group is for some to talk and others to retire or be silent. Some conflict of opinion may arise between spouses and bring this into a new context: The couple displays who wins most decisions. The dominant person will ask the most questions, analyze problems the most, and tend to reward and punish others in the group. The submissive person may agree simply, or disagree simply, and if angry may deflate his partner or another by his aggressive acts. Cultural differences will determine whether partners are concerned with genuine equality—that is, making their arguments come out evenly. A couple from an authoritarian home will make the husband dominant; those from a democratic home will strive for equality within the group.[10]

The group goes through phases of problem-solving, particularly with a client-centered leader who has planned an unstructured group. The

---

[9] Mudd, *et al., op. cit.,* p. 322.
[10] See F. Strodtbeck, "Husband-Wife Interaction over Revealed Differences," Hare, *et al., op. cit.,* pp. 464-72.

first phase is the orientation, when the group asks, "What is the problem?" The problem may be the handling of money, but this is merely the magnet around which attitudes, feelings, and activity are drawn from the couples in the group. As the group settles down to honest work on the problem, they pass to the second phase: "How do we feel about the problem?" As the members become comfortable in each other's presence, they feel free to express both positive and negative reactions to one another. This may be through wit—some of it barbed—which releases tension among members, but also often gets a point across. When members throw up resistances or blocks to the expression of feeling, the group may be pushed back to the orienting phase again.

The third phase is control of the problem: "What shall we do about it?" Solutions to the financial problem are not made out of whole cloth, but they are suggested tentatively by one member to another, as they know their basic feelings about not only money, but marriage, and life itself. Members are able to help each other as they find they can honestly express how they feel and as they are able to accept what another says without getting defensive. If frustration occurs at this level, the group may need to backtrack to the evaluation phase or even to the level of orientation.

As the group nears the end of its life, the members express gratitude to one another for what they have meant—not just for helping in the solution of problems, but for the experience of genuine *koinonia*, Christian fellowship. They realize that they would like to continue meeting, but in the economy of life's plans and purposes, they have had unforgetable moments of confrontation of themselves and other human beings and must now separate. The minister-leader may want to gather up these feelings in prayer at the close, and express heartfelt praise, either silently or out loud. Prayer at this level becomes more than rote learning or verbalization; rather it is bedrock communion, springing from the depths of spirit.

METHODS OF OBSERVATION
OF GROUP BEHAVIOR
BY RECORDER-OBSERVER

Just as there are many areas of information about group behavior, so there are many possible guides and scales for observation. Frequently groups develop such scales to fit their particular needs. Three techniques of observation are given, each useful for collecting a different kind of information.

1. Who Talks to Whom:

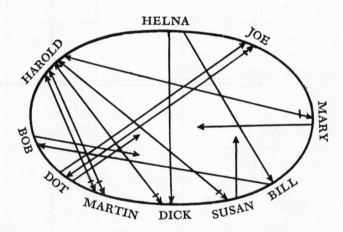

The number of lines made by the observer on this form indicates the number of statements made in a fifteen minute period. Four of these were made to the group as a whole, and so the arrows go only to the middle of the circle. Those with arrows at each end of a line show that the statement made by one person to another was responded to by the recipient.

We see that one person, Harold, had more statements directed toward him than did anyone else and that he responded or participated more than anyone else. The short lines drawn at the head of one of the pair of arrows indicates who initiated the remark. Harold, the leader, in other words had remarks directed at him calling for response from four other people.

2. Who Makes What Kinds of Contributions:

177

Member No.	1	2	3	4	5
1. Encourages					
2. Agrees, accepts					
3. Arbitrates					
4. Proposes action					
5. Asks suggestion					
6. Gives opinion					
7. Asks opinion					
8. Gives information					
9. Seeks information					
10. Poses problem					
11. Defines position					
12. Asks position					
13. Routine direction					
14. Depreciates self					
15. Autocratic manner					
16. Disagrees					
17. Self-assertion					
18. Active aggression					
19. Passive aggression					
20. Out-of-field					

3. What Happened in the Group:

   A. What was the general atmosphere in the group?

      Formal————   Informal————

      Competitive————   Co-operative————

      Hostile————   Supportive————

      Inhibited————   Permissive————

Comments:———————————————————————————

   B. Quantity and quality of work accomplished:

      Accomplishment:————————————High————Low————

      Quality of Production:——— ————High————Low————

      Goals:————Clear————Vague————

      Methods:————Clear————Vague————

              Flexible————Inflexible————

Comments:———————————————————————————

   C. Leader behavior:

      Attentive to group needs————

      Supported others————————————————

      Concerned only with topic————Took sides———— . . ..

      Dominated group————Helped group————

Comments:———————————————————————————

   D. Participation:

      Most people talked————Only few talked————

      Members involved————Members apathetic————

      Group united———— Group divided————

Comments:———————————————————————[11]

[11] *Understanding How Groups Work* (Chicago: National Education Association of the U.S. [Adult Education Service Division]), pp. 43-46. Used by permission.

XIII

A Pastoral Counseling Center

Pastor Paul is sitting in his study on a Tuesday morning. He is tired and more than a little perplexed. Though his church is not large—about five hundred souls, more or less—he has found himself besieged with marriage and family problems. He thought that putting young Smith on as an associate would lighten his own pastoral load, but the people want to see him when they are in trouble, they say, and so things have not let up. Why yesterday when he tried to slip off to play a little golf his secretary reported two couples called for appointments, and when he returned, a distraught mother was waiting at the office to discuss the difficulty she is having with her sixteen-year-old son. He saw her, of course, and worked until ten last night with the two couples. But where can he turn for relief from this crushing burden? He must preach sermons and administer a church and make some routine calls, not to mention reading some new books which remain unopened on his desk.

Guiltily and with some hope for relief, he picks up the phone book and turns to "Marriage." He notes that there are three agencies that deal with marriage problems listed in this town. He calls each one in turn. The secretary at the other end of the line replies, "Sorry, we have a backlog of cases at Family and Children's Services for six months. It will be January before we could see the couple." He tries Planned Parenthood and the secretary tells him essentially the same thing, except that their executive is so busy with consultations around problems of parenthood and with speaking about town that he hesitates to begin counseling. The third agency is the Jewish Family Agency and their executive states that his agency only has time to see referrals from synagogues and Jewish societies: "Sorry, but that is how it is."

Pastor Paul is a little crestfallen by now, but he continues his search in the yellow pages of the phone book. There under "Marriage Counseling," he finds three names listed. He calls each one in turn, and each reports that he is willing to accept referral immediately. He feels somewhat better, but on second thought he decides to call his friend Dr. Brown, a clinical psychologist, to check the qualifications of the three. Brown reports quite candidly, "Two of these people have little to qualify them except their say-so. In fact, they could be guilty of breach of the medical practices act by what they are doing. I know of the results of some of their work and it leaves much to be desired. The third, Mrs. Jones, is a psychiatric social worker, now in private practice; but she has no staff contact, and though she is competent, she is pretty isolated in her work." Pastor Paul unburdens himself over the phone to his friend about the number and complexity of his cases. "Where can I turn for help?" he asks. "I can't afford to put a counseling minister on my staff or to hire a marriage counselor to work with these cases." "A good question for which I don't have a good answer," says Dr. Brown.

In the past decade the establishment of pastoral counseling centers has provided a unique answer to the overburdening, pastoral counseling task of the parish. These centers do not restrict themselves to marriage and family problems, but reports from various executive directors indicate that the presenting problems of clients involve marriage difficulties from 30 per cent to 90 per cent of the time. In fact one director, Dr. James E. Doty, says, "I think we are safe in saying that the majority of all our work in the counseling centers is in the field of marriage counseling." [1] The pastoral counseling center uses pastors as counselors. For that reason it is of central importance for our attention in indicating this community approach to the pastoral counseling of marriage and family problems. What we propose to do in this chapter is to investigate how such a pastoral counseling center is established, how it can be financed, and how it is staffed and operated.

THE STRUCTURE AND PERSONNEL OF THE CENTER

A. Steering Committee

The first requirement is an interested group of pastors and laymen. The need for counseling may be painfully obvious in an urban area, but

---

[1] For mimeographed form used by Dr. Doty in establishing pastoral counseling centers, write to 324 Chamber of Commerce Building, 320 North Meridian, Indianapolis, Indiana.

until a group of citizens becomes aroused, nothing will happen. Unless one church is strong enough to bear the personnel and financial load, the group will need to be organized along district, synodical, or presbytery lines. If the group concerned is interdenominational, they may approach a council of churches in the city for support and sponsorship. Another approach is to go directly to a theological school and approach the faculty, in particular the professor of pastoral care and counseling. In the survey reported at the end of this chapter all three approaches will be indicated and found successful.

This concerned group will form itself into a steering committee with a chairman. They will meet regularly and begin to scout out the possibilities of such a center within the community. The group should be representative of some of the best executive minds and socially concerned persons in the community. This means that lay persons and not just pastors should be involved in the planning and discussions right from the beginning. These discussions should center first upon the purpose of the center with the goals as well as the limitations of pastoral counseling spelled out. This will enable other professional persons in the community to know at the start what you are about. The purpose and policy of the group may be set down in the incorporation papers. The group will be incorporated through the state as a non-profit organization. The steering committee will begin immediately to seek financial support for the center —before the door is open for counseling. They should know where money is available and how to go about budgeting the first year's operation with some realistic knowledge as to where the money will be obtained. When the time comes to open the center, the steering committee will dissolve itself and take the necessary steps to select a board of directors. Some of the steering committee will become board members, but more than likely the representation on the Board will include those from the wider community and body of the church.

B. The Board of Directors

The board of directors is elected according to the bylaws of the center to serve for a specific number of years. They may also be limited as to the number of years they can serve in succession. As indicated above, they should be broadly representative of the community. They should be willing to give the necessary time to handle the business of the center —this hardly needs saying.

The responsibilities of the board are similar to those of the official board of a church. Let us enumerate them briefly, and do this with the knowledge that each center will work out a different pattern so far as board duties are concerned:

1. To make and to review the policy of the center.

2. To raise, receive, and to disburse the funds of the center.

3. To employ the director of the center and to approve the employment of counselors. A personnel committee which has some professional experience in counseling may have to screen applicants and recommend them to the board.

4. To publicize the center through a brochure, letters, and through the media of press, radio, and television. The best publicity, however, is a satisfied client and a satisfied referral person. Added to this, however, must be the public image projected through mass media.

5. To secure memberships and sponsorships to the center if such be a means of financial and community support.

6. To be the liaison with the community and the church in interpreting the counseling center and in sponsoring workshops and conferences to aid in that interpretation.

The center will depend on two primary sources for its strength: the board of directors and the counselors of the center. Both are absolutely essential for a smoothly running organization.

C. The Professional Advisory Committee

The professional advisory committee is made up of those persons in the community who deal with personality and marriage problems, and who bring strengths from a particular profession not represented by the counselors of the center. Their purpose is to consult with the staff of counselors and to advise them concerning problems which touch their respective disciplines. At the very least, the fields of psychiatry, clinical psychology, psychiatric social work, law, medicine, and education should be represented on the advisory committee. Care should be exercised to secure the best qualified person from each field to sit with the committee. In a small committee one from each profession may represent the discipline. This is the practice of a number of counseling centers as indicated

183

in the survey to follow. In this case the advisory committee may meet weekly with the staff for a case presentation or at least monthly for such consultative work.

When the advisory committee is larger, so that several members of each profession are present, it may be necessary for the committee to meet with the staff at particular times to discuss problems which touch their respective fields. One can think of the meeting with lawyers to discuss divorce or separation agreements, or a meeting with gynecologists to discuss the ethics of vasectomies. The entire group can be called periodically to be briefed as to the philosophy and procedure of the counseling staff. However, these meetings would occur only when guidance is being sought on essential matters in professional relations with the entire field. One needs to do this certainly ever so often, to allay the fears of some that ministers are practicing psychiatry or are doing psychotherapy beyond their competence.

The professional advisory committee does not establish the policy of the center. This is the business of the board of directors. However, in matters pertaining to the relationship of the staff to a particular field, they do give their experienced and studied opinion. For example, if the lawyers have a particular way they want a referral made, their representative reports it at a staff meeting. If a staff person appears guilty of a breach of ethics or conduct in the eyes of the professional, he may report to the board of directors and have the matter reviewed. The professional advisory committee performs a real service to the staff for this kind of interprofessional consultation. They serve the board in relieving its collective mind of concerns about the staff's counseling procedure and conduct.

D. Pastoral Counselors
The staff of a pastoral counseling center are pastors who are fully qualified professionally; that is, they are seminary educated, they have been ordained, and are in good standing with their church. In addition they have had experience in pastoral care and counseling: the equivalent of three years in a parish. A third qualification which should be insisted upon in this context is a year of supervised clinical experience. This may be obtained in a hospital, prison, or welfare institution. In this setting the pastor's counseling is supervised by a clinically trained teacher. The

program of the Council for Clinical Training, the Institute of Pastoral Care, and other groups provide such experience. In addition in the field of marriage and the family, training may be obtained through the Marriage Council of Philadelphia, the Merrill-Palmer School of Detroit, the Menninger Foundation at Topeka, the American Foundation of Religion and Psychiatry, and the American Institute of Family Relations. (See Appendix for descriptive listings and addresses.)

The executive director of the staff should be the most highly qualified person in view of his training and experience. He, with the personnel committee from the board, should select the counselors. In a training situation in which the counselors are also in graduate school at the time, the clinical year can be waived. However, each person should counsel under supervision by a psychiatric supervisor and a pastoral supervisor. If the center is staffed by pastors in the field, the supervision should come directly from the advisory committee. Even though clinical training experience is a part of the counselor's equipment, he needs continuing supervision while he is doing his work. Only in this way can he continue to grow in his understanding of the dynamics of personality and of the complexities of the counseling relationship.

Each counselor must guarantee that he will see clients a certain number of hours a week for counseling and that he will attend supervisory conferences and staff meetings when they are held. It is a signal honor for a pastor to be selected for such a counseling center; however, he needs to free his schedule enough to be able to meet the responsibilities that counseling involves. He will be paid for his counseling work, unless he is in training, and this makes the responsibility carry additional weight. The counselor's work should be subject to periodic review, perhaps yearly, and consideration given to whether he will continue on the staff.

E. Counseling Rooms and Secretary

A suite of rooms within a church or college or seminary or even in a separate building should be provided before counseling begins. These should be equipped for counseling, that is, one room should be furnished with desk, chairs, lamps, and tables arranged tastefully as a counseling room. The second room is equipped for a secretary with desk, telephone, record files, dictaphone, safe, etc. Chairs should also be available in the

185

secretary's office in case clients must wait for several moments for their counselor. The secretary has as her job the processing of incoming phone calls—answering questions about the center, arranging counseling hours for the client—typing cases, keeping records, and carrying on correspondence for the center. In addition she meets each client as he comes to the center and may introduce him to his counselor. In a beginning operation a church secretary may serve the center part time in this role.

FINANCING THE CENTER

Every budget will vary from every other and so for that reason we can only deal with broad generalizations in talking finance. However, the board of directors needs to have a workable budget right from the beginning so that the center can open its doors with some assurance of not going into debt. The budget should include the salary for the secretary, the salaries for the executive director and the counselors, and fees for such consultants as are used, the rent for the office space, and such office supplies as are needed—brochures, letterheads, files, etc.

As our survey indicates below, there are several ways to support a center. Let us examine each way which can be used as a single means of support or in concert with other means.

1. Support the program from the fees paid by clients and from honoraria paid the personnel for community services, that is, lecturing to high school and college classes, and speaking to ministers at counseling workshops and pastoral care conferences. If this is the sole means of support, the program of the center will be limited in its scope and its possible outreach over a long period. One must be aware that fees and honoraria do not come in until the program is started, so that unless the counselors and consultants agree to work gratis for a preliminary period the center cannot begin to operate at all.

2. A more satisfactory way to finance the center is to obtain a grant from a foundation or a gift from an interested benefactor for one year to five years in order to underwrite the budget of the center. Foundation grants are awarded to community service organizations if the board can show that grants can be matched by other money, and that they will decreasingly need such support as the community or church provides

186

its backing. The benefactor's gift may be a continuing means of support to the center's budget, particularly if it is left in an annuity.

3. In a pastoral counseling center support may be obtained from the church conference if its service covers the area bounded by conference lines, or from smaller areas such as districts if that is the area of service. An interdenominational center will find some of its support through the budget of the council of churches.

4. Memberships and sponsorships are further means of obtaining support from the community if the board choses to make its appeal in this direction. The Marriage Council of Philadelphia is an example of a counseling center which has used this method over nearly a thirty-year period.

5. Finally, if the center engages in a research project, the board may seek out specific foundation help to underwrite the research over a specific period. Some foundations in particular encourage religious groups in their research; others are amenable to research into counseling functions. The United States Public Health Service may also be approached if the research area has a training aspect, that is, if it concerns education broadly conceived.

Let it be said again, lest the counseling staff be overconcerned about finances, that the board of directors has the responsibility to raise, disperse, and audit the budget of the center. The executive director may be concerned with finance, but the counselors should be relatively anxiety free in this matter so that they may do the best counseling job.

OPERATING THE CENTER

The secretary of the pastoral counseling center receives phone calls from inquirers, makes appointments for the counselors to see clients, meets the individuals when they come to the office and keeps records of counseling interviews which the pastoral counselors either dictate to her or provide her in tape recording or note form. Each counselor sets up his own hours when he will see individuals and/or couples. For example, if he plans to counsel four hours a week he may arrange his counseling schedule from six to ten on Tuesday. He is at the center during those hours whether his client appears or not. Each counselor keeps the secretary informed when a client terminates or is referred so that he can keep a full case load.

The hours for professional consultation are worked out to the mutual satisfaction of the counselor and psychiatrist and/or pastoral supervisor. This is ideally a weekly consultation, particularly if training is being obtained by the counselor. The staff meeting is held regularly either weekly or monthly. This can be the most significant experience for the counselors in the week. The focus of the meeting is a case presentation by one of the counselors, and the various counsultants discuss the case, drawing out the psychodynamics of the client and the various aspects of the relationship which the counselor has established with the client. If two counselors are involved in a marriage counseling case, each may report, and the various attitudes and behaviors of the respective mates analyzed and a continuing plan worked out. The counselors always have opportunity to comment on the case also, so that the staff becomes a learning experience for all attending, pastors as well as consultants.

Referrals to other agencies, to individual lawyers, psychiatrists, or community workers are made with the help of the consultant and through the means of the secretary. A good list of referral agencies and professional people should be in the possession of the counseling center.

The center is publicized by an attractive brochure which lists the purpose of its counseling operations, the place in which it is located, the time it is open, and the phone number and address so that prospective clients may reach it. The brochure also lists names of counselors, the board of directors, the professional advisory committee, and sponsors if such are a part of the center. A convocation program held upon the opening of the center and suitably publicized and with an outstanding speaker for a drawing card is suggested as a capital method of beginning. In addition the holding of an annual pastoral counseling workshop at the center can be a means of informing the churches of the activities of the pastoral counseling program. This practice by the Boston University Pastoral Counseling Center over an eight-year period has developed its workshop until it attracts more than three hundred pastors yearly. The workshop idea, says Dr. Paul E. Johnson, Director, is one of the best means of publicizing the center's activities to the church.[2]

[2] Brochures from the various centers can be obtained by writing their respective directors.

A SURVEY OF FIVE PASTORAL COUNSELING CENTERS [3]

	Center A	Center B	Center C	Center D	Center E
1. Sponsor	Foundation	Foundation	Church Conf.	Large Church	Fees and Board
2. Staff	Clinically trained pastors	C.T. pastors	C.T. pastors	Multi-staff	Social workers
3. Client hours	1200/year	280/6 months	481/year	9847/year	1708/year
4. Percentage of Marriage Problems*	PM 10% M 40% F 15% T 65%	PM 0% M 20% F 14% T 34%	PM 0% M 33% F 27% T 60%	PM .01% M 25% F 5% T 30.01%	PM 10% M & F 80% T 90%
5. Method of Counseling	Eclectic	Eclectic	Client-centered	Psychoanalytic	Casework Relationship
6. Fees	Fee scale $0–10	Voluntary	Voluntary	Fee scale $3–12.50	Flat fee $10
7. In-service Training	Theological students on grad. level	Theological students on grad. level	Pastors	Theological students Pastors	Social workers
8. Consultants	Psychiatrist Psychologist Social worker Teacher	Psychiatrist Psychologist Social worker	Psychiatrist Attorney Social worker Physician	Psychiatrist Attorney Social worker Physician Businessman	Psychiatrist Physician Casework supervisor
9. Research	Ph.D. Candidates	None yet	Analysis of Center	Several under grants	Several under grants

[3] Conducted summer, 1959.

* PM (*premarital*), M (*marriage*), F (*family*), T (*total*).

XIV

Family Life Education in the Church

Counseling with few exceptions is a second-best operation. Except for the work a pastor does with couples before marriage, what we have been talking about is the binding up of wounds suffered in marriage and family relationships. What has been painfully apparent is that this is often too late in the day to do more than a salvage job. Sociologists and psychologists join with religious teachers of marriage and the family to recommend an extensive program of family life education. In the counseling room you may think, "If only I could begin with the previous generation, this couple would not be here for help!" Mature marriages and mentally healthy families are a product of growing up with mature parents a generation ago. To do the job effectively the minister and his parishioners need to think out and plan a family life education program that will help couples and families grow in Christian attitudes and behavior. Nothing short of this total approach to the task is worthy of our consideration.

PRINCIPLES AND GOALS OF A FAMILY LIFE PROGRAM

The orienting principle in family life education is the building of healthy families within the community. This kind of training can be done within the schools, the Y.M.C.A. and Y.W.C.A., or service clubs. However, the church with its basis in ethical and spiritual values is in a unique position to train young people, couples, and families in the essentials of mature and healthy family life. That the church in recent decades has increasingly accepted this responsibility is to its credit.

The goals of family life education include: (1) Training young people for marriage before the premarital interviews take place. Youth from

190

junior high years on up need training in forming relationships with the opposite sex. (2) Training young marrieds for parenthood. This training can begin before marriage;[1] however, the young marrieds are particularly ready to learn the mysteries of parenthood both before and after the first child arrives. (3) Training "mid-marrieds" and adolescents in interdependent living. The changes brought about by puberty create a new situation to which parents and youth must adjust. Parents need to "untie the apron strings" and youth need to learn how to be independent without total rebellion. (4) Helping older adults to adjust to life with children "flown from the nest," and to the new role of in-laws and grandparents. Family life education follows the couple into these important years. (5) Creating a "Church family" within the constituency that makes a place for single persons, widows, and divorcees. Too often in the zeal of family life education, this important group of people is forgotten. They have needs for the support and warmth of fellow feeling that can be obtained in the church. These problems usually need attention and inclusion in family life education.

The minister's role in family life education needs discussion before we go on to specific details of a program. By reason of his focal position with respect to families in the church (see Chapter I), he should be aware of the example and influence of his relationships with his own family. The parsonage has been called a "goldfish bowl." Surely the public character of the minister's marriage and family life has its drawbacks on openness and spontaneity, but it also has some advantages. Young people who come to the parsonage for youth fellowship planning and discussions are introduced to a marriage relationship other than their parents which influences them. Some pastors invite engaged couples to dinner in order that they get acquainted with his wife and family before counseling. The couple's eyes and ears are certainly open during such a social occasion. The writer has had several couples become engaged formally after dinner at the parsonage and likes to feel they became more "sold on marriage" as a result of the occasion. Too, married couples in and out of the parsonage look to the minister, his wife, and family for examples in Christian living.

It should be pointed out that the minister can escape his responsibility

[1] See my article, "Preparation for Parenthood," *Christian Action*, May, 1960, pp. 54-63.

as a husband and a father by preoccupation with church work. Marriage counseling can of itself draw the minister away to the office so much that his own marriage and family life suffers. The case of Dana and Lucy, reported in a popular magazine, clearly points to this tendency of clergymen to neglect their own families while engaged in helping others.[2]

The minister bases his family life program upon the steady and competent pastoral care which he renders his parish. He builds the necessary rapport that gives support to a learning situation within marriages and families. The parents of his parish will become aware of his genuine interest and concern to improve the job the church is doing in the area of family life. They will gladly become a part of a program that seeks to impart sound sociological, psychological, and religious knowledge and skill in marriage and family life. In fact, if certain key leaders in existing groups are perceptive to this need for family life education, they can be enlisted in making such a program a reality.

THE STRUCTURE OF A FAMILY EDUCATION PROGRAM

Each church must adapt any program to its own situation. Better still the program should grow out of the felt needs of the couples and families in the group. An excellent questionnaire to help an interested group discover the needs of families in a local church has been prepared by Edward D. Staples.[3]

A Family Life Committee can be appointed through the commission on education (or similar church school body) to meet and discuss the needs made apparent through the survey or questionnaire. They may after regular and lengthy consideration develop a pattern which they think will most adequately meet the problems.

Several possibilities are open to the committee:

1. The problems can be faced within existing groups. For example, a course on boy-girl friendships can be devised within the junior and intermediate fellowship: or a course on "Dating and Going Steady" in the youth fellowship; "Preparation for Marriage" is a ready-made course for young people, as "Building a Christian Home" is for the young mar-

---

[2] Paul Popenoe, "Can This Marriage Be Saved?" *Ladies Home Journal*, May, 1957, pp. 91 ff.

[3] *The Church and Families*. Write The Department of the Christian Family, P.O. Box 871, Nashville, Tennessee.

rieds. And the men's club and women's group can meet together to consider some of the problems of mid-marrieds. So existing groups can be used.

2. Home discussion groups can be organized over a short period of time. The topic of discussion is of immediate interest and can be dealt with in one, two, or three months. For example, couples within a certain age group come together to discuss problems of "discipline" with their children. Or parents and children can come together in a church school demonstration in order that the parents understand how their religious teaching supplements the Sunday morning session. Parents and teen-agers can meet together to discuss a "teenage code," as they have through various Parent-Teachers' Associations in the last decade. Such meetings have the advantage of enabling genuine interaction to take place between the parties concerned.

3. Group counseling can be organized when a significant number are facing the same problem area (see Chapter XII). It should be said that a family life program differs from group counseling in that it is education, whereas the latter is more "re-education" for those who have developed problems.

CASE STUDY: SEX EDUCATION IN THE CHURCH

Family life education is a total program whose ramifications and complexities would require more consideration than we have time for in this writing. The reader is encouraged to consult the various texts in the bibliography in working out a well-rounded program. What we propose to do is to look at three specific groups and to inquire as to how a program of sex education might be introduced and carried out in these groups.

It must be stated at the outset that the minister will meet reticence and resistance on the part of some people in dealing with sex in the church. Not only in rural areas is this so, but also in some city churches. Prudishness and puritanical shame die hard, even in post-Kinsey America. *The place of sex education is in the home.* The church and the pastor merely help parents to meet their responsibility to their children. When parents default, the school may try to meet the need for imparting the physiological facts about sex, or the basic sociological information about boy-girl relations. However, when both home and school default, the

church may need to impart this fundamental information to its young people. At any rate the church needs to interpret the sexual information and the heterosexual relationship from a religious perspective. No other community agency does this but the church, and it will miss a real opportunity if it also defaults its responsibility. Now to the three groups:

1. Engaged Couples

Perhaps the best place to begin family life education is with the group of young people who are immediately facing marriage. The engaged couples—and even in a small church at some times of the year there are two or three at one time—can be brought together to face in a group some of the questions couples have before marriage and to do this in Christian context. Planning for marriage should be a part of the Family Life Committee's task. The minister may be one resource person, but he does not bear the total task as he does in premarital counseling.

One church entitles their course, "Four Evenings with Marriage," and uses a physician, social worker, home economist, and minister to talk to the couples about the sexual, sociological, budgetary, and spiritual sides of marriage. This is surely the way to approach the subject. As Dr. Theodore Bovet points out, "all too often what is called sexual education restricts itself to anatomy, physiology, and pathology, and omits psychology." [4] And one might add religion. To educate couples sexually, one must go beyond the marriage-manual approach, where techniques are discussed and attitudes and motivations are left to chance.

Such discussions with engaged couples should be carried on by mature, religiously well-integrated individuals who will steer a clear course between prudishness and laughing mockery. Too often a person with some knowledge in the area will try to shock without concern for the feelings of the group or will cover up without allowing members to ask questions which are burning to be answered. The religious dedication of persons like Evelyn and Sylvanus Duvall shines through when they are dealing with couples in the area of sex.

Key questions which may become the focus of discussion are:

1. What is the difference between the sexes? This thrusts one into not only physiological differences but also psychological ones. John may have been puzzled by Mary's blue period just preceding her menstrual

---

[4] *Love, Skill and Mystery* (New York: Doubleday & Company, Inc., 1958), p. 24.

period; and Mary may have been confounded at John's intensity after a period of hugging and kissing. These questions need discussion. Too, the differences between the sexes brings one to the sociological definitions of male and female roles. If, as Bovet points out, the male is the "head" of the home and the female the "heart," how is this worked out in a democratic society with the woman working and away from the house ten hours a day? John and Mary are both enlightened as they hear other couples bring up problems in understanding one another because of sex differences.

2. What is the purpose of sex in human life? The Christian perspective differs here from a strictly biological point of view. Biologically, the couples may say, sex is for the purpose of procreation: the creation of children. But they also mention the fact that sex expresses the deep feelings of love and companionship they have for each other. The difference between lust, *eros,* and *agape* can be fruitfully discussed: lust (satisfaction of desire); *eros* (the companionship of being together); and *agape* (the self-giving side of the relationship where the other's happiness becomes your pleasure). It is gratifying to note how a group of young couples who have grown up in the church can generalize their learning from other areas to the sexual area with a little drawing out.

3. What is meant by sexual harmony and how is it achieved? This particular question needs discussion, and it is often best handled by a physician. The Planned Parenthood Association can be asked to provide a lecturer who will not only explain the process of contraception, but using their scale models do a great deal of teaching regarding the process of sexual intercourse. Here again attitudes are of the essence. One may discover fear or guilt displayed by certain members of the group, and individual counseling sessions may be arranged with those persons. The inability to accept sex as a part of one's make-up may be a harbinger of frigidity or impotence in the marriage union. If these attitudes can be perceived and worked through before marriage, the couple will face fewer problems within marriage. Though some in the church have tended to make of sex something corrupt, the wise leader of this discussion can show the natural place of sex in God's creation, and the complementary side of men and women's make-up in working toward sexual harmony.

4. What is the relationship between faithfulness and a happy married life? In a period when many couples, even church couples, face

marriage with a "trial concept" in mind, this subject needs talking through again at the level of attitudes and basic values. Faith is intimately related to faithfulness, and commitment to the loyalty of his mate. Surely, all of us are attracted to other members of the opposite sex, and in times of stress or separation, the attraction may tempt one to unfaithfulness. However, more than a matter of following one's conscience is the faith one has in God and the commitment to do his will in all things— particularly in this most intimate of relationships. It is distressing to find ministers of the gospel who in periods of alienation from their wives seek the companionship of other women. However, they often find that their marriage is weakened and their spiritual resources impoverished by these attempts at dual living. Couples who are most romantic about their marriage need to face these problems honestly and sincerely.

5. What is the spiritual interpretation of the sexual relationship? The minister should surely want to face this question with his engaged couples. This relationship of the couple's faith to the heterosexual re- lationship has been intimated all along in the discussion, but it needs to be drawn together so that the couples have a well-rounded view toward the physical aspect of marriage. Says Henry Bowman, "The couple's bodies will permit them to establish a sexual, a procreative relationship. Their God-centered orientation will permit them to establish a spiritual, a creative relationship." [5] To show the *agape* nature of the union of the sexes is of primary importance. That sex may be a bridge across which the deepest meanings of life can be conveyed and the most unselfish feelings expressed brings such a discussion to its high point.

Vital study is essential for such a class. One may use a text or draw from several books to plan for the class. Let us look at several books which may be used for this purpose:

Bowman, Henry A. *A Christian Interpretation of Marriage.* Philadelphia: Westminster Press, 1959. This book would make an excellent text for eight sessions. Questions for discussion on sex, marriage, premarital sexual re- lations are particularly relevant, as are the topics for panels and suggestions for the use of films.

Bovet, Theodore. *Love, Skill and Mystery.* New York: Doubleday & Com-

---

[5] *A Christian Interpretation of Marriage* (Philadelphia: Westminster Press, 1959), p. 22.

pany, Inc., 1958. This is an excellent discussion by a Swiss doctor blending the psychological, sociological, and theological aspects of sex.

Bertocci, Peter A. *The Human Venture in Sex, Love, and Marriage.* New York: Association Press, 1950. This psychologist-philosopher has done an excellent job of correlating the place of sex within the whole of life.

Cole, William G. *Sex and Love in the Bible.* New York: Association Press, 1959. A biblical theologian with excellent background in psychiatry examines the practices of love and marriage in the Bible and shows what they say to us today.

Hamilton, William. *Faith, Sex, and Love.* National Student Council, Y.M.C.A-Y.W.C.A. This booklet is a popular treatment by a theologian that should appeal to college-aged young people.

Hiltner, Seward. *Sex Ethics and the Kinsey Reports.* New York: Association Press, 1954. A pioneer study following the stir caused by Kinsey's studies. The Christian faith and ethic are shown as critical of Kinsey's results.

2. Parents of Young Children

This group within the church are in a particular quandary about sex education. By rights they are the ones who having received a helpful start in the premarital instruction want to do a better job of sexual training with their children. They want to avoid the mistakes which bound them in fear and ignorance and help their children to grow in this area as in other areas of life in a healthy Christian way.

The purpose of such a group would be to help parents anticipate the questions which children ask and to enable them to deal with sexual curiosity and sexual experience maturely, without shame or emotional bias. Lester Kirkendall states that sexual education needs broadening from the limited answering of children's questions to a matter of imparting attitudes and guiding behavior.[6] To do this parents need to be relieved of their numbing fear of sex and the consequences of sexual involvement. They need to come to terms with their own sexual concerns and their own sexual adjustments. Before children's urges and drives can be properly dealt with, parents may need help, lest they project feelings that the "body is evil" and "sex is nasty."

"True sex education begins at birth,"[7] as Ackerman reports. The mother is involved in sexual education as soon as she nurses the child.

[6] "Helping Parents Become Better Sex Educators," Vincent, *op. cit.,* pp. 80-87.
[7] Ackerman, *op. cit.,* p. 223.

The father helps the child accept his body as soon as he begins participating in the child's daily bath. How parents react to the child's exploration of the genital area, their mode of toilet training, their bathroom and dressing habits are all a part of the normal preparation of the child for his sexual role. Some psychoanalysts say categorically that basic sexual training has been accomplished by the time the child is five or six, largely by the mother. Without accepting this early conditioning theory completely, we can agree that the training is done unconsciously as well as by imparting information, and that it involves these early childhood years as well as the juvenile and adolescent stages.

Dorothy Baruch simplifies the sexual education of children to ABC's.[8] These are: (1) attachments, (2) bodily sensitivity, and (3) concepts. The child forms certain significant attachments to another person. There follows an orderly sequence from mother to father to playmate of same sex to a person of the opposite sex. The male child loves his mother and from this love knows the joys of such an attachment. He breaks the solitary attachment in identifying with the father to learn the male role. He learns to attach himself to a boy chum before adolescence, then he reaches out toward a girl friend in a love relationship. A girl child follows a similar pattern. At each stage sex education takes place as parents help children with their attachments.

Baruch goes on to point out that the sensitivity with which a child reacts to bodily contact helps him to learn he is loved. This bodily contact may be with various parts of his body but it centers in the genital area as he develops. How the parents react to bodily exploration and how they accept his feelings toward his body helps him to grow toward channelized expression of sexual feelings.

The *concepts* of sex education follow these other learnings. The question of "Where did I come from?" is asked by the child of four. The primary child is interested in "How was I born?", whereas the question of the place of the father in the birth of the baby is not asked until the child is nine or so. These questions are generally more than queries for information; they involve phantasies and feelings the child has about his attachments and his bodily sensitivities. The wise parent is not frightened by outright questions so that he clams up. Nor does he get out charts and

[8] Dorothy Baruch, *New Ways in Sex Education* (Toronto: McGraw-Hill Co. of Canada, Ltd., 1959), pp. 8-19.

biological data beyond the child's grasp at the first query. He answers what the child asks and waits to explain the next step until he is ready to go further.

When treated in an atmosphere of acceptance and love, this area as well as that of discipline or sibling relationships can be met adequately by parents. Within a Christian group the meanings and values of God's plan for procreation need emphasis. The basis of sexual union in love and the miracle evident in the birth of a child can be brought out. The love between a man and woman can be "caught" by the example of parents in the home. By taking time with a child, parents can encourage discussing questions and explorations regarding sex, God, and the wonders of life. These can be vitally related by an alert and understanding parent.

The reading of books with such a parents' group is a necessary supplement to discussion. The books recommended for such a group are:

Dorothy Baruch. *New Ways in Sex Education.* Toronto: McGraw-Hill Co. of Canada, Ltd., 1959. This is an excellent book for parents at all stages but particularly for parents of small children.

Karl de Schweinitz. *Growing Up.* New York: The Macmillan Co., 1953. A non-technical book for use with young children.

Manwell and Fahs. *Growing Bigger.* Boston: Beacon Press, 1942. A religious interpretation for use with Juniors.

Margueritte H. Bro. *When Children Ask.* New York: Harper & Bros., 1956. An excellent book combining sexual education with other areas of religious education.

Roy E. Dickerson. *Teaching Children About Sex.* Pamphlet available through Box 871, Nashville, Tennessee.

Roy E. Dickerson. *Sex Education for Children Series.* Pamphlets for use with each age group. Order from: American Institute of Family Relations, 5287 Sunset Blvd., Los Angeles 27, California.

See also audio-visual materials for family-life program, Department of Christian Family Life, Box 871, Nashville 2, Tennessee.

3. Parents of Teenagers

If ever there is a worried group in the church, the parents of teenagers are one. The problems of childhood just appear to have been faced successfully by parents when puberty explodes and a whole new set of problems emerges. Even the most mature parent finds his ingenuity taxed. A study group for these harried mothers and fathers can help them to face their problems together and to arrive at some common understandings within a religious framework. The purpose of such a group would be to help these parents face the sexual changes of puberty their child is undergoing and the whole range of situations which dating, going steady, and becoming engaged foist on their child and themselves. But primary is the matter of keeping communication lines open between themselves and their youth so that problems can be talked through.

Ideally such a parents' group should meet with their teenage counterparts. Suppose that the teenagers have been studying boy-girl relations in the high school youth fellowship; the parents' group has also been meeting to discuss their concerns regarding the sex education of their youth; then, several joint meetings of youth with parents should be encouraged (as happens through Parent-Teachers' Associations) to arrive at mutual agreements. For the purposes of simplicity, however, at this point we shall deal only with possible directions which the parents' group might follow. And we shall do this as we did with the engaged group, by suggesting certain key questions for discussion:

1. What about the ground rules for dating and intimacy between boys and girls?

No matter how sophisticated the present American generation of parents has become, when their teenagers begin to date, they feel they are one generation behind, and their children will add to this feeling that they are "out of date." Particularly is this so when sex values are in such flux as they are today.

If parents have helped their child mature in sexual attitudes and behavior, they will quite naturally talk to them about the pubertal changes, that is, menstruation or the seminal emission. Without frightening the youth, the parent can help them understand their sexual feelings and the relationship between lust, the desire for companionship with the opposite sex, and the duties and rights of sex within marriage. All of this may come to the fore when the ground rules for dating are discussed between parent and child.

Ruth and Walter Vernon give parents some guidelines for dating rules: (1) See that you know the boy or girl your child is dating. (2) Have agreed upon regulations, but do not be legalistic in enforcing them. (3) Know where your boy or girl will be on a date. (4) Make available helpful books in the area. (5) Face realistically the question of going steady.[9]

2. How soon should they go steady and should I have a voice in this?

"Going steady" means different things to different ages of adolescence and in different parts of the country. It's best for parents to talk this through with their young person. The mother may have been "pinned" in college and considered it as good as an engagement ring—it was engagement to both her and her sweetheart. At age fifteen little Janie goes steady with Johnny this month and Billy next. It's "date insurance" for her. Later at seventeen taking a fraternity pin means she's "engaged to be engaged" and she breaks this relationship much easier than her mother would. Parents need to have a voice in their youth's "steady" behavior, but more of an understanding voice lest they misinterpret the seriousness of the relationship. In the present *dating-rating* scheme young people are working out, their behavior may be far less ominous than the parents believe.

3. What about early marriage? And how early is early?

Even having said the above, we should take account of earlier marriages among our teenagers. In two high schools in a large city teachers report not only a high incidence of marriage but an equally high incidence of divorce. Certainly when teenagers contract marriage because of pregnancy outside of wedlock or infatuations without serious responsibility or to escape their parents' authority, these problems need consideration.

However, parents may need help in understanding their children's earlier maturity and their need for the security of marriage while going on to college and graduate school. Financial support may be necessary from the parents for a longer time to enable this marriage to take place.

4. What stand should parents take toward premarital chastity? "To wait or not to wait," that is the teenagers' question, and it is rewarding to face the questions with parents. Sociologists like Kirkendall, Bowman, Ellzey, and Baruch point out that the important thing is the relationship between teenagers, and whether sex is used as a thing in itself or as

[9] *The Christian Home*, August, 1957. See also R. R. Bell, and L. Blumberg, "Courtship Intimacy and Religious Background," *Marriage and Family Living*, XXI (1959), 356-60.

a channel to express the finest feelings and meanings between a couple. Teenagers can manipulate another person's feelings without necessarily "going all the way." In fact, often among middle-class youth, petting to orgasm is a "moral" way of enjoying sex. The important thing for parents to face with youth, and young men to face with young women is how to make sex experiences good experiences. The Christian view of the dignity of the person and one's responsibility to relate to another as a *Thou* may cause him to put off sexual experiences until marriage, or to enjoy them only with his fiancée. This is not to make the old absolute stand relativistic but to do as Jesus did: to see the spirit behind the social regulation. If the young person learns to be responsible in his sexual conduct, it will be as he integrates his behavior with a faith in a God of *agape* love who can be found in deepest communion between man and wife. Let it be said that the continuing love relationship between a father and mother through these growing questing years can teach youth more unconsciously than can ten lectures. If sex is a meaningful means of communion for parents, the children will not see it as a means of power or humiliation. As said before, the feelings about this important area often come before the teaching of facts or values.

5. How can I keep the confidence of my teenager so that we can talk and have understanding on these sexual matters? This question will most certainly be asked in such a group and the person who asks it needs help desperately, but the aid comes most beneficially through personal counseling. Because the teenager is prone to defy his parents, many times the lines of communication are broken. To re-establish them requires the parent to understand what he is doing to drive his youngster away, and how he can change so as to re-establish confidence between them. The group leader can meet this parent's need most effectively in a counseling session.

Here are some useful resources for group leaders, teens, and their parents.

Baruch, Dorothy. *New Ways in Discipline.* New York: McGraw-Hill. 1949.

Bowman, Henry A. *A Christian Interpretation of Marriage.* Philadelphia: Westminster Press, 1959.

Duvall, Evelyn. *Facts of Life and Love for Teen-Agers.* New York: Association Press, 1956.

Duvall, Evelyn and Sylvanus. *Leading Parents' Groups.* New York: Abingdon Press, 1946.

Lerrigo, Marion O., and Southard, Helen. *Learning About Love.* New York: E. P. Dutton & Co., Inc., 1956.

———— *What's Happening to Me?* New York: E. P. Dutton & Co. Inc., 1956.

Schultz, Gladys. *It's Time You Knew.* New York: J. B. Lippincott Co., 1955.

Weis, Frank. "Old Drive, New Slant." *Workers with Youth.* XII (1959).

Wittenberg, Rudolph M., *Adolescence and Discipline.* New York: Association Press, 1959.

Eighty-five percent of the parents of today have never read a book on child care or child psychology, says Edward Staples of the Methodist Department of the Christian Family. This is not only pitiable but a symptom of a gaping need. These parents know their limitations and most of them want to do something about it. The church as a custodian of values in family living needs to take the lead in this preventative and educative task. Other groups in the community will surely be involved— such as the school, the Y's, and service clubs—in this important effort of education for marriage and family living. But the church should be at the center of this enterprise and through her message provide the heart and conscience of the effort. Counseling with marriage and family problems will become a secondary effort only as family life education assumes a place of primary importance in the program of the church.

XV

Epilogue

The institutions of marriage and the family have greater possibilities in the United States today but they also face greater hazards. Because of the rapid cultural changes we are experiencing in our complex organizational society, there has been a decrease in some functions of marriage and the family which has tended toward looser integration. As Professor M. Nimkoff among others, points out:

The functions of economic production, education, protection, control, and *religion* have diminished while social-psychological functions relating to affection, fellowship, and recreation have increased. . . . There are those who think that in time the personality or social-psychological functions . . . will prove to be more binding than were the traditional economic, political, educational, and religious functions of the family. But in the first phase of industrialization, at least, the effect of change has been to make the family more unstable.[1]

Marriage and the family are always changing, not only from epoch to epoch in history, but also from one period to another in the life of the individual couple. The tensions and countertensions felt between a man and his wife and parents and children—as we have observed in the case studies—are some of the most dynamic and intricately complex realities one can imagine. No one, not even a solitary bachelor, escapes his family's influence. In fact, one may remain a bachelor because of an unresolved relationship with his mother. The Communist Russian and Chinese nations have discovered that they legislate the family out of existence at the state's own peril. Group survival demands the institu-

[1] "The Family in the United States," *Marriage and Family Living*, XVI (1954), pp. 390-96 (italics mine).

tion of the family—in some form at least—to insure the nurture and early education of children, even though that form may differ radically from the traditional patterns of the past.

The high incidence of marriage and family difficulties in the United States today is directly correlated to the social changes and flux in morals. The minister may confront in the parish the destructive, tearing effects of conflict, hatred, jealousy, cruelty, and unfaithfulness. He may also perceive the manner in which role ambiguities and the breakdown in communication led to conflict and misunderstanding between spouses. He believes that love, concern, patience, and forgiving acceptance for the erring—the values implicit in Christ's teaching—can become explicit in the relationships between husbands and wives, parents and children. He looks to counseling as a means to help counter the destructive forces so that the constructive values may grow. This represents a high goal for counseling and a positive motivation for becoming a counselor.

However, as we have discussed in this study, the minister is foolish to attempt to salvage marriages and families as though he were a Messiah working alone against the social currents. There are other agencies and groups in the community concerned with healthy individuals living in healthy families. The minister will do his best work if he joins with them in community associations and professional consultation. Moreover, he can work concertedly with others, if the steps are taken, in a pastoral counseling center where counseling is adequately supervised and followed through. There will certainly be a greater need for such centers in the years ahead and for more ministers to be trained to work part-time in such centers.

One of the most important conclusions we have discovered is that marriage and family counseling are not enough. True, it will suffice to help some couples through marital difficulty and some families to weather a crisis. But with the tremendous changes happening to the institutions of marriage and the family, it is necessary to educate and inform couples and families, to help them think through various vital issues confronting their lives before they are at the breaking point. As we have indicated, it is most important to begin with the previous generation to help prepare children and youth for life in a modern family. Professor Henry Bowman discovered in a 1948 survey that of 1,370 schools and colleges only 632 (49.8%) of them offered courses in the area of marriage education, whereas, 638 (50.2%) offered none.[2] We might well raise the question: What would a current survey of Protestant churches show as to their program of education for marriage? For example, though the Methodist church has a Department of Family Life on the national level, and sponsors a National Conference on Family Life every four years, and publishes a family magazine, *The Christian Home,* would half of their churches have an organized family life committee and an active educational program?

Though the influence of religion and of the church is minimized by some writers, they fail to recognize that religion has a dynamic as well as a conserving function. It is well known that the church, like the school and the state, operates as a conserving force within the social structure. The church's stand on divorce, on sexual morality, and on parental authority can be listed as evidence of its value-binding character. Its teachings and the social pressure it has exerted has tended to slow down social change. However, one must take into account the dynamic nature of religion as well. Many of the values toward which the new society is tending are inherent in the Christian Gospel.

Democracy in the family is one example. It is true that the patriarchal and puritanical image of the family was fostered and furthered by the colonial church. Victorian revivalism tended to make of sexual relationships something to be hidden and denied, and channeled religion into moralistic and individualistic avenues of Sabbath-keeping and piety. However true that may be, inherent in the gospel is a respect for the rights of women and children and a dynamic of love and sharing. The contemporary writing coming from Christian scholars like Seward Hiltner, William Cole, and Peter Bertocci, shows that when this dynamic is released it tends to move the marriage and the family into life-affirming and democratic patterns.

In this new family emphasizing the personal, sociological, and psychological functions, the dynamic of the Christian faith can move individuals to grow within the context of a harmonious social group. Each can count for one, and the household will not be run for the sake of the parents nor for the sake of the children, but for each in turn. Faith

[2] "Collegiate Education for Marriage and Family Living," *The Annals of the American Academy of Political and Social Science,* (1950), 272, pp.148-55.

will not be something tacked onto the family as prayers may be at the start of the meal. But rather, faith will grow out of the trusting environment of parents and children living together. Tension will be experienced between personal growth on the parts of individuals and family harmony. However, rather than splitting the family, this tension may be the occasion for growth of each person involved to a new level of insight and relationship. If the husband and wife come to the minister with a problem, he may well consider counseling with them. If they raise the question in a group at church, this may be the occasion for group counseling or family life education. However, they may call a family council with mother, father, and children meeting around a table and talking the problem through to each member's satisfaction. The reaching of understanding so that growth can take place in the family setting is the important consequence. However it happens, if the church is willing to lose its life organizationally and institutionally, so that couples and children may find themselves, it will be performing a real service. Christianity may in this way again become a "house church" and multiply the forces making for Christian maturity within homes a hundredfold.

The minister may feel an acute sense of dissatisfaction, even frustration, after reading one book or taking one course in marriage and family counseling. This is a good consequence; better this than to take an Olympian stance of knowledge and skill which will blind him to his own weaknesses. In closing we might make certain recommendations which the counseling minister may follow in continuing to counsel with marriage and family problems.

First, *continue to learn the skills of counseling by engaging in counseling under supervision.* One can learn in no better way, whether in a summer course of clinical pastoral training, or in a year-round course at one of the marriage counseling training centers. Ten percent of our clergy trained to handle marriage and family problems is not enough! Either the minister obtains this training or the counseling will go to others by his own default.

Second, *secure some means of self-evaluation of counseling methods,* either in a graduate school, or, if you possess the tools, on your own. There is a paucity of follow-up studies of clients and evaluative research data in marriage counseling. Some of the reasons are the effect which research intrusion has upon the counseling relationship, and the difficulty to recruit and finance researchers. Some of this research needs to be done in the graduate schools of the church and is beginning to emerge at the present time.

Counseling of all kinds requires that a person be willing to grow, to try new approaches, to learn by his mistakes, and to be willing to let the humblest client teach him something about life. Counseling is re-education of the client when the first attempt by parents or teachers has failed. In the religious context it helps individuals to find a frame of orientation —a faith to give their lives anchorage—and a scale of values—some goods beyond mere need-satisfactions—to live for. The counseling minister may never build a cathedral, but if he has helped one couple to find their moorings and to work through misunderstandings to acceptance of themselves under God, he may close the door of his study feeling a little more a pastor to his people and a shepherd of God.

APPENDIX

A LISTING OF TRAINING ORGANIZATIONS
FOR THE MINISTER

I. *Clinical Pastoral Training*
  a) Council for Clinical Training
    Interchurch Center
    Riverside Drive
    New York 27, New York
  b) Institute of Pastoral Care
    Box 57
    Worcester, Massachusetts
  c) Institute of Religion
    Texas Medical Center
    Houston, Texas
  d) American Foundation of Religion and Psychiatry
    3 West 29th Street
    New York 1, New York
  e) Washington School of Psychiatry
    1703 Rhode Island Avenue, NW
    Washington 6, D.C.
  f) White Institute of Psychiatry and Psychology
    12 East 86th Street
    New York 28, New York

Clinical pastoral training is an intensive training in pastoral counseling under supervision, generally over a twelve weeks' period, although the Institute of Pastoral Care has six weeks' courses. The three latter groups have training in a psychiatric setting and are open to clergy who desire training in psychiatric methods and procedure. A training analysis is recommended in some instances.

II. *Marriage Counseling Training Programs*
  a) American Institute of Family Relations
    5287 Sunset Boulevard

Los Angeles 27, California
Dr. Paul Popenoe, Director
Training consists of workshops in the summer of two weeks and of a
period of in-service training covering a year.

b) Marriage Council of Philadelphia
1422 Chestnut Street
Philadelphia 2, Pa.
Dr. Emily Mudd, Director
In-service training for physicians covering a year; also training for allied
professions from six months to a year.

c) Menninger Foundation, Marriage Counseling Service
Topeka, Kansas
The Rev. Thomas Klink, Acting Director
Applicants must have a Ph.D. degree in social work, psychology, medicine,
child development and family relations or a related field. Period of training,
one year.

d) Merrill-Palmer School, Institute of Human Development and Family Life
71 Ferry Street
East Detroit 2, Michigan
Dr. Aaron Rutledge, Director
Graduate students in the social sciences are admitted for a year's course
and a year's supervised counseling.

e) Graduate Schools of Social Work at the various universities throughout the
nation.
Masters and Doctors degrees in marriage counseling are now being offered.
It is best to write directly to the registrar of the university for information.

SELECTED BIBLIOGRAPHY

BACKGROUND IN MARRIAGE AND FAMILY LIVING

Anshen, Ruth N., ed. *The Family, Its Function and Destiny.* New York: Harper & Bros., 1959.

Baruch, Dorothy W. *How To Live With Your Teen-Ager.* New York: McGraw-Hill Book Company, Inc., 1953.

Bossard, James H. S. *Parent and Child.* Philadelphia: University of Pennsylvania Press, 1953.

Deutsch, Helene. *The Psychology of Women.* 2 vols. New York: Grune & Stratton, Inc., 1944-45.

Duvall, Evelyn M. *Family Development.* New York: Lippincott 1957.

————. *In-laws: Pro and Con.* New York: Associated Press, 1954.

————, and Hill, Reuben. *Being Married.* New York: Association Press, 1960.

Kirkendall, Lester A. *Sex Education as Human Relations.* New York: Inor Publishing Company, 1950.

Mace, David and Vera. *Marriage, East and West.* New York: Doubleday & Co., Inc., 1960.

Piaget, Jean. *The Language and Thought of the Child.* New York: Meridian Books, 1955.

Ribble, Margaret. *The Personality of the Young Child.* New York: Columbia University Press, 1955.

Winch, Robert F. *The Modern Family.* New York: Henry Holt and Company, Incorporated, 1952.

Winter, Gibson. *Love and Conflict.* New York: Doubleday and Co., Inc., 1958.

COUNSELING, PRINCIPLES AND TECHNIQUES

Psychiatry and Psychology

Fromm-Reichmann, Frieda. *Principles of Intensive Psychotherapy.* Chicago: University of Chicago Press, 1950.

Kahn, R. L., and Cannell, C. F. *The Dynamics of Interviewing.* New York: John Wiley & Sons, Inc., 1957.

Rogers, Carl R. *Client-Centered Therapy.* Boston: Houghton Mifflin Company, 1951.

Sullivan, Harry Stack. *The Psychiatric Interview.* New York: W. W. Norton & Company, Inc., 1954.

Marriage Counseling

Marriage and Family Living. 1219 University Avenue, S. E., Minneapolis 14, Minn.: National Council of Family Relations (Journal).

Skidmore, Garrett, and Skidmore. *Marriage Consulting.* New York: Harper & Bros.,1956.

Vincent, Clark E. *Readings in Marriage Counseling.* New York: Thomas Y. Crowell Company, 1957.

Pastoral Counseling

Hiltner, Seward. *The Christian Shepherd.* Nashville: Abingdon Press, 1959.

———. *Pastoral Counseling.* Nashville: Abingdon Press, 1948.

Johnson, Paul E. *Psychology of Pastoral Care.* Nashville: Abingdon Press, 1953.

Oates, Wayne E., ed. *Introduction to Pastoral Care.* Nashville: Broadman Press, 1959.

Wise, Carroll A. *Pastoral Counseling, Its Theory and Practice.* New York: Harper & Bros., 1951.

PREMARITAL COUNSELING

Bertocci, Peter A. *The Human Venture in Sex, Love, and Marriage.* New York: Association Press, 1950.

Bullock, Henry, ed. *In Holy Matrimony.* Nashville: The Methodist Publishing House, 1958.

———. *The Pastor's Manual for Premarital Counseling.* Nashville: The Methodist Publishing House, 1958.

Butterfield, Oliver M. *Planning for Marriage.* Princeton, New Jersey: D. Van Nostrand Company, Inc., 1956.

Duvall, Evelyn M., and Hill, Reuben. *When You Marry.* Revised Edition. New York: Association Press, 1953.

Duvall, Sylvanus. *Before You Marry.* New York: Association Press, 1949.

Ellzey, W. Clark. *How to Keep Romance in Your Marriage.* New York: Association Press, 1954.

Landis, Judson T. and Mary G. *Building a Successful Marriage.* Second edition. New York: Prentice-Hall, Inc., 1953.

Lewin, Samuel A., and Gilmore, John. *Sex Without Fear.* New York: Medical Research Press, 1950.

Mace, David. *Whom God Hath Joined.* Philadelphia: Westminster Press, 1953.

Morris, J. Kenneth. *Premarital Counseling: A Manual for Ministers.* Englewood Cliffs, N. J.: Prentice-Hall, Inc., 1960.

Pike, James A. *If You Marry Outside Your Faith.* New York: Harper & Bros., 1954.

Popenoe, Paul. *Preparing for Marriage.* Los Angeles: American Institute of Family Relations, (no date).

Stone, Abraham and Hannah. *A Marriage Manual.* New York: Simon and Schuster, Inc., 1952.

Westberg, Granger. *Premarital Counseling.* New York: National Council of Churches of Christ in U.S.A., 1958.

MARRIAGE AND FAMILY COUNSELING

Ackerman, Nathan Ward. *The Psychodynamics of Family Life.* New York: Basic Books, Inc., 1958.

Bergler, Edmund. *Unhappy Marriage and Divorce.* New York: International Universities Press, Inc., 1946.

Eisenstein, Victor W. *Neurotic Interaction in Marriage.* New York: Basic Books, Inc., 1946.

Goode, William J. *After Divorce.* Chicago: The Free Press of Glencoe, Illinois, 1955.

Guiding Family Spending. U.S. Department of Agriculture, Miscellaneous Publication, 661.

Hill, Ruben. *Families Under Stress.* New York: Harper & Bros., 1949.

Howe, Reuel. *The Creative Years.* New Haven: Seabury Press, Inc., 1959.

Landis, Paul H. *For Husbands and Wives.* New York: Appleton-Century-Crafts, Incorporated, 1956.

Leonard, Vandeman, and Miles. *Counseling with Parents.* New York: The Macmillan Company, 1954.

Mudd, Emily H., ed. *Marriage Counseling, A Casebook.* New York: Association Press, 1958.

————, and Krich, Aaron, eds. *Man and Wife.* New York: W. W. Norton & Company, 1957.

Pilpel, Harriet, and Zavin, Theodora. *Your Marriage and the Law.* New York: Rinehart & Company, Inc., 1952.

Stewart, Maxwell S., ed. *Problems of Family Life and How to Meet Them.* New York: Harper & Bros., 1956.

Taft, Julia Jessie. *Family Case Work and Counseling.* Philadelphia: University of Pennsylvania Press, 1948.

Wynn, John C. *Pastoral Ministry to Families.* Philadelphia: Westminster Press, 1957.

GROUP COUNSELING

Bach, George R. *Intensive Group Psychotherapy.* New York: The Ronald Press Company, 1954.

Driver, Helen Irene, ed. *Counseling and Learning Through Small-Group Discussion.* Madison, Wisconsin: Monona Publications, 1958.

Group Psychotherapy. Beacon, New York: Beacon House: American Society of Psychotherapy and Psychodrama (Journal).

Hare, Borgotta, and Bales. *Small Groups.* New York: Alfred A. Knopf, Inc., 1955.

How to Use Role Playing. Adult Education Pamphlet No. 6.

Slavson, S. R., ed. *The Practice of Group Therapy.* New York: International Universities Press, Inc., 1947.

Understanding How Groups Work. Adult Education Pamphlet No. 4.

FAMILY EDUCATION

Fallaw, Wesner. *The Modern Parent and the Teaching Church.* New York: The Macmillan Company, 1947.

Eakin, Frank and Mildred O. *Your Child's Religion.* New York: The Macmillan Company, 1942.

Groves, Ernest R. *Christianity and the Family.* New York: The Macmillan Company, 1942.

Maynard, Donald. *Your Home Can Be Christian.* Nashville: Abingdon Press, 1952.

Miller, Randolph C. *Education for Christian Living.* Englewood Cliffs, N. J.: Prentice-Hall, Inc., 1956.

Trueblood, Elton and Pauline. *The Recovery of Family Life.* New York: Harper and Bros., 1953.

Wynn, John C. *How Christian Parents Face Family Problems.* Philadelphia: Westminster Press, 1955.

Wittenberg, Rudolph M. *Adolescence and Discipline.* New York: Association Press, 1959.

Yeaxlee, Basil A. *Religion and the Growing Mind.* Greenwich, Connecticut: Seabury Press, 1952.

INDEX

According to Size (film), 164
Accreditation of marriage counselors, 28
Ackerman, Nathan, 140, 143, 146 156, 197
Adaptability, family, 138
Adolescence, 154-55, 156, 191, 192, 193, 199-203
Adoption, 22, 155, 157
Agape, 195, 196, 202
Age difference of marriage partners, 54
Alcoholism, 54, 98, 138
Alexander, Franz, 82
Alexander, Paul, 112
Allport, Gordon, 34
"Alter ego," 164
American Association of Marriage Counselors, 19, 27-28
American Institute of Family Relations, 57, 185, 209-10
American Theater Wing, plays for role-playing by, 164
Annulment, 11, 23, 116, 119
Antenuptial agreement, 72
Anxiety, 23, 53
Astley, M. R. C., 115
Attachments, personal, 198
Authority problems, 13, 144; *see also* Discipline

Baruch, Dorothy, 148, 198, 201
Bedwetting, 147, 152

Bernreuter test, 57
Berreman, 19
Bertocci, Peter, 206
Bible, divorce and, 116
Birth control, 56, 64
Black, Algernon D., 73
Books
  in premarital counseling, 58-59
  for sex education, 196-97, 199, 202-3
Boston University Pastoral Center, 188
Bovet, Theodore, 194, 195
Bowman, Henry, 117, 196, 201, 205
Boy-girl friendships, 192
Bridgman, Ralph, 112
Budget
  adolescent needs and, 155
  in marriage, 61, 65-70, 164
  and the pastoral counseling center, 187-88
Burgess-Cattrell-Wallin Schedule on Marriage Adjustment, 57
Burke, Louis, 109, 112
Burkhardt, Roy, 17

Cannell, Charles, 31
Character, individual, and family integrity, 138
Chastity, premarital, 201-2
Child counseling, 135, 153-54, 159
Children
  adopting of, 155

Children—*cont'd*
confusion in rearing of, 29, 153
delinquency of, 138, 143
of divorce, 121, 124-25
education of, in mixed marriage, 72
illegitimate, 22, 156-57
inconsistent handling of, 154, 155-56
marriage plans of, 155
placement of, for adoption, 22, 157
planning for, 63-64
religious education of, 72, 74
young, and sex education, 197-99
see also Adolescence
Church
decline of authority of, 13
family life program in, 190-203
influence of, 206
place in, for single persons, widows, divorcees, 191
position of, on divorce, 116-18
relationship of counselees and, 51, 75, 123
Client-centered counseling, 32-35, 36, 52
Clinical training, 185, 209
Cole, William, 206
Common interests and activities, 110
Communication
breakdown of, 89-90, 205
client-counselor, 37
emotional, 82
parent-adolescent, 200, 202
Companionship, 97, 195
Compatibility, 51
sexual, 64, 195
tests of, 56, 57
Compulsory counseling, 112
Concepts of sex education, 198
Confidentiality, 44
Conflicts, methods of resolving, 70; see also Problems
Contraception, 56, 64
Cook, Joseph E., 120
Cooling-off period, 108

I Corinthians, Pauline Privilege in, 116
Counseling
client-centered, 32-35, 36, 52
compulsory, 112
counselor-centered, 30-32, 34, 36
goals and methods of, 30-40
group, 126-27, 156, 160-79, 193
pastoral counseling centers, 181-89
relationship-centered, 8, 35-40, 157
rooms and secretary for, in pastoral counseling center, 185-86
supervised, 20, 207
using two counselors, 146
Counselor-centered counseling, 30-32, 34, 36
Courts
divorce and, 119-20
reconciliation and, 112
Courtship, 24, 110
Crane Tests for Husbands and Wives, 57
Crittenton, Florence, Homes, 22
Cross-referral plan, 84, 85
Cruelty, 25
Cultural differences of marriage partners, 175
Custody of children, 121, 124-25

Dating, 24, 63, 192, 200-01
Delinquency, 138, 143
Democracy
in family file, 15, 206
practiced by leader, 162-63
Denney, Reuel, 13
Dependency feelings, 31, 32, 98, 99, 164
Depersonalization, 29
Desertion, 11, 25, 119, 143
Direction, family sense of, 142
Directors for a pastoral counseling center, 182-83
Discipline, child, 154, 155-56, 193
Doctrines and Discipline of The Methodist Church, 117

Discussion
  group, 161-79, 193
  variations in, 174
Disillusioning process, 94, 109
Dispensation from nonconsummated
    marriage, 116
Divorce, 11, 25, 82, 115-18
  children of, 121, 124-25
  "emotional," 95-96
  grounds for, 120
  high-school, 201
  legal aspects of, 119-20
  "poor man's," 119
  "psychological," 11
  reasons for, 114-15
  and reconciliation, 112
  religious view of, 81, 116-18
  responsibility of counselor in, 118-
    21
Divorce counseling, 121-31
Divorcee, ambiguous role of, 118,
    123
Divorcees Anonymous, 126-27
Dominating personality, 70, 175
Doty, James E., 181
Driver, Helen, 163
Drug addiction, 54
Duress, 54
Duvall, Evelyn, 115, 194
Duvall, Sylvanus, 194

Economic side of marriage. *See* Bud-
    get *and* Finances
Education
  of children of mixed marriage, 72
  differences in, of marriage part-
    ners, 54
  for marriage, 17-20, 51, 52-53,
    190-91, 206
  for parenthood, 191
  religious, of children, 74
  sex, 193-203
  see also Training
Educational adviser, counseling by,
    23
Ellzey, W. Clark, 201
Elopement, 54
Emotional communication, 82

Emotional cost of divorce, 121
Emotional disintegration, 140
Emotional divorce (estrangement),
    95-96
Emotional immaturity and maturity,
    25, 51, 97
Emotional security, 15
Empathy, 37, 53, 84
Engagement, 24, 70
Eros, 195
Estrangement, 95-99, 105-6
Evaluation of counseling, 48-49, 207
Executive director, pastoral counsel-
    ing center, 185, 187
Extramarital interest, 25

Face, losing of, 92
Failure, sense of, 122, 133, 152,
    153
Faith
  and faithfulness, 196
  in the family, 142, 157-58
  in God, 202
  and growth, 206-7
  hidden from marriage partner, 98
  meaning of, 51
  privilege of, 116
Faithfulness, 195-96
Family
  changes in, 12-15
  crises in, 25, 137-40
  democracy in, 15, 206
  functions of, 14-15, 204-5
  instability of, 204
  minister's, relations in, 18, 20, 93,
    191-92
  organization of, 138-39, 140
  relations with, 63
  relations within, 141, 151
  religion in, 142, 157-58
  roles in, 12-13, 35-36, 135, 136-
    37, 141, 153, 154
  urban, suburban, and rural, 14-15
Family council, 207
Family counseling, 21, 22
  cases in, 132-35, 146-49
  defined, 135
  flow of, 150-58

Family counseling—*cont'd*
  form for, 158-59
  goals of, 140-43
  group approach to, 135-37
  role of minister in, 143-44
  structure of, 145-46
Family Life Committee, 192, 194
Family life program
  case study in, 193-203
  principles and goals of, 190-92
  structure of, 192-93
Family Life Publications, 56
Fatherhood, 153
Fees, 43
Finances
  family, 25, 61, 65-70, 155
  of pastoral counseling center, 187-88
  and reconciliation plan, 110
Flexibility, family, 138
Florence Crittenton Homes, 22
Forgiveness, 111, 122-23, 157-58
Fox, Ruth, 98
"Freedom within limits," 154
Freud, Sigmund, 29
"Friend of the court," 112
Friendships
  boy-girl, 192
  new, after divorce, 123-24

Galvin, James A., 8
Gaskill, Mrs. Evelyn, 8, 161
God
  faith in, 202
  forgiveness and support of, 111-12, 123, 158
  and pastoral counseling, 34-35, 75
  procreation plan of, 199
  and the quest for meaning, 14
  and the realm of values, 18, 36
Going steady, 192, 201
Goode, William J., 69
Grandparents, 25, 152, 156, 191
Griffith, Mrs. Ethel, 8
Group counseling, 126-27, 156, 160-61, 193
  case study of, 165-73
  of a family, 135-37

Group counseling—*cont'd*
  methods of observation in, 177-79
  role-playing, 163-65
  structure and flow of, 173-76
  theory of, 161-63
Guidance
  child, 135, 153-54, 159
  desire for, 13
Guilt, 56, 122
Guldner, Claude, 8

Harper, Robert, 82
Health certificate, 64
Helper role, 37, 42-43, 82, 153
Hill, Reuben, quoted, 137, 138
Hiltner, Seward, 17, 42, 206
Hobbies, mass-produced, 13
Home visit, 18, 143, 146
Hostility
  in divorce, 122
  expression of, 107, 164
Housing, 68

Identification figure, 37
Identification of problems, 89, 176
Illegitimacy, 22, 156-57
Immaturity, emotional, 25, 97
In Holy Matrimony, 58
Incompatibility, 115, 153
Infatuation, 38
Infidelity, 25
In-laws, 25, 136, 155-56, 191
"Inner release" theory, 34
Insight, 33, 54-55, 82
Installment buying, 66
Insurance, 68
Integrity, family, 138
Intelligence, family, 138
Intercultural marriage, 73
Interdependence, 97-98, 191
Interfaith marriage, 54-55, 71-73
Interpersonal interaction, 51-52, 66, 84, 92, 141, 151
Interpersonal needs, 97
Interprofessional consultation
  in marriage counseling, 25-26
  in pastoral counseling center, 183-84

Interracial marriage, 73, 170, 173
Interview
 flow of, 46-49, 61-75
 record of, 44-46, 75-78
 structure of, 41-44, 60-61
Intimacy
 covenant of, 111
 ground rules for, 200-1
Intrafamily crisis, 25, 132-40
Intrapersonal and interpersonal oriented categories, 36
Isolation after divorce, 124

Jesus
 and divorce, 116-17
 and the spirit behind social regulation, 202
 values taught by, 205
Johnson, Paul E., 8, 188
Johnson, Roswell, quoted, 118
Johnson Temperament Analysis, 57-
 58

Kahn, Robert, 31
Kargman, Marie, quoted, 36
Karpf, M., 175
Kinsey, 13, 65
Kirkendall, Lester, 197, 201
Koinonia, 176
Koos, Earl, 18, 139, 140

Lawyer, counseling by, 23-24
Leisure, uses of, 13
Life insurance, 68
Living standard, 67
Loneliness, 122
Love, 82, 83, 195, 198, 199, 202
Lust, 195

Mace, David, 11, 17
Mace, Vera, 11
McNeill, John, 29
Magoun, F. A., 115
Marriage
 as a block to wholeness, 81
 books to read before, 58-59
 dissolving of, 115-18
 early, 201

Marriage—*cont'd*
 economic factors in failure of, 69
 functions of, 204-5
 growth in, 94
 in middle and later years, 191
 mixed, 54-55, 71-73, 170, 173
 "neurotic," 80, 98-99
 parental acceptance of, 155
 poor risks for, 54
 preparation for, 17-20, 51, 52-53,
  190-91, 206
 problems before, 24
 problems in early years of, 24-25,
  160, 191
 religious side of, 61, 71-74, 97-
  98
 rupture of, 25, 81-82
 screening of applicants for, 53-55
 second, 55, 124, 125-26
 sexual side of, 64-65, 97, 110
 social system of, 39
 tests preceding, 55-58
Marriage ceremony, review of, 74
Marriage Council of Philadelphia,
  185, 187, 210
Marriage counseling
 cases in, 15-16, 85-88
 defined, 21-22
 differences between personal
  counseling and, 79
 flow of, 88-93
 goals of, 80-84
 group, 160-79
 interprofessional co-operation in
  25-26, 183-84
 problems in, 24-25
 professional standards in, 27-28
 structure of, 84-85
 workers in, 22-24
Marriage manuals, 58-59, 194
Masturbation, 56
Maturity
 emotional, 51
 family, 207
 and self-acceptance, 70
Meaning, search for, 14
Menninger Foundation, 185, 210
Mental illness or deficiency, 54, 138

Merrill-Palmer School, 185-210
Messianic complex, 80, 205
Methodist Church, position of, on divorce and remarriage, 117-18
Minister
  burden of counseling on, 180-81
  and family, as models for parishioners, 20, 191
  focal place of, in marriage, 16-20, 24
  relation of, with own family, 18, 20, 93, 191-92
  role of, in family life education, 191
  role of, in marriage counseling, 91-93
  similarity and differences of social worker and, 142-43
  self-projection of, 93
  therapy for, 40
Minnesota Multiphasic Inventory, 57
Mittelmann, Bela, 98
Mixed marriage, 54-55, 71-73, 170, 173
Mobility, social and geographical, 12
Morals and mores, changes in, 29, 205
Moreno, Jacob, 37, 161, 162, 163
Mosaic law, 117
Motherhood, 152-53
Mother-in-law, 133, 136, 155
Mudd, Emily, 57, 161, 175
Mutuality of marriage goals, 83

National Council on Family Relations, 26
Needs, basic, 95, 97, 98-99, 124, 141
Neurotic marriage, 80, 98-99
Neuroticism, 20, 138
New Ways in Discipline (Baruch), 148
Nimkoff, M. F., quoted, 125-26, 204
Normative patterns, 36

Oates, Wayne, 17
Objectivity, 92-93

One Foot in Heaven (Spence), quoted, 50
Onsgard, Carol, 8

Packard, Vance, 12
Parental counseling, 135
Parent-child relationships, 154-55, 156, 164
Parenthood, training for, 191
Parents
  as example for children, 199
  and grandparents, 155-56
  living with, 68
  loss of authority by, 13
  relations with, 63, 137
  roles of, 153, 154
  of teenagers, sex education and, 199-203
  of young children, and sex education, 197-99
Parent-Teachers' Association, 193, 200
"Participant-observation," 146
Pastoral care, 29
Pastoral counseling centers, 205
  counselors in, 184-85
  financing of, 186-87
  operation of, 187-88
  structure and personnel of, 181-86
  survey of, 189
Pastoral Psychology, 52
Pauline Privilege, 116
Permissiveness, 81, 107
Personal counseling, 79, 83, 145
Personality differences, adjustment to, 70, 82-83
Personality tests, 56, 57
Petting, 202
Physician
  counseling by, 22, 23
  premarital visit to, 65
Pike, James A., 73
Planned parenthood, 63-64
Play therapy, 154
Prayer, 75, 111-12, 123, 158, 176
"Pre-counseling," 42
Premarital counseling, 21

Premarital counseling—*cont'd*
flow of, 61-75
goals of, 50-52
position of minister in, 17-20
record of interviews in, 75-78
screening aspect of, 53-55
structure of, 60-61
teaching aspect of, 52-53
use of books in, 58-59
use of tests in, 55-58
Premarital relations, 13, 56, 65, 201-2
Problems
authority, 13, 144
before marriage, 24
dependency, 164
in early years of marriage, 24-25, 160, 191
identification of, 89, 176
interpersonal, 79-80, 82
solving of, 70, 94, 162, 163, 175-76
statement of, 47
Professional Advisory Committee, pastoral counseling center, 183-84
Protestant position on divorce and remarriage, 116-18, 125
Prudishness, 20, 193
Psychiatry, 23, 31-32, 34, 36, 99
Psychoanalyst, 38
Psychological tests, 55-58
Psychologists, 27, 34
Psychopathic personality, 54
Psychosis, 99
Psychotherapy, 27, 31-32, 44
during seminary training, 40
group, 161-62
Public Health Service, 187

Quarreling, 94, 96

Random Target (film), 164
Rapport, 18, 53, 62
Reconciliation, 99-105, 158
and the courts, 112
process of, 106-12
rules for helping to bring about, 105-6

Reconciliation agreement, 109
Recording interviews, 43
Recreation, commercialized, 13
Referral, 43-44, 84, 85, 99, 146, 150, 188
Rejection, case study in, 146-49, 153
Relationship-centered counseling, 8, 35-40, 157
Religion
and divorce, 122, 123
in the family, 142, 157-58
influence of, 206
in marriage, 61, 71-74, 97-98
meaning of, 98
minister as symbol of, 38-39
Religious education of children, 72, 74
Religious resources in counseling, 39, 111-12, 208
Remarriage, 25, 55, 124, 125-26
Research projects, 187
Resentment, expression of, 107
Roche, Phillip, 155
Rogers, Carl, 32, 33
Role
ambiguity in, 29, 205
distortion of, 19, 108
fluidity of, 12-13
realistic, 137
rejection of, 153
understanding of, 83, 91, 92, 108-9
Role behavior, 36, 38, 90-91, 92, 146, 196
Role expectation, 35, 36, 68-69, 92, 108-9, 137
Role image, 19, 35, 36, 37, 83, 92, 96, 153
Role interaction, 35, 83, 141
disturbances in, 96-97
realism in, 108-9, 10
Role-playing, 163-65
structured, 164, 165, 174
unstructured, 164, 165, 174
Roman Catholic Church
position of, on divorce and remarriage, 116, 125

Roman Catholic Church—*cont'd*
    strictures of, on education of children, 72
Romantic role, minister in, 38
Rubber Budget Account, 68
Rural family, 14

"Safety valve," 71
Schedule E, Marriage Council of Philadelphia, 57
Screening of couples in premarital interviews, 53-55
Security
    emotional, 15, 63
    need for, 141
Seeker role, 37, 42-43
Self-acceptance, 70
Self-concept, 92, 96, 153; *see also* Role image
Self-esteem
    loss of, 121
    need for, 156
Self-evaluation of counseling methods, 207
Self-fulfilling prophecy, principle of, 152
    Sensitivity, bodily, 198
Separation, 25, 119, 120, 122
Serologic testing, 64
Sex (es)
    differences between, 194-95
    groups divided according to, 160, 193
    purpose of, in human life, 195
Sex education
    case study in, 193-203
    for engaged couples, 194-97
    for parents of teenagers, 199-203
    for parents of young children, 197-99
Sex-knowledge inventories, 55-56
Sexual deviant, 54
Sexual harmony, 64, 195
Sexual needs, 97, 124
Sexual relations
    compatibility and, 64, 195
    discussion of, 64-65
    embarrassment in discussing, 59

Sexual relations—*cont'd*
    in marriage, 64-65, 97, 110
    premarital, 13, 56, 65, 201-2
    and reconciliation, 110
    spiritual interpretation of, 196
Sherman, Edward, 8, 120
Shirey, Arthur E., 8
Sickness, 71, 100, 101, 102, 138
Silence, wall of, 90
Social changes, 205
Social class difference of marriage partners, 67
Social mobility, 12
Social worker
    counseling by, 22-23
    similarity and differences of pastor and, 142-43
Sociodrama, 162, 164
Sociometric instruments, 57
Spence, Hartzell, quoted, 50
Standards, of American Association of Marriage Counselors, 27-28
Staples, Edward D., 192, 203
Status
    desire for, 148
    loss of, 121
Status Seekers (Packard), 12
Steering Committee, for a pastoral counseling center, 181-82
Stewart, Catherine and Peter, 8
Stone, Abraham, 60, 175
Structured discussion, 174
Structured role-playing, 164, 165, 174
Submissive personality, 70, 175
Supervision of counseling, 20, 207
Supportive therapy, 82, 83

Teenage code, 193; *see also* Adolescence
Tele, 37
Terman, Lewis M., 114
Termination
    of counseling, 43-44
    of interview, 47-48
Tests
    personality, 56, 57
    psychological, 55-58

Tests—*cont'd*
serologic, 64
Thorman, George, quoted, 119
Thrift, 66-67; *see also* Budget
Thurber, James, 94
Training
for counseling, 26, 28, 40, 209-10
professional, minister's lack of, 18-19
required to administer and interpret psychological tests, 55
Transference, 38, 39, 44

Uncovering therapy, 82
Under-age marriage, 55
United States Public Health Service, 187
Unstructured conversation, 174
Unstructured role-playing, 164, 165, 174
Unwed mothers, 157
Urban and suburban families, 14-15

Values, 66, 68, 97-98
in the Christian gospel, 206
in family life, 142, 157-58, 205
the minister and, 18, 34-35, 38
taught by Jesus, 205
Vernon, Ruth and Walter, 200-1

Wade, 19
Westberg, Granger, 17
What Did I Do? (film), 164
Wholeness, 81-82
Winter, Gibson, 111, 157-58
Women, working, 69
Wood, Leland Foster, 17, 18
Working wife, 69
Workshops, counseling, 188
Wynn, J. C., 17

Youth counseling, 156; *see also* Adolescence *and* Child counseling